SENTIMENT, REASON, AND LAW

A VOLUME IN THE SERIES

Police/Worlds: Studies in Security, Crime, and Governance

Edited by Kevin Karpiak, Sameena Mulla, William Garriott, and Ilana Feldman

A list of titles in this series is available at cornellpress.cornell.edu

SENTIMENT, REASON, AND LAW

Policing in the Republic of
China on Taiwan

Jeffrey T. Martin

CORNELL UNIVERSITY PRESS **ITHACA AND LONDON**

First published 2019 by Cornell University Press

Library of Congress Cataloging-in-Publication Data
Names: Martin, Jeffrey T., author.
Title: Sentiment, reason, and law : policing in the Republic of China on Taiwan / Jeffrey T. Martin.
Description: Ithaca [New York] : Cornell University Press, 2019. | Series: Police/ worlds : studies in security, crime, and governance | Includes bibliographical references and index.
Identifiers: LCCN 2019002354 (print) | LCCN 2019004774 (ebook) | ISBN 9781501740060 (pdf) | ISBN 9781501740077 (epub/mobi) | ISBN 9781501740046 | ISBN 9781501740046 (cloth) | ISBN 9781501740053 (pbk.)
Subjects: LCSH: Police—Taiwan. | Law enforcement—Political aspects—Taiwan.
Classification: LCC HV8262.A2 (ebook) | LCC HV8262.A2 M37 2019 (print) | DC 363.20951249/09045—dc23
LC record available at https://lccn.loc.gov/2019002354

Contents

Acknowledgments

I spent eight wonderful years living in Taiwan. I met some of my best friends there, along with many cherished colleagues and teachers. I have been the grateful recipient of hospitality from hundreds of Taiwanese people. This book is based on things I learned from them. However, out of an abundance of caution, I will not mention anyone in Taiwan by name here for fear that the sensitivity of the topics I discuss might somehow bring negative repercussions. It is also appropriate to state that all names in the text (except, of course, those of public figures) are pseudonyms, and I have fictionalized all descriptions of illegal activity, preserving only enough empirical truth to substantiate my theoretical argument.

There are a number of people whom I can safely thank by name. This begins with my father, Michael Martin. I would also like to thank David Leung and Nicolas Spaltenstein, two people who taught me how to take learning seriously and changed my life for the better. I would like to thank Anya Bernstein for a detailed reading of the manuscript, which significantly improved the final draft. Generous mentoring, assistance, friendship, and collegiality have been gratefully received from Nancy Ablemann, Mike Adorjan, Borge Bakken, Jeff Bennett, Kirk Black, Avron Boretz, Kevin Caffrey, Jessica Cattelino, Kai-Wing Chow, Lily Chumley, Jerome Cohen, Jean Comaroff, Jenny Davis, Jane Desmond, Virginia Dominguez, Prasenjit Duara, Brenda Farnell, Judith Farquhar, Chris Fennell, Paul Festa, Katja Franko, Douglas Howland, Fu Hualing, Will Garriott, Maria Gillombardo, Alma Gottleib, Jessica Greenberg, Shane Greene, Eric Haanstad, Faye Harrison, David Hopkins, Julia Hornberger, Cris Hughes, Bea Jauregui, Brian Jefferson, Kevin Karpiak, Craig Koslofsky, Karen Joe Laidler, Erika Robb Larsen, Paul Liffman, Peter Manning, Alexander Mayer, Ellen Moodie, Andy Orta, Elizabeth Oyler, Jerome Packard, Gian-Piero Persiani, David Peterson, Gilberto Rosas, Jacqueline Ross, Brian Ruppert, Misumi Sadler, Mike Schlosser, David Schrag, Shao Dan, Chilin Shih, Michael Silverstein, Georgina Sinclair, Eric Lee Skjon, Krystal Smalls, Colin Smith, Meg Stalcup, Michelle Stewart, Ling-yun Tang, Bob Tierney, Rod Wilson, and Jane K. Winn.

Research funding was received from the Center for Advanced Studies, University of Illinois; the Funding Initiative for Multiracial Democracy, University of Illinois; the US Department of Education, Fulbright–Hays Research Fellowship; the Chiang Ching-Kuo Foundation for International Scholarly Exchange; the Taiwan Foundation for Democracy; the University Grants Committee of Hong Kong; and the University of Chicago's Center for East Asian Studies.

SENTIMENT, REASON, AND LAW

INTRODUCTION

What are police for? The question can be addressed in different ways. Individuals might describe their personal experience with police, and reflect on what those police did to them or for them. The chief of a local police department, by contrast, would tend to speak in terms of the rationale he or she provides for the political patrons who fund the department's operations. The content of the chief's account would minimize qualities of personal experience and valorize statistical indicators of the sort that matter to administrative bureaucracies. Finally, in counterpoint to both the personal and the professional account, a social theorist might try to develop a critical perspective that could illuminate what the institution in the abstract does for society in general. This book, an anthropological study of a police department, combines elements from all three types of narrative—ethnographic, institutional, and theoretical. My participant-observation in a Taiwanese police station brings the data of personal experience to bear on my sociological study of the institutional history of policing in Taiwan. And, on the basis of these two bodies of evidence, I propose a general theory of the way Taiwanese policing has been structured by certain cultural values.

One of the more enduring general theories of what police are for is Egon Bittner's essay "The Functions of the Police in Modern Society" ([1970] 1990a). Bittner proposed "to explain the function of the police [by reference to] what their existence makes available in society that, all things being equal, would not be otherwise available" (233–34). This produced a much-quoted definition of police as "a mechanism for the distribution of situationally justified force" (123), which Bittner took as a basis to advocate for the development of a professional ideal of police as experts in necessary violence. "Using force is to the policing profession what curing illness is to the medical profession" (127). This idea remains influential to the present day, baked into the foundation of the so-called medical model of police professionalism (Thacher 2001).

Actually existing police institutions remain notorious sources of inexpert, unprofessional, and unnecessary violence. Clearly, Bittner's hoped-for model of police reform has not succeeded. Nonetheless, the fact that an ideal is unrealized is not, in and of itself, an argument against the ideal. Indeed, it is the nature of hope to stand willfully against reality. It is perfectly logical to condemn the woeful state of actually existing police institutions while still believing that, because violence is a constituent element of human worlds, the best we can hope for is to be governed by powers that will try to take responsibility for doing violence right. Indeed, that was precisely Bittner's argument. And his unrealized medical model remains a canonical expression of the basic aspiration driving liberal police reform.

The theoretical content of this book is a critique of Bittner's ideal of policing. Unlike most recent critical literature on policing, however, this book does not criticize Bittner's vision by pointing out its empirical failures. Rather, it holds up an alternative vision of success, arguing that it is possible to imagine police as something other than a violent supplement to the rule of law. I develop this argument empirically, on the basis of an ethnographic and historical study of policing in a context where many of the liberal presumptions on which Bittner's theory was founded do not hold. That context is Taiwan.

Taiwanese police have an illiberal history. The institution took shape through a century of service to colonial and dictatorial regimes and was only recently reconditioned as an element of democratic order. This reconditioning did not change the basic architecture of the bureaucracy, which continued to use a registry system to organize neighborhood policing as a project defined by the surveillance of the general population. My ethnography shows how the persistence of this illiberal institution kept policing political, preventing it from redefining its mandate as apolitical "law enforcement." I describe the practical mode of policing that emerged from this as an enterprise of "political curation" or "administrative repair," and argue that its illiberal qualities are vital to the way police maintain Taiwan's democratic order with relatively low levels of violence. Comparing this situation to mainstream theories of a policing studies literature shaped by Bittnerian sensibilities shows the degree to which the fetish of violence at the heart of the "medical model" is generated by liberal axioms concerning the nature of the human subject, the meaning of law, and the purpose of the modern state. Other axioms, other historical and cultural conditions, create other possible formulations of "the best we can hope for" from our police.

Taiwan is a mountainous island, about fourteen thousand square miles in area, inhabited by twenty-three million people. It has a developed late-industrial economy with annual GDP per capita of US$22,000, slightly higher than Europe as a whole. Most of its population is crowded into a string of cities on the alluvial plain that stretches down its west coast from Taipei in the north to Kaohsiung in the south. One hundred miles to the west of those cities, on the other side of the Taiwan Straits, is China.

Taiwan is governed by an entity called the Republic of China (ROC), which memorializes the Chinese Revolution of 1911 as its founding. Taiwan joined the ROC as a province in 1945. This ended the fifty-year period of Japanese colonialism (1895–1945), which first established modern government on the island. After World War II destroyed the Japanese empire, the Pacific Rim was reconfigured by the geopolitical dynamics of the Cold War. A central event in this reorganization was the triumph of the Chinese Communist Party (CCP) in the Chinese Civil War (1927–1950), which established the People's Republic of China (PRC) in 1949. The losing side of that war, the Chinese Nationalist Party (the Guomindang, or KMT), was not completely vanquished. Its leaders fled across the Taiwan Straits, bringing with them some two million soldiers and clients, and most of the governing apparatus of the Republic of China.

Thus did the Republic of China survive the loss of its national territory by collapsing into the physical space of a single province. It was not a comfortable fit. The ROC had acquired Taiwan only four years earlier, and had a poor relationship with the people living there. Although the initial incorporation of Taiwan into the ROC was peaceful, predatory misrule by the new government led to conflict, and the ROC's position on Taiwan was soon reduced to the terms of a military occupation. This position was consolidated in 1950, when the Korean War sent American troops into the Taiwan Straits. Taiwan became "Free China" in American propaganda, and, under American patronage, the ROC continued to hold the UN's China seat until 1971. The boundary line established by American interests, which separated the Republic of China from the People's Republic of China throughout the Cold War, remains to the present day.

One of the first things a student of Taiwan learns about its history is that it spent four decades under martial law (1949–1987). This historical fact is the basis of a conventional formula for talk about Taiwan's democratic present. Martial law was a primary enabling factor for the "White Terror" perpetrated by the KMT's Leninist party-state. Martial law is, thus, metonymic for Taiwan's autocratic past. The definitively undemocratic arrangement that subordinated judicial power to military command, and subjected civilians to courts-martial, supplies a dark background against which the democratic features of the present are clearly visible. Whatever topic may be at issue—whether a concrete institution like the police, or something more abstract like literature or religion—its relationship to democracy can be conveniently described by reviewing its trajectory through the complex political and legal transformation Taiwan underwent after the end of martial law in 1987.

The formula holds true in each individual case. However, as a literature-wide historiographic convention it creates a kind of distortion. It projects artificial coherence onto the historical relationship between autocracy and democracy. That is, it makes the end of martial law appear as the inflection point in a kind of categorical inversion, whereby liberal democracy overcame and displaced its antithesis. Historical reality is never so tidy. The past does not pass, it endures: as infrastructure, as memory, and as debris. Taiwan's contemporary democracy embodies and exemplifies the human capacity to found new beginnings. But at the same time it is equally a legacy and continuation of certain autocratic precedents.

This is perhaps nowhere more true than in policing institutions. Making sense of this is difficult. It means reconciling the conservative and the progressive, as broadly countervailing aspects of modern history (Eisenstadt 2000). In Taiwan, there is a movement to do just this. Politically, it takes the form of a campaign for transitional justice, working to excavate repressed memories and recover suppressed evidence, that Taiwan's future might be shaped by a fuller and more accurate understanding of its past (Stolojan 2017; Hwang 2016). Intellectually, a new wave of political and legal scholarship has drawn on these emergent archives and audiences to develop new historical understanding of the state and its law (Yeh 2016; Greitens 2016; T.-S. Wang 2016). However, despite the centrality that institutionalized state repression holds for all these projects, little of this new work has addressed "policing" per se. And no one has yet explored how Taiwan's *longue durée* history of colonial and dictatorial policing institutions has shaped the quality of policed life in its democratic present.

Filling that gap is the ambition of this book. Its empirical core is an ethnographic portrait of a neighborhood police station (a *paichusuo*) during the first change in ruling parties after the end of martial law (which occurred in 2000). I focus on the everyday routines of the institution, and how those routines fit into the sociopolitical life of the local community. I pay special attention to the persistence of historical elements in those routines, and the effect those continuities have on the meaningful qualities of policed life. This leads me to a somewhat paradoxical conclusion about the role police play in Taiwan's democracy: the *strength* of Taiwan's flourishing democratic political system is, I argue, positively correlated with the continuing *weakness* of its police powers. I explain this paradox through a theory of jurisdictional pluralism, organized by a cultural distinction among sentiment, reason, and law (*qing*, *li*, and *fa*). Each category, I argue, marks out a distinct "ritual center" of authority, legitimacy, and power (Briggs 2018).

Within the triadic distinction among sentiment, reason, and law, I am especially interested in the category of *qing*. Most policing ethnography written since the 1950s focuses on discretion, as a mode of practical reason through which agents make decisions about when and how to apply the law (Ohlin and Remington 1993). In other words, it is an accepted axiom of policing studies that police work sits at an intersection between reason and law. But this has not been connected to any systematic theory of "sentiment" per se, except in studies of racism as implicit bias. The illiberal history of Taiwanese policing puts the significance of *qing* explicitly at the core of the institution. Overt, organized interest by police in *qing* was institutionalized during the martial law era, through the *qingbao* ("*qing*-reporting" or "intelligence") system, when police served as an instrument for the cultivation of properly nationalistic political sentiments. My fieldwork demonstrates how the politics of sentiment that took shape under autocratic rule continued to operate in everyday policing in the early phase of the democratic transformation, even as a more democratic mode of public reason and the ultimate power of legal right were becoming more significant.

To account for the sociocultural dynamics of police power in this pluralist political environment, I draw on a theory of "jurisdiction" as a form of power that acts (or "speaks") on the basis of an exclusive claim to professional expertise. I look to two literatures for this theory. The first is Andrew Abbott's sociology of professions, in which "the link between a profession and its work [Abbott calls] jurisdiction. . . . The interplay of jurisdictional links between professions determines the history of the individual professions themselves" (Abbott 1988, 20). By Abbott's account, modern professions emerge from a history of jurisdictional disputes over the nature and boundaries of the problems they claim to solve. The definition of a problem is the object of struggle between occupational groups, who compete to establish their exclusive control over the supply of expert labor required to solve that problem. In other words, the functionalist question of "what a profession is *for*" follows in the wake of a historical struggle to define what an institution *is*, by distinction from other institutions competing for the same social resources. Putting historical ontology before functionalism is useful in disentangling the kind of path dependency created by powerful institutions like the police, which look at the world with the eyes of a "hammer searching for a nail" (to borrow a hoary cliché familiar in policing circles). Abbot's idea of jurisdiction gives a useful perspective on how the Bittnerian idea of police as experts in violence could emerge as the contingent outcome of a historical struggle over institutional resources, then coalesce into a naturalized ideological rationale for self-justifying behavior. As I show in chapter 2, Taiwan's modern history never put its police institutions into the position of justifying their existence on the basis of a claim to exclusive authority over violence. Rather, the existential "unique value proposition" of police power in Taiwan has taken historical shape as a capacity to mediate between the unruly political energies of spontaneous solidarity and the orderly ambitions of central administration. This conjuncture is occasionally violent, and Taiwan's police have historically relied on violence to do their job, but they have never grounded their authority in a claim of privileged access to some kind of ultimate, sovereign, "law-giving" violence (Benjamin [1921] 1996). My ethnographic materials show street-level patrolmen yielding, quite openly and systematically, to a superior capacity for violence by other players in their city's political landscape. I show how this position of structural weakness is rationalized in the pedagogical materials through which the rank-and-file are taught to respect the balance of sentiment, reason, and law.

To answer the question of how such policing is possible—how police could function if they are not, as Bittner thought, professional experts in violence—I turn to a second theory of jurisdiction, developed by lawyer and linguistic anthropologist Justin Richland (2013). This approach begins by taking the word itself at face value—"juris-diction"—and proposes to understand law's force through speech act theory. This gives rise to an empirical concern with the institutional structure of a government, exploring how it makes certain speech acts legally effective by supplying an infrastructure of perlocutionary conditions that activate the illocutionary force of legality within a given statement. Richland is especially interested in the dynamic by which subaltern legal actors represent their powers as *delegated*, when in fact their performances actually *constitute* the higher authority they claim to represent. This is an application of the semiotic theory of "authorizing discourses" (Asad 1993; Caton 2006) to the issue of legal sovereignty, showing how the ostensible *presupposition* that a court acts as a delegated agent of sovereign power is, in actual practice, *entailed* as an outcome of performances staged within that court. A similar dynamic, I argue, can be observed in the way Taiwanese policing acts under the authority of *qing*—that is, in claiming to defer to the sentimental imperatives of a particular situation, police are in fact (re)*constituting* the affective solidarity of policed order. To adapt Richland's frame for textual analysis of law to the extralegal dynamics of the street, it is necessary to consider the field of authorizing discourses as embedding legality per se in a wider pluralism, and consider how the category of *qing* has been institutionalized in this plurality as the ritual center for a jurisdictional power defined in contradistinction to legal sovereignty.

My ethnographic material shows how the capacity of Taiwan's police to give legal commands is systematically frustrated by the existence of competing grounds for politically effective speech, including, notably, a practice known as

"speaking *qing*" (*shuoqing*, discussed in chapter 3). The practice of effective policing at the street level is predicated on engagement in this pluralistic political
field, not its violent rejection in favor of the liberal fetish of sovereign law. To
understand this kind of policing it is necessary to have ways of talking about the
relationship between law and politics that go beyond simply positing their opposition, to supply a detailed vocabulary for articulating the qualities and degrees of
their distinction and/or conjuncture. A good beginning is Randall Peerenboom's
(2004) idea of "thinner" vs. "thicker" versions of rule of law. Thinness corresponds to the formal autonomy of legal procedure; at its thinnest, the rule of law
collapse into the principle of legality. Thickness corresponds to the substantive
values people associate with law; at its thickest, rule of law discourse expands
to a consideration of moral action in general. Actually existing legal regimes sit
somewhere between the two extremes, and different cultural traditions "thicken"
the principle of legality in different ways. Looking at Taiwanese history through
this lens exposes an interesting contradiction. On the one hand, at the macro-
institutional level, the island's transition to democracy was accompanied by an
increasingly "strong judicial and political commitment to a liberal-democratic
'thick' version of the rule of law" (Cooney 2004, 417). At the same time, the
ground-level, micro-institutional practices inhabiting this judicial and political
infrastructure continue to marginalize the significance of law per se, reproducing
a social order organized around an alternative set of cultural values (Potter 1995;
Winn 1994a, 1994b). In other words, in democratic Taiwan it appears that the
complex set of practical and symbolic relays integrating the spheres of state and
society somehow allow the rule of law to flourish in the former even as the "order
of custom" is retrenched in the latter (Diamond 1971).

Another useful idea comes from Christopher Tomlins's (2007) discussion of
the historical basis for the "relative autonomy" of legal institutions. Building on
theoretical debates between formalists (who argue that law is an autonomous
sphere of logic) and instrumentalists (who argue that law is overdetermined by its
context), Tomlins proposed a research program focused on the question of what
it is that a given invocation of law seeks to gain its autonomy *from*. In other words,
accepting the thin/formalist principle that legality is a distinct kind of power
opens up empirical questions about "law's relational other." How does law coexist
with the counterpowers against which legal actors must actively work to maintain
the supremacy of legality as the determining basis of consequential event?

Tomlins's idea of law's relational other is helpful for clarifying the historical
dynamics by which policing powers take shape in relation to legal institutions.
Police institutions are connected to the courts, but they stand at a distance, mark-
ing a kind of perimeter or margin in the process through which social problems are
transformed into legal problems. Following Abbott, this distance from law—this

proximity to law's relational other—defines the kind of claims police make to their own independent professional jurisdiction. For Bittner, law's relational other was a supplement of violence: "In order for [legal] process to enjoy an atmosphere of calm deliberation, where everything that needs to be accomplished can be accomplished by mere talk, logical inference, and careful assessment of facts, it is necessary to expel from its purview all those exigencies that are incompatible with it. [That residue of] violent and intuitive action [becomes] the exclusive monopoly of the police" ([1970] 1990a, 118–19). Taiwan's illiberal history provides a stark contrast to Bittner's liberal imaginary, which figures law and violence in binary opposition. Taiwan came to modern law through a *Rechtsstaat* version of law as the instrument by which Japanese colonial authority was imposed by force on its subject population. This established a historical approach to legality (which remained active through Taiwan's authoritarian era, into the 1990s) in which there was no ideological basis for distinguishing between law and violence as a matter of principle; they were fused elements of central power. From the perspective of a police station within this regime, law's relational other was not violence but rather the forms of local solidarity that central authority sought to subordinate and subjugate beneath its modern legal-bureaucratic authority. Thus, the Taiwanese *paichusuo*, as a historical institution, calibrates its distance to law by reference to the complementary category of *qing*, conceptualized as a political sphere defined by the spontaneous and unruly politics of human connection. Over the *longue durée* history of modern policing in Taiwan, this category has come to stand as the ritual center of an independent "jurisdiction," or authorizing discourse, which speaks for local community against central power (Briggs 2018).

This book provides an ethnographic portrait of a police station practicing a historically distinctive form of policing, a form of policing conceptualized as the project of mediating between local politics conducted in the register of *qing*, and central authority projected through the form of law. I begin with a chapter describing my own ethnographic trajectory through the policed sociality surrounding and infusing the *paichusuo*. This trajectory brought a change in perspective. When I first set out to study police, I assumed patrol was the primary mechanism by which police power was projected through society. Accordingly, I took observation of patrol as a primary objective for my fieldwork. But my attempts to observe patrol were chronically frustrated by a logic of host-guest relationships. I was a guest in the police car, police were treated as guests by the political elites of the city, and, as the guest of a guest, I was unable to refuse invitations to leave the police car and engage in other activities. Through my inability to control my own movement, I began to see control over movement as an aspect of police power distributed through the political landscape in a manner that effectively embedded formal police operations into the wider political economy.

Chapter 2 provides a historical sociology of the *paichusuo* as an institution, describing how it has been shaped by the jurisdictional qualities invested in the category of *qing*. From the initial formation of modern policing under the Japanese, through mobilization for fascist total war, across the rocky transition to Chinese rule, through forty years of dictatorship, and into the democratic era, I inventory the multiple meanings that have been bundled into the engagement neighborhood police are expected to maintain with the *qing* of their local community. This history, I argue, has configured the contemporary *paichusuo* as a political arena used for the work of cultivating the collective will to live together.

Chapter 3 returns to the topic of patrol, using ethnographic descriptions of patrol practices to illustrate the ways Taiwanese policing emphasizes a politics of social networks over the control of physical space. This leads me to a general critique of functionalist policing theory, suggesting that some of the most important aspects of Taiwanese policing arise from the value of participating in a meaningful world rather than instrumental concerns with enforcing law or maintaining order. The value of policed order lies as much in its quality as an experience as it does in its functional contribution to other ends.

Chapter 4 describes the routine work of *paichusuo* patrolmen, presented with the theoretical goal of specifying their particular contribution to the city's order. I develop a characterization of their unique professional competence as a kind of "administrative repair," which deploys the power of inscription to facilitate the political processes by which people curate their common world. Chapter 5 takes up the issue of how a police power defined, in practice, by the dialogical accommodation of disorder can effectively uphold a solidary political community. I argue that this is done by valorizing an ideal of balance among sentiment, reason, and law, and using this ideal to continually renew attunement to the potentialities of worldhood emergent from the natality intrinsic in human togetherness.

In chapter 6 I explore the connection between this mode of policing, the ideal of democracy, and the nature of Taiwan's sovereignty, as these connections were revealed by the Sunflower Movement of 2014. This leads me to my counterargument to Bittner's medical model. What Taiwanese police "make available . . . that, all things being equal, would not be otherwise available" is a bureaucratic route through which to channel certain forms of political conflict corrosive to the status quo. The *paichusuo* is the front line of this system, providing an institutional arena for mediating antagonism between local political powers and articulating the resulting compromises with the demands of central administration. The role of *qing* in this process ensures that the institutional operations of policing serve as a cultural mechanism for aligning individual will and collective solidarity along the axis of imagined cosmic principles. This cultural dimension is effective in curating a general will to continue living together in spite of the disorder, contradiction, and crime that generate ceaseless demands for police assistance.

I conclude the book by reflecting on what the Taiwanese police reveal about the liberal fetish of autonomy and its pernicious effects on policing. The idea of autonomy is a central theme in intellectual traditions associated with a classical Greek concept of human flourishing as a matter of accessing a self-given *nomos* that allows people to overcome the limitations of their individual experience and attain a "perspective of universality and objectivity" (Hadot 1995, 95; cf. Durkheim 1973). According to Habermas, this classical ideal was an important source for modern republicanism. It supplies the logic that allows the "private autonomy" of bourgeois subjects to aggregate into a public that approximates the Kantian ideal of universal reason better than an aristocracy can (Habermas 1991; Kant [1784] 2012). This modern ideal of republican power presumes the existence of a kind of authority that is "wholly autonomous, which exists to regulate the public affairs of an independent community, and which brooks no rivals as a source of coercive power within its own *civitas* or *res-publica*. It is here, in short, that we first encounter the familiar understanding of the state as a monopolist of legitimate force" (Skinner 1989, 107). Liberal legal philosophy then proposes law as an instrument for approximating the autonomy of public reason in actual practice, realizing republican government by constraining the sovereign power of state decision making entirely within the form of law. In sum, then, the ideal of autonomy aligns three elements of modern liberal ideology: the subject, the state, and the law. And political flourishing happens when all three sit on the same side of the distinction between autonomy and its logical negation as "heteronomy," suggesting a kind of foundational binary between a desirable political situation in which state law empowers individual subjects to flourish, and an undesirable one in which state power acts as an external force on individual free will. The idea of police I propose in this book—in which police function as political agents curating the will of the policed—sits on the wrong side of this binary. What allows this illiberal form of policing to operate as an element of a flourishing liberal democracy, I argue, is the entrenched institutional legacy of the first hundred years of Taiwan's modern history, combined with the cultural tradition of mutualist ethics that has been incubated within this field of governing technologies.

BACKSTAGE PASSAGE

We arrived at dusk. A pig was roasting on a spit outside the police station's front door. People were sitting at tables in the street. Before we sat down, Ahe took his guests—his wife, her sister, his children, and me—to meet our hosts. The banquet was a fund-raising event, paid by the table. Each table featured its sponsoring patron, who sat as host for the group gathered there. Some of those guests had, like Ahe, invited their own friends or family. This created a hierarchy of hospitality, guest-of-a-guest dynamics within the dozen or so people seated around each table. Above those diverse table-internal hierarchies, the assembly as a whole was integrated through the singular recipient of the funds being raised that evening: the neighborhood police station, represented by its commanding officer, who sat as host for the overall event.

Ahe was a patrolman in the station. I had known him for years, among the earliest friends I made when I arrived in Taiwan for the first time in 1997. But before this event, the Mid-Autumn Festival of 2001, I had not visited this particular police station. Ahe valued propriety. Reckless sociality grated against his character, and he invested considerable care in the invitations and introductions he managed. Indeed, the greetings we made on our initial circuit through the banquet were carefully arranged in accordance with the complicated obligations of his personal network. Ahe's social life was systematically articulated into the clientage network assembled at the police station that evening. He was the unit's *zongganshi*—its "general secretary." Unique among the thirty-odd patrolmen in the station, he held no formal patrol duties. Instead, he carried responsibility for keeping the quotidian bureaucratic affairs of the station in order. This involved things like managing the flows of official communication (still paper-based at the time), paying the utility bills, keeping the lights on and the cafeteria operational, etc. But the primary weight of his position was informal, consisting in the labor required to manage a fabric of relationships known across Chinese-speaking communities as *guanxi*. Ahe served as the station's social fixer, its raconteur-in-chief, and, not incidentally, its "white gloves" (*bai shoutau*—i.e., bagman). Keeping the station's complicated institutional economy running smoothly was an endless enterprise of social hygiene, grooming the fractious collection of patron-client relationships entangled in the multiplex processes by which police power circulated through the life of the local community.

The round of greetings Ahe provided began with the commanding lieutenant himself, sitting at a table directly in front of the station's doorway. Then we met a few local chapter heads in an organization called the Police Friends' Association (Jing You Hui), some members of civil defense (*minfang*) and volunteer police (*yijing*) groups, an alderman (*lizhang*), the secretary of a temple management committee, and some businessmen. After this lengthy observation of etiquette, we finally sat down, joining a throng of people happily eating and drinking. There were hundreds of people there, including, beyond the figures mentioned above, a range of municipal and county government workers, officials from the centralized police bureaucracy, wives, children, and an eclectic collection of neighborhood residents. Almost all the attendees wore civilian clothes. Their identities, and their relationship to the police institution, could be discerned only through moments of ritualized narrative, like Ahe's introductions, or the convention of making a few statements about oneself by way of a toast before draining a glass with a group of interlocutors.

There was a lot of toasting going on. One of the party's many sub-hosts had stocked it with a truckload of Heineken beer. As the banquet proceeded, the distinctive green-and-red cans began to mark an increasingly disordered landscape. Piles of empties collected under the tables. Half-full cans moved into the station as uniformed policemen on duty, called out to join in a round of toasting, carried them back inside and set them on the desks where they processed paperwork. Clusters of men stepped into the station's reception room to talk, leaving it littered with beer cans and plastic cups of blood-red betel spit mixed with cigarette butts. Drunkenness followed the cans. A couple of hours into the feast, someone vomited in the bathroom and plugged the drain. The bathroom was in heavy use, and a puddle of filthy water trickled under the door down the hallway toward the reception desk. Citizens arriving to take care of police business (the station was still open) had to navigate a shouting throng of drunken revelry and running children, and make their reports to a smiling man holding a can of beer.

Alcohol loosened the atmosphere. The formal introductions of our arrival were replaced by casual gestures of shared inebriation. People began walking from table to table, toasting one another as groups and individuals, collapsing the table-organized hierarchies of clientage into an egalitarian space of *communitas*. I joined one such patrol, and ended up seated next to a man who introduced himself as an auto mechanic from up the street. We fell into conversation, and he narrated our surroundings through the social categories that organized the local world. Befitting his vocation, his reflections began with the cars parked around us on the street. The stubby blue work trucks, he said, are driven by "little old hundred-names" (*xiao laobaixing*), the working class, who depend on them for their livelihood. They bring their car into the shop with the urgency of life itself. Sedans, by contrast, like the one I had arrived in with Ahe, are vehicles of the middle class. They are more easygoing; it's no big deal for their owners to lose a car for a few weeks. And then there are cars like that, he said, gesturing to a black Mercedes-Benz nearby. Those are driven by "the boss." His voice lowered to a conspiratorial whisper, and he raised one hand to mark off the channel of communication connecting his lips to my ear. "Sometimes," he said, "a boss from the 'Black Society' [*hei shehui*—i.e., the mafia]." I looked at the owner of the car in question, sitting as the host of another table. He was a big, well-oiled man, accompanied by a remarkably attractive woman who lit his cigarettes. We had been introduced as I arrived. According to his business card, he was the head of a chapter in the Police Friends' Association.

A World of *Yuanfen* (Fated Relationships)

Ethnographic fieldwork involves movement through a world. An individual fieldworker's trajectory combines elements of contingency with forms of institutional determination. Ethnographic writing, impelled by its genred aspiration to describe a world, pushes the institutional dimensions of the journey into the foreground. This sleight of hand, however, reverses the relative primacy that contingency holds in the actual fieldwork process. Studying Taiwanese police required navigating a social environment of overwhelming complexity. Under such complicated conditions, my consciousness became attuned to a register of contingency that my interlocutors figured in a language of fate. This discourse was exemplified by something they called *yuanfen*, "fated relationships." *Yuanfen* came to me as an almost magical word: a reflexive label that could emerge in the course of a developing relationship to mark its passage across a qualitative threshold of intimate solidarity. To discover *yuanfen* with another person was to recognize that the apparent contingency of your situated encounter was not random, but rather a sign of higher-level cosmic intention. My attendance at the banquet was, in retrospect, a sign that I belonged there.

The etymological meaning of the term combines the "dependence" (*yuan*) in the Buddhist concept of "dependent arising" (*yuanqi*) with the quantum "allotment" (*fen*) through which shares in corporate bodies, like families and business corporations, are figured. *Yuanfen* is a quantum of mutuality, a destined interdependence, a solidarity solidified by cosmic powers that transcend strictly rational accounting (Hsu and Hwang 2016). My movement through the social world of the police turned so systematically on *yuanfen* that it was impossible to explain any other reason for what happened to me. I was, as every invocation of *yuanfen* reminded me, dependent on fate.

Movement through policed space is organized by police powers. Few things display these powers more concretely than arrest and custody—the special authority police have to hold and move people against their will. Navigating the penumbra of sociability that surrounds and suffuses the work of professional coercion is an enterprise of managing tension. One of the insights I gained from my fieldwork was learning how people used historical and cultural resources— idioms of friendship and fate, for example—to manage these tensions. As I gained access to the substation and began to circulate more and more widely through its routine operations, I began to perceive the process of moving and being moved through its orbit as "policing" itself, organized in a systematic way by various idioms of virtue, ethics, and care.

Invocation of *yuanfen*, for example, drew on a vaguely traditional, explicitly theological register of common sense to endow institutionally inconvenient (or worse) situations with the ostensible legitimacy of a transcendent order. Such vernacular metaphysics play a significant role in the overall organization of policed order. It was not just me; *everyone* in Taiwan depended, to some degree, on fate to help navigate the policed aspects of daily life. Which is to say, the "order" maintained by the police institution was *defined* in part by this vaguely traditional, explicitly theological, substantively historical common sense. The people who attended the banquet all belonged there. Fate brought them together. Their community was cosmically ordained.

The formal pretext of the banquet was Zhongqiu Jie, the Mid-Autumn Festival. This is a state-approved "traditional" holiday that has been celebrated in a recognizably consistent form since the Tang dynasty. Zhongqiu Jie is conventionally understood, in the contemporary Republic of China, as a time for family. It is set aside to convene, reflect upon, and consolidate the institutions of intimate solidarity that underwrite the structure of everyday life. The stereotypical activity of this festival is gathering the "whole family" (*quanjia*) for a barbecue outside under the harvest moon. The cosmic foundations of intimate order are renewed as a reflection of the fullness of the moon above in the wholeness of the family below. The police banquet borrowed this customary pretext for a family dinner and repurposed it as a rationale for bringing the station's jurisdiction together in a collective gesture of financial tribute.

It was a ritual event, consistent with Victor Turner's (1967) model of "ritual process." That is, the gathering operated as a cultural technology for managing the movement of people across boundaries that, in normal times, defined the status distinctions of the constituted social structure. This movement is achieved by staging a theatrical moment of disorder as a means of disaggregating, then recomposing, the conventional social order. In this case, the central "liminal" phase involved inverting conventional normative expectations of police decorum. The police got drunk in public, allowed their facility to become slovenly, and their unit to be overrun by a company of civilians with reputed gangsters in prominent positions. This momentary rupture of conventional norms softened the constraints that defined social difference, facilitating readjustments that could establish new relationships (as well as consolidate old ones). In the drunken euphoria at the banquet's core, its moment of raw *communitas*, the gathered crowd mixed and mingled with relative freedom, micromanaging the free creation of new relationships through the ritual etiquette of toasting and introductions. The instituted order that reaggregated as people sobered up the next morning was structurally identical to the one that disaggregated the night before, except that certain individuals had changed their positions in the social field. In this case, the group of ritually transformed individuals included myself, a hungover ethnographer, who had moved from the anonymous space of the general public into the first ring of familiarity with a neighborhood police station.

As I reflected on the unexpected wildness of the party, I was intrigued by the application of a ritual formula for kindred reunion to police business. This seemed to push the figurative language of tradition across an important modern boundary: the line that prevents the principled autonomy of state power from collapsing into the divisive solidarities of intimate partiality. What legitimate business could a police station possibly have renewing its intimate wholeness with a collection of parochial elites? This question led me back to the station.[1]

The following week, I made an appointment to visit Ahe on duty. He met me at the door of the station and led me to a long low table in the corner of the main case-processing room. He then brought over his commanding officer, who sat with us while Ahe made tea. The three of us chatted about the banquet, how I knew Ahe, and my interest in Taiwan. The lieutenant soon had to return to the stack of paperwork sitting on his desk at the far corner of the room, but he excused himself politely by welcoming me to drop by anytime. Several other patrolmen I recognized from the party were working at other desks in the room.

They came over one by one, greeted me, sat down and shared tea or cigarettes, then excused themselves and went back about their business. After a while, Ahe himself left to take care of business outside the station. He indicated I could sit and watch TV there as long as I liked. I sat for a while, watching the business of a police station: a half dozen men writing quietly amid a haze of tobacco smoke and the drone of television news. It was a scene far removed from the images of action and adventure popularly associated with police work.

My curiosity about the police party and the social dimension of policing that it seemed to expose continued. I took at face value the lieutenant's formulaic statement that I was always welcome, and began to visit the station regularly. After my initial visits I stopped making appointments and simply dropped by. There was invariably somebody on duty who recognized me from an earlier visit. And I would always end up at the tea table, watching television and chatting with other people sitting there. As it turned out, the table was intended for people like me. A sign hanging from the ceiling designated it as the station's official "reception area" (*jiedaiqu*). This sign marked the table as the focal point of an absorptive arena through which a broad spectrum of the station's activity was routed. People waiting on bureaucratic procedures sat there, as did personal visitors waiting to speak with individual policemen. Groggy patrolmen stumbling downstairs from their sleeping quarters sat there to button up their uniforms and smoke the day's first cigarette. Members of the diverse entourages that accompanied people to police-mediated negotiation held in the station would sit there when their counsel was not needed. Relatively civil lawbreakers—people entangled in the myriad problems of licensing and registration that provide the bulk of Taiwanese substation business—were invited to pull up a chair and have a cup of tea while they waited on the outcome of a case in process. Occasionally, people on their way to jail sat there too, despondently sharing in the tea-drinking formalities as they waited for transport to arrive.

Host Power (*Zhuquan*)

My fieldwork in the station thus began by paying attention to what was going on at the tea table. The station's kettle provided a physical medium through which the work of sociality was materialized in the formal etiquette of sharing tea. To be sure, this was a "formality" so casual and ordinary that it operated almost beneath the level of conscious reflection. In Taiwan, where unboiled water is considered a health risk, drinking tea is the conventional way to stay hydrated. I don't think it is an exaggeration to say that, for the Taiwanese, sharing tea is as familiar as drinking water. The difference between tea and water, however, is that tea is "cooked" rather than raw. Socioculturally speaking, this is a difference that makes all the difference; for cultural beings, the social dimensions of sharing are at least as important as the physical properties of the thing being shared. Moreover, there is *technology* involved in drinking tea—kettles and pots and cups and trays and so on. These technical instruments and the skills involved in using them are the basis for a consciously cultivated aesthetic through which people perform the quality of their character as social beings—*gongfu cha*, "skilled tea." You can, according to the Taiwanese police, learn a lot about individuals from the way they drink tea. I sat through many disquisitions on the "way of tea" (*cha dao*) as a mode of self-cultivation (and one especially suited to police life).

The formality of this mode of cultivation is worth studying. It embodies an ideal of the values at stake in proper host-guest relations. There is an extensive literature on "guest ritual" in China, in part because it supplied the formal idiom through which diplomatic relations were conducted in Imperial times (Hevia 1995; L. Liu 2004). Indeed, the complement to guest ritual, "host power" or *zhuquan*, became the modern Chinese word for sovereignty.[2] The making of worlds is entangled with the meaning of words; politics has a poetic dimension. The Weberian approach to understanding this, known as historical sociology, looks at how regionally distinctive versions of modernity come into being as the development of institutions—in this case, the police—finds a historical grounding through "elective affinity" with the cultural sensibilities that precede those institutions (Eisenstadt 2000; K.-H. Chen 2010). Taking this approach, I argue that the host-guest dynamics that are materialized through drinking tea in a police station manifest, at the microcosmic level of casual relationship-work, an understanding of "the political" derived from the larger historical processes through which the constitution of modern statehood in China has unfolded on the basis of preexisting cosmology and tradition.

Drinking tea in a police station is intrinsically political. It is, I will argue, an instance of what Hannah Arendt (1958) called a "space of appearances." The material aspects of boiling and steeping and pouring tea provide a medium of visibility that people use to enact sociality through "ritual appearances" (*limao*— the term is used as the standard translation for "politeness"). In the police station, the ritual gestures embedded in the movement of tea around the table were used to maintain surface decorum over what were sometimes deeply conflicted relationships. People who were being subjected to police-administered punishments, ranging from paying fines to going to jail, were routinely invited to drink tea with the processing officer as they waited. In its ordering intent, such gestures of superficial politeness were aligned with the functional purpose of police station itself as a node of ordering force. The performative dimension of ritual formality operates through a kind of moral force, which although superficial is nonetheless

constitutive of social order (Seligman and Weller 2012). The etymological resonance of the English terms polite/police is no coincidence, nor is the parallel
resonance in Chinese between *limao* and *li*. Modern ideals of politeness, police,
and "polished" behavior come from the same historical source. It was only in the
modern period that new ideas about the autonomous nature of state sovereignty
generated an idea of police powers as an objective force categorically distinct
from inner subjective orientations to politeness and the aesthetics of polished
decorum (Elias [1939] 2012; Brodeur 2010; Silver 1967).

The labor of keeping an ethnographic notebook anchored in a situation of
frequent ritualistic tea drinking attuned me to the sociocultural poetics of guest
ritual. I began to notice this poetics at work in other settings as well. The relational idiom between host and guest provided a general formula for the performance of civil power. Host and guest were mutually constitutive categories,
inherently dialectical identities. A host hosted by relation to those who received
and consumed his or her tea, and thereby accepted the positioned identity of
guest. At the station house tea table, host power could be performed by anyone
who brewed and served. This position could be occupied by a number of different people, which included beyond the resident policemen a group of nonpolice
persons known in the station as "friends of the station" (see below). There were
requirements for hosting, of course; not just anyone could take up the kettle of
station house "sovereignty." So, how did one qualify for the role? In my notes, I
distinguished three requirements. The first was obvious: one had to have something to give one's guests. You can't serve tea without tea. Policemen kept bags
of tea in their equipment lockers, sometimes dozens of bags, as tea was a stock
item in the gift economy that circulated through their social world.[3] But just as a
gift is constituted as such by its acceptance, one could not successfully play host
without recognition by one's guests, manifest as they received the offered cup.
This second requirement—recognition—carried a set of normative expectations, which imposed the third and most institutionally significant requirement
for playing host in a police station.

This final normative expectation revolved around the host's responsibility
for managing conversation around the table. To play the host well depended on
one's capacity to make a positive *representation* of one's guests in their relations
to one another. Introductions were very important. Which meant one had to
possess local knowledge adequate to provide auspicious narrative introductions
between any unacquainted people sharing your tea. It was this display of caring
social mastery that authenticated the true host as an authentic representative
of the place where the tea was served. The knowledge associated with this version of host power is an intrinsically particularistic, *intimate* form of knowledge.
This was as true in the police station as it was in a family home. The capacity to

perform intimate familiarity with everyone who can enter a given space with the legitimate expectation of being hosted there is a core element of the skills required to play the host. Serving a police station's tea, in other words, requires a certain depth of historical engagement with the community under its jurisdiction.

After I had spent some time hanging out with police, I was occasionally asked to make tea. This was more difficult than it appeared. Attention to the physical properties of tea had to be combined with attention to the social properties of the assembled group of tea drinkers. The physical side of things consisted of bringing a large kettle of water to a boil, packing a small clay teapot full of tea leaves, rinsing and warming the leaves with boiling water, then brewing successive "steeps" of tea in the teapot and straining them out into a serving pitcher at the point of maximum fragrance (*xiang*) prior to bitterness (*ku*). When the serving pitcher contained enough for all present, small cups were poured and presented all around, in order of most-important guest to least-important guest. Meanwhile, steeping continued indefinitely, repacking the pot with fresh leaves as the flavor began to diminish. The quality of the host's character is revealed by a capacity to ensure that every individual member of the group always has a cup of hot, properly steeped tea. This involves calibrating production to differential rates of consumption in a socio-material assemblage of time, heat, and sociality—an acquired skill I found roughly as difficult as learning how to drive a car.

The work of hosting is not done for nothing. It is a means of producing good relationships. Next to my notes on the three requirements to play host are notes on the two dimensions of its social productivity. Again, these were not unique to tea-mediated interaction. They were basic conventions of social interaction, which just happened to be conveniently tangible when expressed through the medium of tea. The first was the production of hierarchies, the "vertical" dimension of the host-guest hierarchy. This was dramatized by attentively supplying and respectfully receiving, or politely speaking and respectfully listening. The second dimension, contrasted with this overt hierarchy, was the egalitarian "horizontal" intra-guest dynamics involved in drinking from the same teapot under the auspices of a shared host.

"Friends of the Station" (*Paichusuo de Haopengyou*)

The host-guest idiom provides a robust analogy for understanding the social dimensions of Taiwanese policing more generally. Police are expected to use the hierarchical leverage of their situated host-power/sovereignty to cultivate and guarantee bonds of lateral trust within the community under their jurisdiction.

As an ideal type, this is the modern "idea of police" itself, true not just in Taiwan but as a general principle. However, the cultural particularity of customary etiquette in Taiwan provides a resource for engaging with this ideal in a distinctive way—for example, drinking tea or holding neighborhood parties.

Indeed, the tea table and the banquet tables were different arenas for doing the same work, two instantiations of the same ritual frame used to manage the productive potentials of the interface connecting "vertical" trust in higher authority to a "horizontal" trust afforded by individuals' shared deference to common authority. The difference between ordinary/everyday tea drinking and occasional/grand banqueting was only a matter of scale. Most concretely, the banquet had more than one table. The individual tables at the banquet functioned *exactly* like the station's tea table. The difference came as their plurality was incorporated into a singular order by a meta-level hosting process through which they were incorporated under the authority of a single common host. This kind of political structure has been described by many ethnographers of Chinese-speaking communities. Its most famous or canonical description is Fei Xiaotong's "differential mode of association." This compares the scalar incorporation of plurality within sovereignty to the concentric rings that spread out from a power source analogized to a rock dropped into a body of water ([1947] 1992; the metaphor is from a Confucian discussion of the concept of *lun*, "human/normative order").

The difference in scale between the station's individual tea table and its multitable banquet was a quantitative difference with a qualitative effect. The banquet, by gathering dozens of small hosts under the aegis of a single big host, elevated the reputation of its big host above the realm of concrete interpersonal connections involved in personal relationships, and endowed it with a more abstract, generalized authority. The banquet revealed the police station as a regional power, aggregated from the multitude of individual relationships coordinated by its subsidiary table hosts cum station guests. This abstract, regional power was implicit within the gathered crowd, a body of people engaged in the full spectrum of enterprises conducted in immediate proximity to police institutions. The banquet made the implicit power of the neighborhood police station explicit. It concentrated a diffuse enduring network into a concrete congregation assembled, for a brief moment, in the same place, at the same time, for the same purpose. They came to know themselves as a group reflecting, in alcoholic effervescence, upon their common relationship by relation to the host that gathered them: the lieutenant in charge of the local police station.

As mentioned, the provision of introductions makes a host a sort of guarantor for relationships that develop between his or her guests. This enables a transitive quality to the modality of trust founded on the idiom of host power, which allows trust to scale up or down according to the dictates of circumstance. The capacity of places like Taiwan and China to organize expansive and efficient economic enterprises with little to no support from formal institutions like banks or courts is attributed to the existence of a distinctive modality of trust or "social capital" associated with *guanxi* networks (Winn 1994a, 1994b). The enforcement of such quasi-contractual relationships through personal connections is at the core of Taiwanese policing, a practice rationalized by the ethics of *ganqing* (discussed below).

In the context of police station sociality, everyday ritual propriety projects trust through social networks in a triadic configuration. The horizontal relationship between two people in a common guest position is linked to the vertical relationship they have with their shared host. This leaves the vertical matchmaker forever implicated in the match. Threads of particularistic guarantee spun by hosted introductions remain active at second- and third-order connections within the networks that propagate through new introductions made possible by old introductions. Thus, for example, Ahe remained something like my original sponsor in all the relationships I subsequently formed within the world of the police station. This was not changed by the fact that he transferred to a different station a few months following the banquet, after which I seldom saw him in person. For years afterward, whenever questions arose about what I was doing somewhere, or whether I could be trusted, my references would be checked. It would occasionally become evident that Ahe was still in the loop and on the hook for any confidences his colleagues might invest in me.[4]

I was not the only civilian who hung out at the police station. It had an established cohort of regular visitors. Some, like retired taxi driver Old Chen, were simply old men with nothing to do. They treated the police station like a temple yard or park bench, a place to bide their time. When I asked Old Chen why he spent his days at the station, he replied, "I don't like to sit at home watching TV. If you go out drinking, you have to drink. If you go out gambling, you have to gamble. Not here. This place is open twenty-four hours a day, and there's always someone to talk to, or something interesting going on." It was true. Taiwan's local police stations are designed as social venues capacious enough to accommodate the social processes involved in the routine management of neighborhood affairs. This leaves plenty of space for recreational or ethnographic activity. For someone as disinterested as Old Chen, the station house tea table provided a stimulating social arena in which to keep up on gossip and enjoy the spectacle of other people's problems. And, by virtue of being both disinterested and wise in the ways of this world, Chen could manage his presence there without being conscripted into the sphere of *yingchou*, "obligatory reciprocity," that made police sociality so complicated.

Most of the people who hung out in the police station were not disinterested observers. They were active participants in arrangements of ambiguous legality that dominated the city's political economy.[5] Their motivations for investing their leisure time in the social work of police reception were not purely recreational. There were interests at play in the cultivation of *guanxi* around the tea table, saturating the "ritual appearances" operating there with sticky, entangling implications in all kinds of trouble. The station's reception area was an absorptive drain for things that passed through the police station without any formal place. As a platform for building relationships, the tea table supplied the formal nucleus of an informal sphere built into the architecture of the police station itself, a ritually structured interface between the police power and the wider community. Sitting there for any length of time pulled one inexorably into the practical side of extralegal policing.

After a month of regular visiting, I knew the thirty-odd patrolmen who lived at the station on a first-name basis and had begun to develop personal friendships with a few of them. To be sure, not everyone in the station liked me. There were a few sadistic individuals I learned to dread, and others who treated my proximity as pure liability. But tolerance for tension was built into the institution, and I was a relatively benign presence by comparison to a spectrum of powers chronically and instrumentally involved in the course of routine police business. Moreover, other aspects of my research outside the station brought me into contact with people at higher levels of the bureaucratic system, making me a potentially useful connection for substation patrolmen. Later, I got a job teaching at Central Police University, the police officers' school. This formally affiliated me with upper management, and profoundly legitimated my presence in the station. All in all, over time, my participation in the little rituals of mundane socializing brought me, slowly but surely, through the informal portal into the station's general operations. Eventually my new status became evident in the term of reference by which I was introduced to people I hadn't previously met. I ceased being "a friend of Ahe" and became a "friend of the station" (*paichusuo de haopengyou*).

Falling into the Ocean (*Xia Hai*)

"Friend of the station" was a conventional term police used to refer to people involved in their everyday working routines who were neither members of the state bureaucracy nor objects of police procedure. The station had many friends. Not all of them warranted equal respect. Akim and I defined the opposite ends of the spectrum. I was nobody, a random foreigner. Akim was an esteemed elder member of the community who had retired wealthy from a construction business and commanded one of the neighborhood's volunteer civil defense teams. He was frequently called upon by police to help manage their informal affairs. He owned a basement apartment near the police station and had converted one of its rooms into a karaoke parlor where policemen sometimes spent their evenings in wine and song. He was a kind of larger-than-life figure, but also quite friendly. A few months after I began hanging out at the station, he decided to take me under his wing.

He wandered into the reception area one night with a bottle of whiskey in a paper bag and invited me to share it with him. Drinking inside the station was technically forbidden, but rules are made to be broken. Indeed, rules against alcohol consumption among the police seemed to function primarily as vehicles for building intimacy through shared violation.[6] Akim and I discreetly finished the bottle, and for the rest of the night our drunkenness provided a source of jokes around the tea table.

The next day Akim showed up again, already well into his cups. To the amusement of the patrolmen I was chatting with, he declared that he had only come by the station to pick me up and take me to the "tea table" up the street. The Taiwanese term *the-to-a* "tea table" is a euphemism for a hostess bar. Sure enough, he put me on the back of his motorcycle, and we drove to a hotel a few blocks away. I knew the hotel from the police station's routine business as a site of frequent prostitution arrests, so I was not surprised that the second floor was decked out in velvet and chrome, the kind of place where groups of men rent private rooms equipped with private waitresses. I was somewhat surprised, however, when I entered the room to which Akim led me and found a group of men that included several of the station's patrolmen, accompanied by their second-in-command (wearing a leather jacket over his uniform), engaged in a raucous party with a room full of naked and partially clothed women.

We joined the group. The men were all police and "friends of the station" familiar from the station house tea table, some of whom, it was now revealed, owned the establishment in which we were drinking. They began instructing me in protocols for interacting with their hostesses. I was averse to sexual contact, and my reticence seemed to irritate the sergeant. After a while he directed all the women in the room to attack me in a concerted mass and strip me naked. This was unpleasant. In an environment where social standing is acknowledged through displays of "face," it was a violent insult, a demonstration of coercive power in which I was pulled from my chair and forcibly relocated from the community of men calling the shots into the space of women on display. I was completely taken aback, and tried to resist without losing composure, but without escalating to actual violence it proved impossible to prevent my humiliation before the audience of drunken policemen. After they let me recover, another friend of the station sitting next to me made some gestures at soothing my feelings, and the party continued.[7]

By the time I returned to the police station the next day, the event had become part of my identity. Police humor tended to be aggressive, and they jokingly named the event an act of "rape" (*qiangjian*). Ever afterward, patrolmen in the substation would find opportunities to refer to that particular hotel when talking to me by saying (mirthfully), "you know, the place where you got raped." In the immediate aftermath, the story circulated widely. I listened to it told repeatedly around the tea table, and I was called to confirm it with patrolmen and friends of the station who brought it up in other places. I eventually began to see the event as a sort of hazing or initiation, as I noticed how the story operated as a marker by which I was being consciously absorbed into the network of those privy to what happened behind the closed door of the hostess bar.

Intimacy is not necessarily friendly. The coercive aspects of police work bring this animus into the foreground. Modern police powers are authorized to operate in a clinical space of exception to certain conventional norms. Just as doctors hold a special license to violate normal expectations of bodily dignity, police hold a license to violate the ordinary boundaries of social autonomy. The act of enforcing a rule or command displaces the consent-based political ideal of self-determination with the overt imposition of an alien will. Liberal democracies suppress this fact under a legitimating ideology that figures law as the expression of an abstract "general will" and thereby transforms the heteronomy of police coercion into putative autonomy, through either the presumptive consent of an artificial "social contract" or the synthetic a priori of a natural law. If you don't want what you should—be it a legally ordered society or the attentions of a naked woman—police intervention to correct your error stands as a legitimately pro-social act.

This kind of ideological legitimation works most effectively at a distance—that is, in the public debates that maintain the institutional "mandate" of police powers (Manning 1997). More immediate experience, including ethnographic participant-observation, disrupts the conventional processes of abstraction that convert particular events into examples of general principles. Indeed, ethnographic methods depend in part on the dialectical tensions between estrangement and familiarity, tensions that register as data through the tangible shock that a neophyte outsider experiences through an unfamiliar encounter with another world (Keane 2003). Firsthand experience of a surgical incision or a contentious arrest can produce poignant experiential insight into the nature of norms and their exception.

The coercive qualities of policing reveal a stratum of heteronomy that lurks, always, just beneath the liberal pretension that civil sociality is properly constituted by consensual autonomy all the way down. Enmity and amity are equally intimate, and one is seldom found without the other. Perhaps the least friendly forms of intimacy are those found in institutions associated with criminal justice, which manufacture punitive suffering by exposing intimate details to legal scrutiny. By the nature of their work, policemen become attuned to social forces generated by the movement of knowledge across the membranes that separate distinct spheres of moral community. Indeed, the energy differentials maintained by these boundaries and released by their rupture provide the motive force driving most of the "disorder" that Taiwanese police are called to manage. As with any profession that works with dangerous forces, attention to self-preservation is fundamental to the job.

In this respect, as one might imagine, my presence as an outside observer inside the police world was not without tension. On the one hand, scholarship is considered a noble vocation in Taiwan; policemen were flattered to be chosen as an authoritative source by a foreign scholar interested in the relation between policing and the democratic transition. On the other hand, within the police station, journalists were regarded with disdain. The less scholarly my interests appeared, the more I looked like a journalist. A clear line in the ethnographic sand was laid down by one patrolman, who after engaging in a detailed discussion of the organization of graft, concluded by saying, "In the abstract, these are things everyone knows. It's no big deal. So long as they do not become attached to specific people and places, it's not a problem."

It was along those lines that the event at the hostess bar made sense as a mode of initiation into a more intimate sphere of police life. It was a way of introducing an outsider to the specificity of certain abstractions in such a way as to fuse my knowledge of those particular facts to *my* specific identity as a person. "Everyone knows" that police are simply men in uniform, susceptible to selfish desires. And "everyone knows" that police work is dirty work, situated in spaces of moral contradiction, unavoidably contaminated by the transgression it is asked to control. Nobody can be surprised that policemen were in a hostess bar. Indeed it is required they routinely inspect such establishments to ensure that they are not employing underage women or illegal immigrants. Nor is it especially unthinkable that, in the lead-up to the New Year's holiday, the owners might politely invite their local policemen to spend some time in the guest position. Nonetheless, the image of uniformed officers sitting with nude hostesses remains publicly scandalous, something capable of making significant problems for the individuals involved. Having entered a private space where policemen discarded their public face, I had been humiliated, forcibly stripped of the dignity to set my own boundaries. As gossip fixed the event into anecdotal form, it made any reference to that afternoon a reference, in the first place, to my presence. The focus on me in my naked embarrassment ameliorated the other specificity of the abstraction: policemen carousing in uniform. If that image was to circulate beyond the closed door of the private room we had shared, their clothing would have exposed them to more publicly consequential shame than everyone else's nakedness.

To conduct a long-term ethnography of policing is to learn to dwell in a world of coercive heteronomy,[8] to live in immediate personal contact with the limits of consent, and navigate the vast and unruly field of sociality that exists on the other side of that limit. Ethnographic theories of policing, following Peter Manning, have relied on Erving Goffman's front-stage/backstage distinction to make sense of this, showing how this marks a line of contradiction running right down the middle of the police institution. My experience has been that every backstage has its own backstage: there is no end to the work involved in staging performances so the right people get the right message. Social control involves situated performances directed to whatever audience is at hand, and every shift in the sociological context introduces another layer of tension between the hidden presuppositions and aspirational entailments of a given performance.

A Taiwanese discussant commenting on the story of my "rape" once characterized it as the moment when I "fell into the ocean" (*xiahai*). This is a euphemism sometimes used to describe acts that produce a permanent change in someone's reputation or status, things like a prostitute's first client or a gangster's first crime. That evening marked a movement in my ethnographic engagement with the police from the relatively controlled space inside their station house to the much more complicated environment outside. "Complication" (*fuza*) is another euphemism. Indeed, among my police interlocutors it was the standard euphemism for ending a conversation. To refer to a situation, a case, or an individual as "complicated" was to foreclose further discussion on the topic, with the implication that there was something dangerous about the knowledge at stake.

There is much to gain by clarifying complicated, dangerous knowledge. Analyzing the event in the hostess bar, for example, reveals something important about the role "host power" plays in the ways people move and are moved through policed space in Taiwan. My physical trajectory through space was determined by the figurative relationship connecting two "tea tables," the literal one in the police station and the euphemistic one in the hotel. Both were arenas for the same genre of social work, namely *yingchou*, or the labor of cultivating business *guanxi*. Both arenas were substantiated by the ritualized exchange of valued substances like food, drink, tobacco, or bodies. As a guest, I was not in a position to control myself. A guest cannot refuse hospitality without insulting the host, and thereby becoming alienated from the community constituted by that host's power. As mentioned, "host power," *zhuquan*, is the Chinese word for "sovereignty." The poetics of sovereignty made evident through my experience with Akim—that is, the way policed space is navigated through the concentric rings of "host power" that Fei Xiaotong described—reveal a cultural fact of practical significance in the organization of Taiwanese liberalism. The mode of popular sovereignty at issue in "democracy" (*minzhu*, literally "common people [as] host") is figured not in the liberal register of contracts, but through the idiom of host-guest relations.

The trajectory that took me from the police station to the hostess bar moved me as an object traveling through networks of exchange that linked the men who hosted me. I passed through a series of three distinct guest positions. I began in the good auspices of "the station" hosted by the neighborhood's *patria potestas* in the abstract. In the months since the banquet, my faithful performance of respectful clientage in the station's reception area allowed me to cultivate a modicum of agency in this position. But the station's table was but one node in a vast and pluralistic landscape of parochial powers. Democratic policing involves leaving the station house and going out into the wider, polyarchic world. My first sortie into this wider world came as Akim's guest, his host power transporting me to the hotel where I became the guest of the station sergeant. The transgressive element of the "rape" was also consistent with this logic. It was a response to my refusal to conform to etiquette and accept what was being offered by my host. Finally, it was the sergeant's position as host of the table that enabled him to command others to act against my will. And it was my position as his guest that made my clearly stated protests irrelevant to their enforcement of the host's command.

In its aftermath, the event took on the qualities of an initiation that changed my status in the community. As the story circulated openly through a closed network, it made it tangibly easier for members of that network to trust and include me in their complicated collective life. It opened the door of the station into the networked circulations of police power that stretched out from the station into the wider community. And it marked a moment of qualitative increase in my capacity to explore the complex world of Taiwanese policing. This informal inclusion in police life eventually allowed participant-observation of the broad spectrum of police work detailed in this book, including the aspects of station house routine beyond the reception room, patrol and incident handling, roadside inspections, household visits, routine investigations, and training exercises.

The form of practice that interested me most at the beginning of my police ethnography was patrol. Based on American pop-cultural representations of policing, like the show *COPS*, I assumed that patrol was the heart of the police function. Although inaccurate, my assumption had a historical pedigree. The movement of uniformed patrolmen through public space has supplied a defining, focal, iconic image for "the thing itself" of police power since 1829, when it was institutionalized as the primary mechanism by which the state would "prevent" crime. As I moved into the project of doing police ethnography, I was oriented by the goal of observing patrol, under the presumption that this was an institutionally definitive site of police action. Getting to go out on patrol took a long time. Only after about a year did patrolmen I had become familiar with begin to invite me to accompany them on patrol. I subsequently spent hundreds of hours trailing motorcycle patrolmen on my own motorcycle, and sitting in the backseat of the station's patrol car.

At first, this felt like a breakthrough; I had managed to access the canonical site of police action. If getting into the patrol car was an achievement, however, it was often beyond my capacity to stay in the patrol car long enough to return to the station at the end of a shift. As I discuss in detail in later chapters, Taiwanese police patrol was a social practice profoundly tangled into all manner of other business. It bore little relation to the experiences I have had on "ride-alongs" with American police. There seemed to be no institutional insulation separating the inside of the car from the outside, no way for me to remain aligned with a police mission categorically distinguished from the social world through which policemen traveled. I was a guest in the patrol car. And this was a transitive role. Wherever the police were guests, I was a guest of a guest, doubly bound to treat the host of my host with respect. This meant I was often unable to refuse invitations to leave the patrol car and engage in other activities. I found this frustrating at first. It seemed that my incapacity to control my own movement was keeping me from observing police work. I gradually changed my perspective to focus on the process of moving and being moved through policed space as the thing-itself to which I should direct my ethnographic attention. My incapacity to control my own movement through policed space *was* the police power at work.

Invitation

One night in 2003, I left the station on patrol with two policemen I counted among my friends. A couple of blocks from the station we were waved over by Atiao, an entrepreneur active in the social life of the station. He was sitting at a roadside café with a group of enormous men I hadn't seen before. When the car stopped they all rushed over, drunk and ebullient. Atiao jumped into the front seat, and three of the burly strangers piled into the back, one of them sitting on my lap. Atiao was ecstatic. He had been coaching an amateur baseball team that had just won its league tournament, bringing him a gambling windfall. One of his coaching innovations had been hiring semipro players to masquerade as amateurs. He was now taking these ringers out to celebrate. The patrolmen drove the packed car to a hostess bar across town, far out of their station's jurisdiction. Atiao would not hear any refusal of his hospitality on that special occasion, and as the baseball players exited the car, they carried me with them. We rented an enormous room and began to drink. Other people showed up, and the party became raucous. I ended up sitting next to a man who introduced himself as a criminal detective from the precinct office, who began asking me questions about Acai, a mutual acquaintance of ours who worked in the station.

That was not a happy topic. Acai was in serious trouble. His wife had been a low-level bookie in a numbers racket known as "Everybody's Happy" (Dajiale) when a bet she took hit the jackpot. The higher-level bookie with whom she placed her bets absconded with the winnings. She was more honorable than he, and paid off the win with borrowed money. To raise the money she leveraged the family's social network to its limit, and made up the difference with a high-interest loan from an underground bank. As these debts began to come due, Acai's family had been all but destroyed. His wife fell into a suicidal depression, they officially divorced, and she went into hiding. The detective expressed sympathy for Acai, saying it was a terrible situation, adding ominously that he (the detective) was also a "victim" of the disaster. I didn't say much. I knew things it would have been impolitic to mention.

Drunkenness made the hired athletes abusive to their female attendants. Animosity escalated until one of them struck the woman sitting next to him, knocking her to the floor. The lights came up abruptly, and the room flooded with in-house security. In a cloud of tension and Atiao's money changing hands, our group was escorted to the sidewalk. There were about twenty of us standing there, which meant multiple taxis would be required to take us to the next bar. As people sorted out, I was helped into a taxi with three men who had been sitting on the other side of the detective. One of them, a fat muscular older man, had been introduced to me as Big Brother Li. The other two, who had not been introduced, seemed to be his subordinates. I found myself in the backseat sandwiched between Brother Li and one of his subordinates, while the other sat shotgun looking back at me with a blank expression.

As we pulled away from the hostess bar, our taxi did not follow the others toward Taipei's red-light district. It turned the other way and began driving toward an industrial wasteland that marked the outer limit of the greater Taipei urban area. I began to get scared. We drove in silence. The streetlights ended. The landscape outside the window was almost pitch black, temporary factories built of corrugated steel around the network of cement ditches that drain the mountains of the Taipei Basin into the Danshui River. The main channel was a huge canal capable of moving typhoons into the ocean. It was haunted by the memory of bodies dumped there, most notoriously that of Bai Xiaoyan, a celebrity's daughter kidnapped and murdered with great spectacle in 1997. A few years later Liao Xueguang, a self-styled anti-mafia crusader newly elected to the national legislature, was taken from his bed at gunpoint one night and left locked inside a dog cage up that road. Driving people up into those mountains was a conventional way to send a message. The silence in the taxi was oppressive, but I had no idea what to say. Then Brother Li reached over and took my hand, held it gently in both of his, and began whispering in Taiwanese into my ear. I couldn't understand what he was saying.

It was terrifying. But, at the same time, I felt some confidence that I couldn't be treated badly with complete impunity. The network that delivered me to Brother Li would be capable of extracting me if the situation got ugly. I had a phone in my pocket with enough numbers stored on it to find somebody with connections to somebody who could call in a favor with Brother Li. I endured in anxious silence, hoping not to escalate the situation into an embarrassing set of phone calls that might lead to the location of Acai's wife becoming an explicit question (she was hiding in my apartment). I said nothing, let Brother Li hold my hand and speak his piece, and waited. He fell silent again. Then the car turned a corner, and streetlights appeared ahead. We were driving back toward the inhabited area of the city. Brother Li suddenly snarled in Chinese, "Why are you holding my hand, you fucking faggot!" and dropped my hand. His subordinates laughed. We arrived at a tavern, and the ride was over. I saw them to the door, excused myself, and went off to find a different taxi back to the police station.

Police Power, Local Counterpower, and Republican Virtue

Acai's family eventually paid off their debts and returned to normal life, their reputation as trustworthy human beings restored by the lengths to which they had gone to avoid default. My ride in the dark fit into the trajectory of that problem as a conventional technique used to circulate a message of mutual responsibility through the social networks implicated in a given situation (cf. Martin 2017). Such is the system of enforcement that secures the informal credit that capitalizes so much of Taiwan's economy. Such is the chain of custody that moves people from the back of a police car into the hands of a debt collector.

Did my ethnographic passage through this fraught space illuminate something that can legitimately be called "policing"? The answer to this question turns, obviously, on the way we define the category. Brodeur's (2010) definition of policing identifies it with any legitimate use of exceptional powers. That is, for Brodeur, policing is the space in which powers normally denied to most people are authorized for use by specific agents for specific purposes under specific circumstances. By this definition, a policeman making an arrest is "policing" because the act of physically seizing and restraining someone is a power denied to most people under most circumstances. By this definition, a father spanking a child is also "policing" in a literal sense, because of the way that form of physical discipline is generally denied to nonparents. This is a definition of policing covering an expansive, eclectic, and internally contradictory collection of activities. The interesting thing, for Brodeur, is the way this pluralistic assemblage of exceptional powers falls into historically routinized patterns. My ethnographic experience illuminates one such historical pattern, generated by a process of democratization following a century of autocracy.

It would be a stretch to claim that the things I described in this chapter enjoyed positive legitimacy in the eyes of Taiwan's general public. That is not my claim. The legitimacy involved in the policed world I describe was not active but *passive*, constituted by the tolerance for a "settled situation" most people are willing to accept without resistance. The legitimacy of the relationships I describe between (for example) gangsters and police in Taiwan is comparable to the legitimacy of the racial inequalities involved in American policing. Polite society expresses shock and dismay when confronted by the unvarnished reality of status quo inequalities. But the perspective of polite society is a point of view situated in a position that carries an overwhelming structural preference for reactionary ignorance over the revolutionary implications of taking an ethical stand against the structural violence of the status quo. The association of police work with corrosive moral ambiguity arises from the incompatibility of police agency with the conventional habits of bourgeois illusion. To move through the policed world is to come face to face with institutional forces legitimated by silent acquiescence rather than positive rationale.

Nonetheless, policed order is still a fundamentally *meaningful* order. The world I passed through in the course of my ethnography cohered as a loose assemblage of divergent powers practically integrated through the idiom of *zhuquan*, "host power." That was the mode of power that moved me from the police banquet into the police station, from the police station into a police car, and, finally into the gangsters' taxi. Host power, in other words, is one of the structuring idioms for the policed order of the world I describe in this book.

To observe policing from the vantage point of someone carried along currents of informal activity that spin and swirl around its formal operations generates a data set different from conventional studies of police. The analysis of policing I develop in this book emphasizes the broad contextual dynamics through which circuits of police power find their social ground. I describe policing as a kind of movement within a social world, a reactionary reflex *of* that world against transgression of its largely unstated rules (cf. Martin 2018). This leads me to a rather critical perspective on the conventional obsession of policing research with patrol. It is more important to understand the cultural idioms of power that structure human movement through policed space than it is to study the way police move through physical space (see chapter 3 for detail).

Conventionally speaking, jurisdiction refers to the "scope of a legal institution's power vis-à-vis other institutions in the system to which it belongs" (Richland 2013, 211). From this perspective, the jurisdiction of a police agent or institution consists in what the agent or institution is legally authorized and bureaucratically required to do. In this chapter, we have seen jurisdictional dynamics manifest as the broad structural background defining the relationship between the *paichusuo* and the neighborhood it serves. The banquet was a party held for a group of people whose political-economic interests were somehow implicated in the records held by that particular police station. But beyond that baseline parameter, the dynamics of the banquet, and everything that followed from it, were structured by forms of power completely invisible to a strictly bureaucratic accounting of jurisdiction.

"Waving . . . the seemingly pre-theoretical wand of 'jurisdiction' . . . instantly sorts governance processes, knowledges and powers into their proper slots as if by magic" (Valverde 2008, 6). This is a misleading impression; the field of governmentality is more complicated than a bureaucratic diagram. What happens in and around a police station is an effect of multiple causes. Police business is overdetermined. To understand the full panoply of forces operating through a bureaucratic system, it is necessary to study the long arc of its historical formation. The next chapter reviews the history of modern police in Taiwan, showing how the *paichusuo* was instituted as a mechanism for cultivating qualities of civic virtue. These qualities have been defined in various ways by the different regimes that have ruled modern Taiwan. In the democratic era, I argue, the jurisdictional focus of neighborhood policing has become grounded in virtues exemplified by the elite figures who "speak sentiment" in the course of police business. It is this mode of civic virtue that upholds and renews shared confidence that the conflict and chaos of ordinary life are contained within bounds of a collective prior commitment to peaceful coexistence. In other words, it is the virtues of *qing* rather than the force of law that secure the peaceful but conflicted sociality of agonistic pluralism, keeping it from degenerating into the zero-sum antagonisms of political warfare (Mouffe 2009).

2

THE *PAICHUSUO* AND THE JURISDICTION OF *QING*

While patrol forms the background of American policing, the *paichusuo* is the backbone of Taiwanese policing.

(Cao, Huang, and Sun 2014, 85)

The *paichusuo* (literally a "dispatch post," generally translated as "substation") is an organizational unit in Taiwan's policing system one bureaucratic step above the *qinqu* assigned to an individual patrol officer. The *qinqu* (literally an "area of responsibility," conventionally translated as a "beat") is the elementary unit of police jurisdiction in Taiwan and has been since 1945 when the Republic of China assumed operational control of its policing system. A single police beat consists of a territorially contiguous group of three to four hundred households, whose records are all maintained by an individual patrolman. These records are part of the *hukou* (also called *huji*). The *hukou*—literally "doors and mouths"—is a registry system (Kuo and Chen 2016; Lin and Tseng 2014; von Senger 2009; F.-l. Wang 2005; Wang F.-c. 2005). A police textbook explains the terminology as follows: "The *hu* is a collective unit, referring to a family or other group that lives and/or manages its common affairs under a single person of authority. *Kou* refers to the population. *Kou* is considered a neutral mathematical term: every natural individual, without regard to gender, is counted as one *kou*. *Hu* are constituted of *kou*. All *hu* contain *kou*, and every *kou* must belong to a *hu*" (Yang 1993, 1). In principle, every one of Taiwan's twenty-three million residents is registered in one and only one police beat, and thereby made the personal responsibility of an individual policeman. The population does not come to the attention of the police as individuals, however, but rather as members of *hu* groupings. This collectivist approach to surveillance, where people are made legible to the state as members of organized groups, is a defining feature of the *hukou* and its associated policing practices. "In sharp contrast [to the individualism embodied by Western system of state identification] the *hukou* system was oriented towards the registration of families" (Torpey 1997, 858).

At the time of my fieldwork, *hukou* records were kept by substation policemen in paper form, organized in color-coded binders stored in their lockers. These lockers were in the substation's main case-processing room, a line of steel cabinets holding the official documents for roughly forty thousand people living in the immediate neighborhood. Where the *qinqu* is the elementary unit of police jurisdiction, the conduct of police work relies on the *paichusuo* as its fundamental operational node. In addition to keeping the neighborhood's papers in order, the substation held a residential barracks where its thirty-odd patrolmen slept, a cafeteria where they ate, and all the equipment they depended on for their working routines.

Most of Taiwan's police serve in *paichusuo* like this. They are home base for the "administrative police" (*xingzheng jingcha*) who work in continuous and direct contact with the general population. The majority of substation police are noncommissioned personnel holding the lowest rank (*yuanjing*). Taiwan differentiates police rank-and-file from commissioned officers as separate career tracks. The line officers in a *paichusuo* take their orders from a lieutenant assigned as station chief (*suozhang*), who depends on two or three noncommissioned sergeants to ensure his directives are followed. Substation patrolmen work outside the *paichusuo* only a few hours each day. They bring any business they can't dispose of in the street back to the *paichusuo* for further processing, and deliver their completed reports to the station chief's desk to be filed under the lieutenant's imprimatur. The *paichusuo* is the front line of Taiwan's policing system. It takes care of everyday policing routines. Anytime substation policemen encounter a situation exceeding the humble endowments of their station, they must rely on assistance from the much larger and better-equipped precinct office immediately above the *paichusuo* in the bureaucratic hierarchy (i.e., the *fenju*). Notably, these outsourced specializations include everything associated with the drama of fighting crime. The routines of ordinary substation policing are handled without involvement of "detectives" (*zhencha*), "criminal police" (*xingshi jingcha*), or "judicial police" (*sifa jingcha*).

The institutional form of the *paichusuo* comes from Japan. The term itself was coined in 1881. This was ten years after the Meiji government initiated its first modern police patrols (through a ward-based system called the *rasotsu*) and seven years after the Tokyo Metropolitan Police Department was established (Westney 1987; Tipton 2001; Umemori 2002). Prior to the creation of *paichusuo* (*hashutsjo* in Japanese), the front-line institution of the Japanese police system was the *koban* ("police box"). Early police boxes were simple shelters where police stood watch in shifts. The *paichusuo* was introduced as an expanded institution, capable of accommodating multiple police officers and a wider range of police business. *Paichusuo* were thus, in a sense, born of the bureaucratic utility afforded by concentrating resources in an administrative node that managed a portfolio of elementary jurisdictional units (Aldous and Leishman 2000; Leishman 1999).[1]

The *paichusuo* came to Taiwan in 1895, when the island became a Japanese colony. This introduced modern police to Taiwan, and the historically distinctive approach Meiji Japan took to modern policing supplied the foundation on which the Taiwanese form of policing took root (Abe 2003; Ts'ai 2009). Meiji modernization had a defensive orientation. Nineteenth-century European imperialists claimed extraterritorial jurisdiction wherever local governments could not guarantee "civilized" treatment of their European residents. The policing system Japan set up after the Meiji Restoration in 1868 was designed, in part, to resist such extraterritorial claims (Lam 2010). The strategy was pursued by studying the conceptual framework through which such claims were pursued, and developing ways to meet and counter them on their own terms. Japan quickly mastered the emerging discourse of international law, as well as the underlying rhetorical "standard of civilization" on which claims to national sovereignty were based (Howland 2016). They used these discursive conventions as a point of reference for their newly created police institutions, placing a civilizing project of moral regulation quite explicitly at the core of the institution's design (Umemori 2002; O'Brien 2003).

In 1870, officers of the Tokyo City Guard commissioned Fukuzawa Yukichi to advise them on modern policing techniques. Fukuzawa produced a translation of an American encyclopedia article describing police as "a judicial and executive system and an organized civil force for the preservation of order and the enforcement of the laws" (Umemori 2002, 45). Fukuzawa's translation included an annotation contrasting the "organized civil force" of modern policing with the pluralism inherent in the traditional use of clan-based militias to keep order. Fukuzawa is most famous for his advocacy of liberal ideas, such as the principle of constitutional rule, and his description of policing emphasized the modern administrative ideal of integrating society around a single political center (Umemori 2002). More extensive empirical investigation of practical policing techniques quickly followed. In 1872 foreign missions were sent to study policing institutions throughout the major countries of Europe and the European colonies of East Asia (Westney 1982). These missions produced a kind of blueprint for Japanese policing with the 1876 publication of Toshiyoshi Kawaji's famous book *Keisatsu shugan* (The hands and eyes of police). This text is the source for many of the ideas that have become associated with a distinctively Japanese or East Asian style of policing. "A nation is a family," wrote Kawaji. "The government is the parents. Its people are children. The police are their nursemaid. Those who have not yet been civilized completely like ours must be regarded as mere infants. It is nothing other than the nursemaid's obligation to nourish the infants" (quoted in Umemori 2002, 112).

Implementation of this civilizing project made *paichusuo* policemen agents of state registration. The overall design of Meiji policing was based on a French model, a nationally centralized bureaucratic organization that distinguished the proactive "administrative police" in the Ministry of Interior from the reactive "judicial police" in the Ministry of Justice. The nourishing/civilizing qualities of policing were located primarily on its administrative side, operationalized through police responsibilities attached to the population registry. Japan has been keeping official state records of its population for well over a thousand years (Cornell and Hayami 1986; Chapman 2008). The version operating at the beginning of the Meiji period recorded households "in a Confucian hierarchy with a ruling male head followed by his male elders and offspring. . . . Female elders, spouses and offspring were enumerated as property" (Winther 2008, 23). To adapt this tradition of state inscription to modern conditions, the lowest-ranking patrolmen working in the front-line institutions of administrative policing were made responsible for keeping these records in order, and the form of the record-keeping was reorganized to foreground the work of modernization.

Japan's first set of *Regulations for Administrative Police* (issued in 1875) gave individual patrolmen the task of maintaining the records for roughly three thousand people. They were expected to know everyone's name and occupation, and submit regular reports evaluating the quality of their behavior (Umemori 2002, 96). A patrolman's manual printed in 1879 provided the following guidelines for evaluating subject quality: "A person who behaves properly, works hard, dutifully helps his or her parents, and fulfills social responsibilities should be defined as a good subject. A person who likes to resist the authorities and eats the bread of idleness without a job and property should be defined as a bad subject" (quoted in Umemori 2002, 96). Front-line administrative patrolmen were, in other words, expected to serve as judges of character; in Kawaji's canonical phrase, they were expected to "hear voiceless voices, and see formless forms" (Umemori 2002, 53). Their role in the larger system was to inscribe these judgments into a standardized accounting system that would, in aggregate, make the quality of national character legible at the level of the entire population. This project of modernizing inscription was the core logic of Meiji administrative policing.

When the Japanese came to Taiwan they brought this idea of administrative police with them. They established two *paichusuo* in Taipei in 1895 and added seventeen more the following year, distributed across several other cities (Li Zhengchang 2007, 47). By 1902 there were more than one thousand *paichusuo* operating in Taiwan, one for every three thousand inhabitants (66). For the remainder of the colonial period, these police substations provided the core institutional interface between the Japanese state and Taiwanese society. However, the *paichusuo* that developed in Taiwan were not identical to those in Japan. The period between 1895 and 1902 involved significant political struggle, and the nature and the function of the *paichusuo* were fundamentally altered by the process through which it was adapted to the political conditions obtaining in early colonial Taiwan (Ts'ai 2009).

China ceded Taiwan to Japan after losing a war fought in Northern China, far away from the island (Lamley 1999; E. Chen 1977). Nobody in Taiwan was happy about this arrangement. Taiwan was Japan's first colony, and it took some time to develop a successful mechanism for colonial administration (Kerr 1974). Its first three Japanese governors were military men, all of whom tried and failed to shift their governing practice away from its de facto organization as a military campaign. They brought detailed blueprints for civil governance and attempted to establish civil police institutions, but every police outpost they set up was drawn into service in fighting an escalating counterinsurgency, becoming military adjuncts without any real capacity for regular police work. By 1898, the Meiji government was struggling to justify its ever-expanding investment of life and treasure into the seemingly hopeless project of extracting profit from a notoriously ungovernable island (Ka 1996).

In February of 1898, Taiwan's fourth colonial governor, Kodama Gentaro, arrived on the island. Like all his predecessors, Kodama was a military general. However, he delegated considerable power to his chief of civil administration, Goto Shinpei, who is widely credited as the architect of Taiwan's colonial policing system (Chang and Myers 1963). Goto was a doctor who first worked for Kodama establishing the Army Quarantine Office during the Sino-Japanese War (the war by which Taiwan was made a colony), then went on to become a sanitation engineer. Kodama and Goto arrived in Taiwan with the colony's financial solvency as their primary concern. They implemented a reform strategy in two phases. The first phase, from 1898 to the end of 1902, focused on shifting away from military counterinsurgency to emphasize civil policing through an "anti-banditry" rationale. The second phase used the new policing system as a foundation on which to build additional capacities for civil administration. This allowed them to complete a cadastral survey in 1903 and implement a new tax system the following year. The overall result of this strategy established a modern police state, in the sense that *all* of Taiwan's administration was channeled through its police institutions. Through this mode of police governance, Goto made the colony not merely financially self-sustaining but a source of increasingly profitable returns to Japanese capital after 1905.

The first phase of reform involved redesigning the *paichusuo* for colonial use. This was achieved by augmenting it with a subordinate institutional system for collective responsibility and surveillance called the *hoko*. During the previous phase of colonial rule, Japanese police had been unable to deal effectively with the political qualities of Taiwanese society. A fabric of traditional self-defensive organization confronted the "civil" pretensions of Japanese policing with forms of resistance that provoked military response by the Japanese. Such escalation secured military victory but prevented movement toward a functional civil administration.

The Taiwanese capacity to resist Japan's initial attempts to establish modern police institutions was a legacy of the way political life in Qing-era Taiwan had been organized. State capacity in Imperial China was quite limited. The lowest-level office in its administrative bureaucracy was the district magistrate, a single individual responsible for managing the affairs of a population numbering in the hundreds of thousands (Ch'u 1962; Djang 1984). The day-to-day operations of the district magistrate's yamen, or office, relied on a network of informal, conventional, and quasi-official institutions, which had developed in historical conjunction with the state and were integrated into formal government operations as a necessary adjunct (Reed 2000). The political rationality of local politics was transactional, a system in which the entrepreneurial performance of governmental services was done in exchange for a quotient of whatever revenues might be extracted in the process. The structural tyranny enabled by this "absence of a practical distinction between public and private" was, as Prasenjit Duara describes it, not "corruption [but rather] a feature of the system itself" (Duara 1988, 47). The tendencies of this arrangement to foster predatory powers stimulated local communities to organize in their own interests. Thus, where the modern world expects to find a state-society "boundary"—that is, a formally intelligible relationship between agents and subjects of the state—Imperial China cultivated a political field in which downward-cascading relations of entrepreneurial brokerage met upward-directed relations of protective brokerage (Duara 1988).

Qing-era Taiwan was an exceptionally unruly part of China. It was first incorporated into the polity in 1683, to suppress rebellious activity in a kingdom established there by Ming-era buccaneer Zheng Chenggong. This established a "quarantine" strategy of governance: the Qing set up a military garrison on Taiwan with the mission of preventing further immigration to the island (Shepherd 1999, 109). Population pressures in southeastern China generated a constant stream of economic migrants, however, and the Chinese settlement of Taiwan was gradually accepted and legalized by the central administration (Shepherd 1999). This led to a sociopolitical order in which most de facto military and judicial power was exercised by landlords. Officers of the state could call up overwhelming force if provoked, but they generally tried to avoid getting embroiled in local problems, rationalizing the island's chronic civil disorder as just another feature of its generally pestilent environment. The state held itself aloof, allowing the Taiwanese to work out their own problems through *sidou*, "private battles." The island was notorious for chronic feuding and vendettas between opposed segments of its political economy (Lamley 1977). For the state to become involved, a private battle would have to escalate to the level of a *xiedou*, or "armed affray"; the largest case of *xeidou* documented in Qing-era Taiwan involved over one hundred thousand combatants (Ownby 1990).

The Japanese troops who landed in northern Taiwan in late May 1895 got a taste of the Taiwanese capacity for defensive mobilization. Over the six months it took them to establish control of the island, they came into contact with the full panoply of militant institutions that had taken shape in Taiwan during the preceding three centuries. The encounter revealed significant obstacles to Japanese plans to institute civil government on Taiwan. As an example, consider the difficulties the first governor-general, Kabayama Sukenori, had in setting up his administration. His troubles began as he waited on a boat off the northern coast for clear authorization to go ashore. Although Chinese officials on the mainland had signed a treaty establishing Japanese possession of Taiwan, the Qing representatives on the island refused to accept its terms. They declared (disingenuously) that the island had undergone a revolution to establish its independent sovereignty as the "Democratic Country of Taiwan," and raised an army to defend their new republic (Lamley 1970; Morris 2002). Kabayama eventually decided to take the island by force and landed on the northern shore. After a four-day battle with the "Republican" army, the Japanese took control of Keelung, Taiwan's northernmost port city, and the erstwhile Qing/Republican officials fled. The capital city, Taipei, twenty miles south of Keelung, then descended into a state of riot. This lasted for days, until a committee of Taipei's merchants opened the city's gates and invited the Japanese to take control as a stabilizing force (C.-C. Chen 1988). Heartened by this turn of events, Kabayama held a ceremony formally inaugurating Taiwan's Japanese government on June 17. It was premature. As he moved south from Taipei, his army immediately began to encounter sporadic harassment, and they got only as far as the next major urban center before getting completely pinned down. For the next six weeks Kabayama's forces fought a general insurrection throughout northern Taiwan, with two thousand of his soldiers trapped inside the walled city of Hsinchu by ten thousand Taiwanese militiamen mustered by the local gentry (Lamley 1970).

It was November before Kabayama established military control over the entire island. After this, Japan's hold on Taiwan was never again seriously threatened by Taiwanese resistance, but the guerrilla resistance that the colonizers met on their arrival persisted in ways that rendered Japan's initial plans for establishing civil government impossible. Everywhere the Japanese regime wanted to put administration, they found politics. It was a tenacious politics of grassroots resistance grounded in long-standing traditions of collective self-defense. The first three governors responded to this militarily, a strategy that proved counterproductive to the larger aims of colonization. Taiwanese traditions of self-defensive organization were too weak to challenge the military might of the modern Japanese army, but they were strong enough to prevent the Japanese from establishing a stable civil government on the island without negotiating some role in it for Taiwanese elites.

The *hoko* provided a way to end to this impasse. Goto created a mechanism for negotiating the relations of administration in a way that effectively captured the self-defensive motivations of local politics and aligned them with central policy objectives. He developed this mechanism through a theory of "biological government," which treated the customs of a colonized people as a constitutive element of their social organism (Chang and Myers 1963, 438). Confident in his racist faith in Japanese superiority, Goto understood his colonial mission as a pastoral intervention toward increasing the subject people's competitive fitness by improving their customary practices (e.g., eliminating opium smoking, queue wearing, and foot binding: Tsurumi 1967). He talked about policing through a medical analogy. The effects of a surgical procedure depend on the cultural physiology of the organism under the knife. Toward understanding the native constitution of the Taiwanese, Goto created a "Committee for the Investigation of Old Customs," staffed by Japanese ethnographers and lawyers (Myers 1971). Their task was to research Taiwanese culture in order to improve the ability of the colonial state to grasp the existing constitution of its newly acquired society (Kyoko 2003). Goto's approach to administrative design was focused on maintaining selected vectors of cultural continuity across the transition to colonial modernity.

As mentioned above, the average villagers in premodern Taiwan did not expect agents of the state to participate in the routines that kept their day-to-day existence in order. The politics of local society constituted what Philip Huang (1996) called the "third realm" of governance. This realm encompassed a diverse collection of people and institutions, operating as a coherent political arena through a hybrid logic emergent from the intersection between the substantive *gemeinschaft* values of intimate community and the long shadow cast by the orthodox forms of state power that towered above local society. The role of the district magistrate, as the local representative of the state, was (ideally) to facilitate the order that existed in this third realm (P. Huang 1996). This approach to local administration produced a literature that theorized the logic of local administrative/jurisprudential practice as an intersection between three distinct elements:

sentiment (*qing*), reason (*li*), and law (*fa*) (Shiga 1998). Goto embraced this for-
mulation as a useful resource for his administrative apparatus, most specifically
as it was articulated in a district magistrate's handbook called the *Complete Book
concerning Happiness and Benevolence* (Djang 1984), which was one of the key
works translated by his cultural research team (Ts'ai 1990).

The *Complete Book* contained a description of an institutional mechanism
called the *baojia*, which was widely used to organize the interface between the
state and local political society in Imperial China. Goto's *hoko* was explicitly conceived as a modern version of the *baojia* system; indeed, the term *hoko* is simply
a Japanese pronunciation of the Chinese characters for *baojia*. The description
Goto found in the *Complete Book* was the conventional model established by
Song dynasty scholar Wang Anshi (1002–1086), who presented it through an
idealized depiction of governance during the Zhou dynasty (771–256 BC) (Kuhn
1979). The Japanese *hoko* system followed its formula, gathering groups of ten
households into units called *ko* (Chinese *jia*) headed by a leader called *kocho*.
Groups of ten *ko* were gathered into units called *ho* (Chinese *bao*), under the
leadership of a *hosei*.

Taiwan's first Hoko Law was promulgated in August 1898. It laid out the
organizational architecture described above, and specified that each layer in the
organization was collectively responsible for the behavior of its entire membership. It also required that each *hoko* publish a substantive Hoko Code—based
on Japanese prototypes and guided by their Japanese superiors—enumerating
local rules and punishments for their transgression (Lamley 1999; Ts'ai 2009).
The Japanese superiors in this arrangement were the police of the local *paichusuo*. In other words, the *hoko* was installed as a layer of local self-governance
immediately subordinate to the police. It provided an arena for the continued
practice of traditional forms of local politics, while containing this arena within
an encompassing shell of modern administrative power. By creating functional
units of collective control, the *hoko* provided Japanese policemen with a manageable interface between their bureaucratized power and the forms of customary
authority extant in local social order. This arrangement allowed Japanese police
officers to adopt the practical attitude of an imperial district magistrate, focusing
on the higher-level political dynamics of the intersection between state power
and the general population while allowing matters of individual-level discipline
to be handled within the governed community. By this arrangement, Goto realized his ideal of "biological government," preserving enough of the native political metabolism to keep the "physiological" bases of customary order viable, while
drawing sharp new lines of control to fragment native authority into tightly constrained arenas of local self-regulation that would be incapable of organizing in
resistance to the colonial state.

The rationale for this arrangement was consistent with the Imperial Chinese jurisprudential logic of *qing-li-fa* mentioned above (which was as important to Japanese legal traditions as it was in China: see Miyazawa 1987; Matsamura 1988). Goto's policing system channeled indigenous politics into the sphere of *qing*—the affective solidarities of kinship and co-residence—while subordinating this sphere to the final authority of colonial *fa*—law. This feature of the *hoko*'s design established the institutional parameters for the enduring significance of *qing* as a jurisdictional sphere within Taiwan's modern division of social control labor. A 1925 poster diagramming the operations of the *hoko* system as a whole carried an aphorism that elegantly summarized the place of *qing* in colonial Taiwanese police governance: "The will [*yi*] of the superior is projected downwards. The *qing* of the subordinate is delivered upwards" (Ts'ai 2013, 78). In the imperial jurisprudence of the third realm, "operationally, *qing* meant the resolution of disputes through mediated compromise" (P. Huang 1996, 12). Goto's policing apparatus ensured that it would continue to play this role across Taiwan's transition to modernity.[2]

Mobilizational Policing

The origin story told above follows the work of Caroline Ts'ai, who used a detailed historical sociology of the Japanese colonial administration to develop a measured argument about exactly where and how policing institutions fit into the longer-*durée* formation of Taiwanese modernity.[3] She describes the original police-*hoko* nexus as an "extra-bureaucratic" political field, created by "grafting" colonial modernity onto Taiwan's preexisting political society. The success of this hybrid formation came as enterprising Taiwanese people began to use the parameters of the police state to organize their own projects: the police bureaucracy took root in local society to become a source of its "vitality" (2009, 71). The most significant and enduring fruit of this vitality came from the way the collective responsibilities of Japanese police governance made the administrative units defined by *ho* and *ko* groupings into communities of common fate. This, Ts'ai argues, is the origin of the significance that the category of "locality" has in Taiwan's modern political discourse.

The political significance of this local identity intensified in the 1930s, as war shifted the orientation of the state from civil administration to political mobilization. Beginning in 1934, Japan established a network of fascist patriotic organizations in parallel to the *hoko* bureaucracy (Ts'ai 2009). As the demands of war penetrated ever more deeply into Taiwanese society, this fascist mobilization apparatus displaced the older policing system, leading eventually to the complete elimination of the *hoko* in July 1945. By then the entire Japanese empire was governed as a command economy under a unified administrative system, and the Taiwanese were being encouraged to take Japanese names and think of themselves as imperial rather than colonial subjects. They were also being conscripted directly into the Japanese army.

Wartime mobilization had a "spiritual" dimension (Tsai 2009, 161–62). This was connected to the category of *qing* in a manner that transformed the practical significance of the category in Taiwan's modern political life. Up until the 1930s, *qing* was most politically consequential in the context of neighborhood policing. People invoked it as a basis of traditional authority, and local communities relied on these forms of authority to negotiate the unified front they were required to present to the police. This use of *qing* was grounded in Chinese political traditions through the administrative handbooks Goto used in designing the *hoko*. However, this drew on but one strand in a much wider field of discourse about *qing*. *Qing* has figured in philosophical discussions about human nature from the classical period, and it provided a kind of hinge through which modern social thought took root in East Asian intellectual traditions (Epstein 2001). As a foundational term through which to account for the practical significance of human affect, it supplied a primary element in various different ways people engaged with modern concepts of identity (Lee 2007; Lean 2007). The concept of nationalism was one: "Ideologically, the nation was organized in emotive terms, emphasizing horizontal identification, egalitarianism, voluntarism, and patriotic sacrifice. Nationalism insisted on a higher, or heroic, mode of activity—national liberation, resistance, revolution—that transcended and subordinated the everyday" (Lee 2007, 10). Taiwan's first sustained experience with this kind of modern *qing*-based national mobilization came through conscription into the front lines of a fascist total war.

Caroline Ts'ai argues that this effectively changed the political significance that "the local" held, as a structure of feeling, for a self-consciously Taiwanese sense of identity. A new appreciation of the geopolitical power of nationalist *qing* was sedimented on top of the historical familiarity with the neighborhood version of *qing* that structured the micro-politics of community order. The relationship between these contrasting versions of *qing* is quite concrete in the institutional structure of Taiwan's modern security state. The *paichusuo* is an institution of neighborhood order. It was designed to serve as a mechanism through which the modern state could cultivate the delicate relationship it has with the autonomous energies of society as a living organism. The meaning of *qing* in the *paichusuo* is grounded in this idiom of grassroots social vitality. At the same time, the *paichusuo* is the capillary base for a state security apparatus with a number of higher functions. At the other end of the state security hierarchy, its ostensible "top" (e.g., the Japanese governor-general's "high police," the generalissimo's National Security Council, or the military's garrison command), are institutions concerned with the *qing* of domestic order at issue in the arrangements of *qingbao* or *qingzhi*—the "*qing*-reporting" and "*qing*-control" institutions that constitute the domestic political intelligence apparatus. The resonance that fascist mobilization established between these two idioms of *qing*—the grassroots and the political vanguard—remained strong through the transition from Japanese to Chinese rule.

World War II ended in August 1945, and Taiwan passed from Japanese to Chinese control. The process by which Taiwan's governing institutions were transferred across this change in regimes was not smooth. Its effects on the organization of local policing are best described in three different stages. The first stage was the process of formal transfer, between October 1945 and February 1947, when policing institutions established by the Japanese were taken over by the Chinese. The Republic of China (ROC) was not a very stable entity at this time. It was aligned with the Chinese Nationalist Party (KMT), who for decades had been entangled in civil war with the Chinese Communist Party (CCP). The civil war had been temporarily halted by World War II, but soon resumed. The ROC's approach to governance in Taiwan immediately after World War II was disorganized and predatory, provoking increasing resistance on the part of the Taiwanese. This resistance led to the second period in Taiwan's postwar police history, beginning when tensions came to a head in the 2/28 Incident, an island-wide insurrection that momentarily overthrew the island's provincial government (Kerr 1965; Lai, Myers, and Wou 1991; Phillips 2003). The KMT's response to the uprising was a ruthless and indiscriminate slaughter of Taiwanese civilians, inaugurating the use of political terror as a policy instrument of the KMT's rule in Taiwan (Kerr 1965). A military-led purge of Taiwan's political elites continued over subsequent years, as the Chinese civil war resumed and the KMT's circumstances became increasingly dire. By the end of 1949 the KMT had lost the war. Chiang Kai-shek fled to Taiwan, bringing two million refugees and the remnants of his failed state with him. Things looked bleak for the continued existence of the ROC when, in June 1950, it was saved by the geopolitical dynamics of an American war in Korea. This reprieve inaugurated the third period of transformation in Taiwan's policing apparatus, in which civil police institutions were repurposed as an element in a military system of "political warfare" that governed Taiwan's domestic security through the 1980s.

Preparations for transferring Taiwan's police to Chinese control had begun before the end of the war, in April 1944, when the KMT first began to formulate a plan for incorporating Taiwan into the Republic of China. They created a two-headed bureaucratic structure for use in the handover: the Taiwan Provincial

Administrative Executive Office would take over civil administration, and the Taiwan Provincial Garrison Command (Taiwansheng Jingbei Zongsilingbu) would handle the transfer of military institutions and the repatriation of Japanese soldiers. The two bureaus were integrated by virtue of being headed by a single individual: Chen Yi, a notoriously brutal and corrupt member of Chiang Kai-shek's inner circle (Kerr 1965).

Police affairs were classified as an element of civil administration. The official tasked with overseeing the process of bringing Taiwan's police apparatus under Chinese administration was Hu Fuxiang, founding head of the Police Bureau (Jingwuchu) within the Taiwan Provincial Administrative Executive Office. Hu was a long-standing subordinate of Chen Yi who had served in various positions in the ROC police bureaucracy, studied in Japan, and written a book on Japanese colonial policing (Chen Chunying 2012, 3). In August 1944, Hu was appointed director of a newly formed Taiwan Police Cadres Training Section (Taiwan Jingcha Ganbu Xunlianban) in the ROC Police Officers School. Classes began the following month, and by October 1945, Hu had trained 932 officers to take over the senior command positions vacated by the departing Japanese (70 percent of whom spoke Taiwanese: Chen Chunying 2012, 5). Hu made his first report on the progress of the transfer to the Provincial Consultative Council in May 1946. He listed the total number of personnel employed as police officers in Taiwan at retrocession as 12,980. Of these, 1,717 were commissioned officers in command positions, 255, or 15 percent, of whom were Taiwanese. The remaining 11,263 were line staff, of whom 5,427, or 48 percent, were Taiwanese. "[These] original Formosan police are being retained for use as far as possible," he stated, "at the same time new Formosan police are being trained to supplement the number" (Kerr, n.d.). Hu's second address to this council, in December 1946, reported that he was now operating a total of 1,462 police stations, including 1,329 *paichusuo* (a reduction of 39 in the total number of *paichusuo* received from the Japanese). He was somewhat short-staffed (by about 400 people), but nonetheless had 1,371 officers (of whom 430, or 31 percent, were Taiwanese) and 7,105 line staff (of whom 6,546, or 92 percent, were Taiwanese). It is clear from these numbers that, despite the notorious purge of Taiwanese civil servants from the overall administration, emphasized by George Kerr and others, the intention of the first phase in the formal transfer of the policing system was to maintain continuity at the level of the *paichusuo* operations.

Beneath the *paichusuo* however, where the *hoko* had operated before the war, the Republic of China introduced something new, the *qinqu* system of police "beats." The motivation for this change came primarily from the history of modern policing in mainland China. Chinese police history has parallels with the Taiwanese experience but diverges in important ways, especially in respect of its street-level institutions. Taiwan's colonial *hoko* was, of course, originally modeled on the traditional Chinese *baojia* system. The development of modern policing in the Republic of China (which drew heavily on Meiji models) also used the *baojia* system to supplement its formal bureaucracy. However, the Republic of China was never able to project central authority very far from its center. The overall balance of powers obtaining between *baojia* and police authority in Republican China as a whole ended up quite different from the relationship between *hoko* and police in colonial Taiwan. As Chen Chunying describes this, "the Japanese made the *baojia* an adjunct to police, using tradition to facilitate modernization, rendering from tradition a design principle by which to successfully plant the roots of a modern administrative system into the ground [of Taiwanese society]." By contrast, in mainland China, "the overall failure to create a functional police force left the *baojia* system as the primary institution for keeping social order in most of the countryside. . . . Local self-defense organizations *replaced* police as primary guarantors of social order, dominating political resources and relegating police to the status of an adjunct to local powers" (Chen Chunying 2007, 48–49, my emphasis). The committee meetings where China's strategy for administering Taiwan was developed in 1944 included arguments against the *hoko/baojia* (the same word, Romanized differently according to its Japanese/Chinese pronunciation). "We must abolish [it]! . . . Not only has [the Japanese administration] achieved policy implementation without relying on the *baojia*, they have established preconditions for self-governance through the street and village offices. There is no need for us to include the *baojia* as a layer in the system" (quoted in Yao 2007, 49).

The Taiwanese *hoko* was a multifunctional institution. It brought an element of quasi-democratic representational authority into the dynamics by which local communities selected leaders responsible for managing their collective subjection to police power. Chinese plans for reconstructing Taiwan's police apparatus separated its multifunctionality into two institutions. Police responsibility per se was channeled into the police beats, replacing the political mediation of local elites with the "mathematical" logic of the *hukou* registry system. The second institution was a system of local elected offices, the *linzhang* and *lizhang*, neighborhood and borough chiefs (a modification of the Japanese street and village offices). It was this second system that accommodated the political function of local elites in "representing popular will" (*minyi daibiao*—as these local elected officials are called to the present day). In principle, separating the executive power of police from the quasi-legislative power of local representation looked like a progressive advance toward self-governance. In practice, however, as the relationship between Taiwanese society and the Chinese state became adversarial, the two institutions folded together into a unitary police function as illiberal and malignant as the Japanese system had ever been.

On February 28, 1947, agents of the Monopoly Bureau assaulted a woman selling untaxed cigarettes in a central Taipei park, then shot and killed a man who came to her defense. This was the last straw for a state-society relationship that had been degrading steadily since the handover. An angry crowd chased the Monopoly Bureau agents into a police station, where they remained besieged as a spontaneous uprising spread through the city, and then to the rest of the island. Between February 28 and March 8, 1947, official representatives of Taiwan's provincial government stayed in hiding while the island was managed by citizens' councils whose primary concern was coordinating an authoritative list of grievances to negotiate with the central government (Kerr 1965; Edmondson 2002). On March 8, Chinese military reinforcements arrived from the mainland, and wholesale slaughter of Taiwanese civilians began. The initial phase of the slaughter resembled a military invasion, but after restoring their undisputed military dominance, the Chinese Nationalist government turned to a campaign of (crudely) targeted assassination that used the island's administrative system as an apparatus of political intelligence. This was described by a Chinese officer as follows:

> We first compiled all the information provided by party officials, intelligence organizations, the military and the police, and from this created a list of all suspects along with their places of residence and activity. At the same time, we convened a meeting with the city's government officers, along with all local district and borough chiefs and some of the neighborhood chiefs, and announced to them our investigative purposes while soliciting their opinions and requesting their assistance. After this we imposed martial law across the whole city, and stopped all traffic. Beginning at dusk, we dispatched infantry units to assist the gendarmes and police who, accompanied by local personages, made a meticulous inspection. By dawn of the second day we had our result. The aggregate result of our inspection was the arrest of over three hundred suspects. Among them six resisted our military units, some with firearms, some with knives. After their arrest, they were given to the military court for hearing, judgment, and formal charges. When carrying out the sentence, they were first paraded through the streets by the military and the police, then taken to the execution ground and shot. (In Li Xianfeng 1998)

The ROC's system of local administration was enlisted in this campaign of political terror in ways that reproduced the most illiberal qualities of the Japanese *hoko*. A set of "implementation procedures for sub-district [political] cleansing" (*fenqu qingxiang shishibanfa*) issued in Kaohsiung, for example, required neighborhood and borough chiefs to conduct inspections of all residents in their areas. They were tasked with certifying the accuracy of the registry records and organizing resident households into units of collective responsibility for delivering "spies, rioters, and gangsters" to the authorities. As with Goto's pacification of the anti-Japanese insurgency fifty years earlier, these groups were compelled to cooperate by the collective punishments they would face if any political dissidents were discovered unreported in their communities (Yao 2007, 49–50). The primary feature distinguishing this Chinese system from the earlier Japanese system was that local political compulsion was organized through a bureaucracy separate from that of the police. Where the Japanese system had operated on the principle that police were the sole agency for domestic security (*annei wei jing*— see Chen Chunying 2007, 48), the KMT created multiple overlapping systems of domestic control. This fragmentation and redundancy would become a defining feature of the domestic security system that took shape under the KMT.

In the years following 2/28, the Republic of China collapsed. Its sovereign pretensions contracted dramatically: in 1947 it claimed a political authority encompassing a continent and a civilization; by the end of 1949 it occupied an island as the rump state of a defeated army. This had a significant effect on Taiwan's policing system. The Police Bureau remained an organ of the provincial government, with its subordinate *paichusuo* structure unchanged. But the provincial government itself was reorganized to become, simultaneously, more accessible to local Taiwanese politicians and less powerful vis-à-vis the central government. At the same time the garrison command, originally created in parallel to the provincial administration, was moved into a superior position as the conduit through which the central government secured its military control of the island. Then, with declaration of the People's Republic of China in 1949, the entire government of the ROC relocated to Taiwan. Taiwan's "central" government became nothing more than a bureaucratically superior layer of administration contained within its only remaining province. This established the redundant, two-tier arrangement that persisted through the authoritarian period. Local (sub-provincial) affairs were promoted as an arena of democratic self-governance (prominently displayed to American patrons of "Free China"), while dictatorial control was maintained in and through the organs of central government (Lerman 1977; Winkler 1981a, 1981b). And the dictator himself, Chiang Kai-shek, held a power transcending bureaucratic concern altogether, legitimated by the "sacred mission" of his noncommunist Chinese revolution.

This set the stage for the third phase in the development of Taiwan's postwar policing system—construction of the security apparatus that gave Taiwan's martial law or "White Terror" period its name. Political conditions adequate to support institution building were established in June 1950, when the beginning of the Korean War secured the ROC's continued existence on Taiwan. The institutional framework of the security apparatus took eight years to find its final shape, completed with the reorganization of the garrison command in 1958 (Chen Chunying 2007).

Updating the security apparatus was only one element of a wholesale reconstruction of the entire government structure, which began with a purge and reorganization of the KMT launched in August 1950 (Myers and Lin 2007). The party was the supreme political institution and remained so throughout Taiwan's authoritarian period. As the guiding slogans of the times put it, "Use the Party to Lead the Government" (*Yi dang ling zheng*), "Use the Party to Lead the Military" (*Yi dang ling jun*), and "Use the Military to Lead the Police" (*Yi jun ling jing*) (Chen Chunying 2007, 51). When it came to political security, the party did more than lead. It was directly involved in the actual work. After Chiang Kai-shek purged the KMT, he rebuilt it, using a party school (the Fu Hsing Kang Political Warfare College) to ensure loyalty and discipline. The founding head of this school, Wang Sheng, summarized the focus of its curriculum as follows: "War is basically an act of violence in which both sides exert maximum effort for the purpose of defeating, subjugating and rendering the other side helpless. . . . At times they resort to nonviolent activities and are able to achieve victory. Political warfare is this type of warfare" (quoted in Marks 1998, 144). Political warfare was a mobilizational project focused on the morale of the general population, deploying education and culture toward the goal of national "revolution." It valorized the "spiritual" dimensions of *qing* in a manner similar to Japanese fascism (Bullard 1997).

By 1952 the party had 282,000 members (over half of whom were Taiwanese), and 30,000 work team units conducting "social investigations" (*shehui diaocha*) designed to ascertain the political quality of the general population and identify potential dissidents (Myers and Lin 2007, 37). These numbers increased steadily, making the experience of party-organized domestic political surveillance one of the signature features of life in authoritarian Taiwan (Greitens 2016, 107–8). The use of political warfare as an idiom for domestic security was consistent with an overall approach to governing that Shelly Rigger (1999) calls "mobilizational authoritarianism." The KMT encouraged or demanded political participation, channeling this mobilization into routes that served its agenda. It used electoral democracy at the local level to recruit grassroots political elites into a clientelistic arrangement that made centrally controlled resources available to people willing to cooperate in securing party power (N.-T. Wu 1987). Party mobilization was the primary axis of government control. The police bureaucracy, historically located within the provincial government and thus associated with the subordinate sphere of local "self-governance," served as a peripheral adjunct to the political security apparatus. Its place in the system was defined by the guiding slogans of the times, which supplemented the above-mentioned principles of "Using the Party to Lead the Military" and "Using the Military to Lead the Police" with a final slogan: "The Police and Population Registry Systems Are Unified" (*Hu jing heyi*). The civil police apparatus was given the primary task of maintaining registry records as an element in the political surveillance system. Which is to say, its basic job was to "report *qing*" (a literal rendering of *qingbao*, the term for a political intelligence report).

The KMT and the Japanese regimes in Taiwan shared the predicament of ruling without benefit of any organic historical connection to local society. This motivated a strategy using a blend of clientelism and repression to engineer a state-society relationship consistent with the government's agenda. Civil police institutions marked a point of contact at which this relationship could be made legible and manipulated. The Japanese concentrated the entire political weight of colonialism in the police, using the *hoko* to graft the command authority of modern police into a subordinate sphere organized by traditional forms of political authority. The Chinese, by contrast, separated the electoral politics of mobilizational authoritarianism from the command authority of police. In this Leninist division of labor, the party did politics, and the police were an administrative instrument responsible for assisting the party's political objectives by supplying reliable information and following commands. The governing practices of the KMT party-state marginalized "police power" per se, subordinating it to the power of the *qingzhi* (literally "*qing*-control," or intelligence) system that secured party dominance in sociopolitical life.

For those who experienced life inside this authoritarian security system, it had "its deepest impact with regard to political offences"—that is, forms of behavior interpreted as "an attack upon the political order of things" (Peng 1971, 474). The autocratic state saw the political order of things everywhere. It was in the stability of commodity prices, in the discipline of school classrooms, in rumor and gossip, not to mention the ideas of the public sphere. To control politics at such a fine grain, state power had to be projected into the deepest interior of private life. Like the Japanese before them, the KMT used the intimate dimensions of *qing* as an instrument for political control. The family was conscripted into the police bureaucracy through the *hukou*, which made the head of a household (*jiazhang*) responsible for the political behavior of its members. On top of the ostensibly natural bonds of kinship captured by the population registry were multiple overlapping mechanisms of administrative review. The head of household reported to a "neighborhood officer" (*linzhang*), and the neighborhood officer reported to the borough or village officer (*lizhang* or *cunzhang*); "each unit has its own head who is responsible to the police and supervises the members of the households under his jurisdiction" (Peng 1971, 488).

A "Regulation for Denunciation of Communist Spies during the Period of Rebellion" (Kanluan Shiqi Jiansu Feidie Tiaoli) made failure to report knowledge of sedition a crime, punishable by up to seven years' imprisonment. This embedded hard-edged political surveillance in the sphere of voluntary association. Permission to join any kind of formal organization—to become a student or teacher, to join a club, become a civil servant, or work in an office—was predicated on passing a political review that "required by law [that the applicant] offer at least two guarantors to the effect that [the applicant] holds and *will hold* 'pure and correct thoughts,' is not and *will not be* engaged in any 'anti-governmental' activity'" (Peng 1971, 487, original emphasis). This guarantee system created a general, defensive compulsion to avoid or denounce anyone who seemed untrustworthy. Failure to proactively denounce a known associate exposed you to punishment for any deviant thoughts or behaviors (real or not) that might become attached to that person by someone *else's* secret denunciations. The compulsion of guarantee made political correctness a prudent civic responsibility. The security apparatus injected itself into the internal dynamics of the collective subjects it punished for the deviation of their individual members. The bonds of intimate solidarity were bureaucratized and objectified, converted into overlapping hierarchies of jurisdictional obligation.

A police textbook published in 1987 (the year martial law ended) contains an overview of the "general population intelligence reporting [that is, *qing*-reporting] system" (*quanmin qingbao zuzh*). The system was organized in two levels. The top level was headed by the military garrison command. Officers from this level had discretionary authority to engage directly with any unit in the lower level. The lower level was composed of five bureaucracies of surveillance: societies and clubs; schools and related organizations; local administration; military reserves; and, finally, the police and civil defense. Each separate reporting line contained five hierarchical levels, beginning with individuals' obligation to report to their neighborhood, classroom, or unit officer (*linzhang, banzhang,* etc.), and moving upward through increasingly larger units before culminating in the county government. The link between the bottom and the top levels of the organization was something called a "base-level mobilization assistance report" (*jiceng zongdongyuan xiehui huibao*), issued by the precinct chiefs in the county police department. These reports were delivered to the county executive, who in turn prepared a report to pass to the military officers of the garrison command (Zhang and Ding 1987, 637–41).

A notable feature of this organizational chart is the way it disregards the separation of powers. Elected representatives fall under the command authority of police officers, who are subordinated to higher-level political appointees, who are in turn subordinated to military officers. The arrangement is consistent with a security state, not a police state per se. Taiwan's authoritarian system, in Chen Chunying's analysis, "used the intelligence apparatus to fracture the police system, and relegate it to a peripheral role in the overall security system" (2007, 45). Japan left a solid police-state infrastructure on Taiwan, but the KMT's approach to national security privileged party and military organization in a way that degraded and marginalized the island's received police institutions. By the time the KMT's security apparatus was fully implemented in late 1958, Taiwan "no longer qualified as a police state" (65). It was a national security state, in which the party was supreme, using the military to control the people. The police had a relatively peripheral role in this larger security system, attached primarily to the population registration system.

Bureaucratically speaking, since the 1930s the Republic of China has had a Bureau of Population Administration dedicated specifically to the management of the population registry and existing separately from its police bureaucracy. Nonetheless, from the moment of retrocession in October 1945 it was considered practically exigent for police to handle the *hukou* records in Taiwan. The rationale for this arrangement was consolidated by the chaos leading up to 1950, and in 1951 Chiang Kai-shek announced his intention to fold the household registry system entirely into the police bureaucracy (Chen Chunying 2007). The realization of his intention took two decades, however, during which time the work of *hukou* surveillance was shared in various ways between *paichusuo* patrolmen and the grassroots officers of electoral representation (a practical amalgamation of the two institutions that the ROC created to replace the Japanese *hoko*). When the formal absorption of the *hukou* system into the police bureaucracy was finally completed in 1973 (the year the National Police Administration was created), the regulations for police registry work described its rationale as enabling police to practice a "three dimensional" mode of "population dynamics" (Xu 2003, 103); the three dimensions at issue were the administrative, the judicial, and the political (103).

Taiwan's authoritarian state was a successful example of the type. "The state machine penetrated every sector of society, eventually exercising comprehensive controls over universities, the entertainment community, farmers' associations, fishermen's associations, labor unions, trade unions and local financial associations" (Yeh 2016, 35). Military institutions of political warfare oversaw a total social mobilization for the war effort, in which all forms of civil organization were to be managed by party penetration, and a political intelligence apparatus added up to a "level of societal penetration historically matched by very few secret police organization—among them those of contemporary North Korea and the East German Stasi" (Greitens 2016, 108). This omnipresent political police force was colloquially known as "thought police" for the way its unashamedly antiliberal logic replaced the dignity of free will with the political necessity of right will (S. Lin 2007, 6). As a technology of control, this jurisdictionalization of mutual responsibility effectively rendered virtue as a policeable object. Care itself, the fabric of mutual concern for shared life, was the object of the authoritarian police apparatus.

The Democratic Transition

Cracks in Taiwan's authoritarian system began in 1971, with the geopolitical shift created by Nixon's détente with China. The ROC was subsequently replaced by the PRC in the United Nations, beginning a process of international isolation that has left the ROC with only a handful of countries willing to recognize it as a sovereign state (seventeen as of this writing). At the same time, good economic policy and preferential access to American markets had transformed the domestic situation by making the country wealthy. Taiwan was a firmly middle-class society by the mid-1970s, and the younger generation were beginning to question the limits imposed on their political lives. The rationale legitimating the authoritarian state was intrinsically temporary, based on an argument that representative democracy was impossible without elections that included the 98 percent of the population who lived in mainland China. Until the mainland was recovered, the nation's parliamentary bodies would remain occupied by the representatives elected in 1947. As time went on, these people grew old and began to die. "Supplementary elections" to maintain the government's nominal parliamentary system became necessary beginning in 1969. This provided a sort of loophole in the single-party system, allowing courageous opposition politicians to stand for office "outside the party" (*dangwai*). This grew into an island-wide Dangwai movement, which declared itself a formal political party in 1986. This was, of course, illegal under the martial law decree, and the following year martial law was canceled, and multiparty competition became the accepted form of politics in Taiwan. In 1991 the "State of Exception during the Communist Rebellion" was finally ended. The liberal-democratic constitution of the Republic of China was allowed to function "normally" for the first time in its history. Between the 1980s and the 1990s, Taiwan changed from a police state every bit as totalitarian as Soviet Russia or contemporary North Korea (Greitens 2016) to one of the freest and most "vibrant" democracies of the contemporary world (Fell 2012; Chao and Myers 1998; Winkler 1984).

This transformed the context of everyday policing. The early 1990s mark a historical inflection point at which police became accountable to the people they policed as one part of a broader "legal awakening" (Lewis 2009). The national security apparatus moved into the background of domestic politics. The garrison command was dissolved in 1992. Constitutional guarantees of rights—in particular those of free speech and political assembly—led to a surge in political activity at the grassroots, which compelled the police powers involved in local life to assume a more definite and visible shape. The previously ubiquitous and amorphous qualities of "secret" policing were pinned down by democratic sociopolitical forces focused through legal form. The place of police power in everyday life was transformed by the democratic project of exposing and adjusting the connection between sovereignty, representation, and administration. "Taiwan . . . successfully made the transition from authoritarianism to democratic governance and correspondingly from a police-centric to a court-centric legal system" (Fu Hualing, in Cohen and Lewis 2013).

The significance of *qing* in policing persisted through the way that police powers had come to be understood as a form of emotional discipline. This was expressed quite directly in the "police punishments" authorized by the Police Violation Code (Weijing Fafa) and the Hoodlum Ordinances (Liumang Tiaoli). Those laws authorized punishment applied at the discretion of the police, including forms of administrative detention that could last for up to two weeks under the Police Violation Code, and up to three years under the Hoodlum Ordinances. The rationale for this detention was its instrumentality as *ganxun*—emotional discipline (Cohen and Lewis 2013, 27). This ideal of emotional correction was consistent with its precedents in the civilizing project of Japanese colonialism and the Leninist idiom of party-led sociopolitical engineering. The institutional basis for these punishments was retained well into the 2000s. Police maintained their "hoodlum registry" until 2009, when the law was finally found unconstitutional. People were classified (by police) as hoodlums on the basis of their *qingjie*—that is, the quality of their *qing* that is generally translated as a "psychological complex."

This realm of police punishments marked a "unique straddling of criminal and administrative law" (Cohen and Lewis 2013, 21). Deviant behavior was treated as a problem for administrative classification, delegated to the discretionary authority of the beat cop who maintained the registry records of the population within his duty area. Just as it had from its origins in Meiji-era Japan, this institutional arrangement treated the custodial authority of the *paichusuo* patrolman as an instrument for the cultivation of positive virtue, empowering him to act on his discretionary judgment about the quality of a person's character. Even as the democratic transition began to impose legal form on police powers, police discretion remained an arena where the spiritual or civilizing role of *qing* in police work was embedded in the documentary process that defined the "kinds" of people brought into view of the state (H. T.-M. Huang 2004).

How police discretion fits into the sociopolitical order of ordinary life is a matter of institutional design. Up until the 1980s, Taiwan's police were weak players in the country's larger security apparatus, subordinated by the architecture of authoritarian rule to military and party-based powers. Outside the state, however, they encountered few limits arising from the social environment in which they operated. "Under martial law, the main function of the police was to protect the KMT's regime rather than serve the people. They were highly politicized with appointments being part of the patronage system that rewarded regime loyalists. In the name of defending Taiwan from communist threat, police officers spent a great deal of time spying on the populace in an effort to unmask political opposition; crime against citizens was less a concern. The police were deployed to hundreds of *paichusuo* and officers were assigned to their beats with instructions to collect information on anti-government activities" (Cao, Huang, and Sun 2014, 29).

The shift to democracy did not strengthen the institutional position of police in their political environment. They remained weak and deferential to the patronage systems that influenced their budgetary and personnel arrangements. What the dissolution of military and party-based systems of rule did to the police was move the political apparatus that controlled their bureaucracy out from behind the democratically inaccessible screen of autocracy and make influence over police part of the spoils of party politics. The police became subordinate to the democratic politics of the social environment in which they operated. This generated a set of problems that came to public attention through a discourse of crisis in the quality of policing, known as the Zhian Ehua Yiundong, the "Corruption (or Degradation) of Policing" movement (Chuang 2013, 43–69; Lin Meiling 1991).

Anxiety about the erosion of public order began in the late 1980s, in the immediate aftermath of the initial contraction of the military role in domestic peacekeeping (Lin Meiling 1991). Political parties multiplied, the ruling party ceased to function as a mediating agent harmonizing the conflicts of factional political culture, and street-level politics began to exhibit elements of violence (Hood 1997, 122). By the early 1990s, concern with declining public order had shifted from its original flashpoint issues (smuggling and street protest) to a general fear that the distinction of the political from the criminal was collapsing (K.-l. Chin 2003). Campaigns for the local elections of 1994 witnessed unprecedented violence, with five incidents of gunfire at campaign offices or candidates homes, while charges of corruption and gangsterism featured prominently in campaign disputes (Hood 1997, 129). In 1995 the speaker of the Kaoshiung County Council, Wu Ho-sung, was assassinated, and the speaker of the Pingtung County Council, Cheng Tai-chi, was convicted of assassinating a business rival. As the campaign began for the historically unprecedented multiparty presidential election of 1996, public anxieties over criminality in politics were high. Papers from the three months prior to the March election were filled with accounts of gun battles between politically connected figures, assaults and assassinations of people in public office or involved in political campaigns, gangster terrorism directed against journalists based on the political content of their stories, and editorial commentary and accusations connecting these sorts of behaviors to political interests active in the struggle for democratic power. In this light, the intervention of the People's Liberation Army, which launched dummy missiles over Taiwan two weeks before the election, came as something of a respite from domestic concerns, and was pivotal in mustering an overwhelming margin of support for sitting president Lee Teng-hui. But domestic social problems soon returned to center stage. In April the Chou Jen-sen scandal broke (when a prosecutor obtained an account book recording the bribes paid by a gambling syndicate), resulting in indictment of hundreds of people serving in the criminal justice system, including two precinct-level chiefs of police and a chief prosecutor.[4] The next month, prosecutors and judges from four different district courts issued a combined public statement accusing the president of interfering in the judicial process. In August the chief executive of Taoyuan County, Liu Bangyou, was indicted in a case related to a local bank failure, then murdered along with seven other people meeting at his house. One week after that, Peng Wanru, minister of women's affairs of the Democratic Progressive Party, was abducted, raped, and murdered after leaving a party meeting.

This was too much. Peng Wanru was not a dirty politician, but an icon of progressive hope. Her murder replaced cynicism with moral outrage. Activists began organizing direct action around victimization issues. A foundation disavowing any connection to established political parties was created in Peng's name, its first project being the drafting of a new domestic violence law. Four months later, in April 1997, Bai Xiaoyan, the teenage daughter of a single-mother celebrity named Bai Bingbing, was kidnapped. The story broke immediately and became the central focus of public attention. Negotiations over the ransom payment were broadcast on live television. When those failed (in part because of media interference) and the girl's corpse was found in an industrial canal, it was the trigger for a cataclysmic public outrage that generated the largest mass political action since the 2/28 incident.

A consortium of some five hundred civil society groups coalesced through the process of organizing three protest marches, on May 4, 18, and 24 of 1997, all of which targeted the presidential office. The intensity of these protests, which brought up to one hundred thousand people into the streets simultaneously, was inversely related to the clarity of their demands. Indeed, the phrases written on banners and projected by laser onto the surface of the Presidential Palace were sublimely simple, single-word statements of emotion, like "Sadness," or "Fury." One year after Taiwan's first presidential election, ten years after the end of martial law, the public stood before the seat of executive power asking for better policing. The ground on which they articulated their appeal was pure emotion. Democracy consolidated the centrality of *qing* in the public's demands on police.

In 2003, Taiwan's police college introduced a course on "interpersonal relationships for police" (*jingcha renji guanxi*). The instructor was a former parliamentary liaison officer of the garrison command, Liu Shengzuo, and the textbook he developed for the course was later published under the title *You guanxi, bie shuo nin buhui: Taiwan jingcha renji guanxi xintan* (There's *guanxi*, don't say you can't: A new exploration of interpersonal relations for Taiwanese police) (Liu Shengzuo 2008). Chapter 7 of Liu's text, "The Principles of Communications between Police and Popular Representatives," introduces prospective patrolmen to the complexities that neighborhood democracy will impose on their work. It begins with a review of the electoral system, describing local political machines generated as clientelistic networks organized by vote brokers. Vote brokers are people who organize voting blocs and derive power by managing the quid pro quo relationship between members of these blocs and elected politicians who rely on their support. These networks of political coordination are connected to financial interests, making the political-economic field of local policing "as well organized as a large corporate enterprise, or a well-disciplined army" (Liu Shengzuo 2008, 115). Appreciating the profound influence of this subterranean dimension of the municipal, says Liu, is necessary for *paichusuo* patrolmen to process the attention they can expect to receive from elected officials (*minyi daibiao*, "representatives of the people's will") concerned with individual cases. Handling such visits are of the highest importance in street-level police work. Local councils set police budgets and review personnel decisions. "Misunderstanding a situation" (*wuhui qingshi*—and note "situation" as *qingshi* could be rendered literally as the "things of *qing*") can have serious consequences for *paichusuo* operations as a whole, to say nothing of an individual's career.

Among the many things Liu's candid discussion of politics illuminates is the trajectory of my own fieldwork, as described in chapter 1. My ethnographic access to policing practice moved through the category of friendship, *youqing*, and the way this category enabled a relationship between individuals to be transferred to the *paichusuo* as an institution. This kind of slippage between the intimate and the institutional exemplifies the affordance *qing* supplies the state-society dynamic in Taiwan's contemporary police-community relationship. "Friends of the station" were a constitutive element of the substation's operational routines. At any given time in the station house a diverse assortment of nonpolice would be sitting around its television, drinking tea and smoking cigarettes, available to help out as need be (on "helping out," *bangmang*, see chapter 4). It quickly became evident that individuals who consistently "helped out" in the station were a class unto themselves, and I noticed police occasionally distinguished them from the general category of "friends of the station" by specifying them as "locals" (*difang renshi*, literally "local figures/elites," or even, wryly, *difang shenshi*, "local gentry"). When I asked a patrolman to elaborate on his use of *defang renshi* as a category, he explained, "It's the vocational participants in local affairs, people who are a bit more enthusiastic about participating in community business—the temple management committees, the village or borough chief, the village secretary, the popular representatives, the ones who are routinely active in the locality. . . . There are even some with no formal status at all [who just] like to participate in 'backstage work' . . . you know, the advisers and the 'pillar feet' [vote brokers]."

The significance of the "locals" in policing exemplified the way democratic citizenship in Taiwan has taken root in the networked idiom of *qing*. A primary mode of assistance provided by the locals was supplying political representation to clients caught up in police action, a form of helping out performed as *jiangqing* or *shuoqing*: literally, "speaking *qing*." People seeking to enlist police services on their behalf (to report a crime or mediate a dispute) brought "locals" with them when they arrived at the station. People finding themselves dealing with the police in the streets used their cell phones to summon their patrons, if not to come to the scene and advocate in person, then at least to have a few words with the policeman over the phone. Such advocacy by the locals was crucial in determining the consequences of police intervention. Having a big man on hand to "speak *qing*" on one's behalf could make the difference between gaining recognition as a subject participating in political discussion, or losing control and becoming classified as an object for police processing. In this role, the locals embodied the complexity of state-society relations defining Taiwanese democracy at its grassroots. They constituted a layer of organized political brokerage that served to weave state action into social life through a fabric of network connections. *Qing* provided the idiom in which this integration was achieved.

The patrolmen to whom *qing* was spoken stood in an institutionally weak position vis-à-vis the locals. Vote brokerage traffics in the currency of electoral power, which determines the membership of the councils that approve *paichusuo* staffing matters and fund their operations. Liu's textbook description accepts the institutional subordination of a patrolman embedded in the field of *qing* and, on this basis, articulates a strategy by which line officers can pursue a degree of relative autonomy in their decision making. This strategy turns on the dynamics of "host power," which I introduced in chapter 1. *Zhuquan* is turned into an instrumental technique to the end of "seizing agency" (*bawo zhuti*), and "seizing agency" is analyzed through the power dynamics of host/guest relationships (*zhu/ke*; it is relevant that in modern Chinese *zhuti* is the "subject" and *keti* the "object" in the subject-object dyad). Liu introduces his practical description of "seizing agency" through an anecdote about Theodore Roosevelt. Prior to any meeting, says Liu, Roosevelt would carefully research the background and interests of his guest and thereby gain the ability to "move their sympathies" (*dadong renxin*). This, says Liu, illustrates "grasping subjectivity" as the basis of interpersonal power. A *paichusuo* policeman cultivates skill (*gongfu*) in this field of power by building a *guanxi* network that spans various social spheres, providing access to the *qing* required to understand the distribution of political sympathies within the political environment of his *paichusuo*. Liu's background in the garrison command is evident in his advice. He connects the meaning of *qing* associated with emotional sympathy to its meaning as political intelligence. Applying the principles of political warfare, Liu advises Taiwanese patrolmen to cultivate *ganqing* (sentimental feelings; see below) across a network, which will allow them to construct a *xulie qingbao* (an intelligence report on the enemy's order of battle) that reveals the points of strategic vulnerability in the political formations whose emissaries will come to him asking for favors. He closes his discussion with a relatively concrete example. Suppose, he says, you are processing a robbery case, and an elected councilor (*yiyuan*) arrives to express his concern for (i.e., alliance with) the accused. A constable in such a situation must receive the political representative with utmost politeness (while immediately informing his or her commanding officer of the situation) and in no way hinder the councilor's access to the case. At the same time, however, the patrolman's control of the situation will depend on being able to represent the status of the case-processing to the politician as having passed the point where it would be convenient to intervene. In this way, concludes Liu, "by paying equal attention to law, reason, and sentiment, one can give face to the representation of popular will while still executing governance in substantive accordance with law" (Faliqing jiangu, ji geile minyi daibiao mianzi, ye shouzhule yifaxingzheng de lizi) (Liu Shengzuo 2008, 79).

As *paichusuo* police looked for ways to adapt to their newly democratic conditions, they found inspiration in the same principle of Imperial Chinese jurisprudence on which the institution was originally founded.

The Jurisdiction of *Qing*

Discourses of sentiment are not merely representations or expressions of inner emotions, but articulatory practices that participate in (re) defining the social order and (re)producing forms of self and sociality.

(Lee 2007, 8)

The long arc of modern history includes a cultural process of "moral regulation" (Corrigan and Sayer 1985). This process makes historically particular ideas about properly "civilized" behavior into hegemonic norms (Elias [1939] 2012). The institution of police figures centrally in this. A population becomes "policeable"—which is to say, civilized and modern—as it learns to take its police institutions for granted, engaging with them on the grounds of unquestioned presumptions about what it means to be human such that a human being can be controlled, corrected, and/or improved by the state (Canoy 2007; Silver 1967). For a policed society to also be a liberal society, the process of moral regulation attached to the police power must create more than mere docility; it must "habituate people into the discipline necessary for liberty to be feasible" (Dodsworth 2008, 600). The long arc of Taiwanese modernity institutionalized *qing* as a focal category in the field of moral regulation. As the institutions of neighborhood policing adapted to their role in a liberal political system, the powers invested in *qing* became a crucial feature of the habits of citizenship that allow liberty to flourish.

Isaac Balbus (2010, xiii) summarized the aspiration to democracy as a hope for "the possibility that the governed and the governing might be one and the same." This ideal appears at the heart of an ideal-typical formula for democratic policing known as "Peel's Principles," in the form of an aphorism characterizing the ideal police-community relationship as one that "gives reality to the historic tradition that the police are the public and the public are the police" (Lentz and Chaires 2007, 73). This is not, in itself, a liberal aspiration. Taiwan's Japanese colonial and Chinese authoritarian governments both championed a similar idea through the propaganda slogan "Massify the police, and policify the masses" (Jingcha minzhonghua; minzhong jingchahua; for Japanese usage see Ts'ai 2013; for Chinese see Chen Chunying 2007). This was a patronizing exhortation, valorizing a civilizing project in which self-appointed elites would make the masses into subjects that, someday, perhaps, would be capable of ruling themselves. When democratic reform came, it replaced the overt asymmetries of tutelary rule with an ideal of civic equality. But policing is a place where asymmetries of power persist in the relationship between state and non-state agencies. Taiwan's transition to democracy turned the fundamental antinomy between equality and hierarchy (or consent and coercion, or autonomy and heteronomy) into a central issue for police legitimacy (Martin 2014). The field of politics anchored to the neighborhood police station looked to the category of *qing* as a resource through which to reconcile these contradictions. This is the context that has pushed *qing* to the center of the state-society relationship embedded in Taiwanese police operations.

Taiwan's colonial and autocratic regimes valorized *qing* as a source of the spontaneous dynamics that condition individual character and generate localized political solidarity. They pursued modern governance by finding ways to accommodate and articulate this power with the countervailing power of law, conceived in its *Rechtsstaadt* version as an instrumentality for centralized administration. Cao, Huang, and Sun (2014, 85) describe the *paichusuo* as the institutional "backbone" through which this articulation was achieved; I would extend the metaphor, comparing the population registry to a nerve bundle ensconced within this spinal formation. The basis for this vertebral arrangement was established when the Japanese grafted a modified version of their metropolitan *paichusuo* onto Taiwanese society, using the neo-traditional arrangements of the *hoko* to create a vital joint, preserving elements of indigenous political metabolism within the hard shell of a police state. They subsequently replaced the *hoko* with a totalitarian mobilization structure, but the *paichusuo* endured, supplying an institutional bridge connecting Taiwan's Japanese and Chinese forms of national-socialist authoritarianism. Through the democratic transition, the population registry continued to structure the routines of police work as a personalistic relationship between individual policemen and the collectively defined units of their beat. The population registry is the bureaucratic anchor keeping issues of personal character at the heart of the police power. The overall effect of this, I argue, is a form of modern personhood in which "police status"—the content of one's records in the police registry—takes precedence over legal citizenship as the primary vector for state-provisioned ontological security.

The cultural aspect of this history has made the category of *qing* into a "boundary object"; it inhabits intersecting worlds, linking them by satisfying their divergent expectations (Star and Greisemer 1989). The meaning of the category encompasses a "bundle" of different ideas, hiding their potential contradictions beneath a unified symbolic surface immediately recognizable in very different contexts (Keane 2003, 414). This facilitates the translation of forms of value across the boundaries separating disjoint contexts, "[maximizing] both the autonomy and communication between worlds" (Star and Greisemer 1989, 403).

The materials presented in this chapter expose at least four different ways that *qing* has historically figured into the meaningful organization of Taiwanese policing. In the first place is the imperial jurisprudence of *qing-li-fa*, which mobilizes *qing* to valorize an approach to governance through mediated compromise. As Kuan-Hsing Chen argues, this meaning is preserved in the contemporary values of *minjian*, which is the dominant idiom of political society in Taiwan's democratic era (K.-H. Chen 2010, 224–54). A second meaning of *qing* lies in its foundational position as the customary basis for "traditional" forms of local authority. This interpretation is preserved in the networked practices of host power described in chapter 1, and is consistent with the "differential mode of association" described by Fei Xiaotong ([1947] 1992). A third meaning of *qing* is its definitively modern valorization as the moral force of nationalist revolution (Lee 2007; Lean 2007). This gives *qing* a hard-edged partisan quality, which was exploited for mobilizational purposes by both the Japanese and the Chinese. Finally, slightly beyond the scope of this chapter, is the position the category holds in various traditions of ethical discourse. *Qing* supplies a language through which Confucian philosophy, Buddhist theology, and the popular discourse of Taiwanese folk religious practices address questions about the nature and practical significance of virtue (Feuchtwang 2007; Fingarette 1972). As the seat of virtue, *qing* provides a robust way to answer questions about what police are for.

The historical intersection of these different genealogies in the formation of modern policing supplies any contemporary invocation of *qing* with at least four distinct frameworks of interpretation, each historically warranted, each potentially divergent from the others. This makes the category of *qing* comparable to the "sincerity bundle" Webb Keane identified as a central element of Protestant modernity (Keane 2002). As later described by Niloofar Haeri, this ideal of sincerity covers an ensemble of concepts, including "inner self, spontaneity, originality or authorship of one's words, agency, autonomy, [and] freedom" (Haeri 2017, 127). This plurality of concepts became combined under the sign of "sincerity" by the historical role that Protestant Christianity played in the formation of modern political institutions, and modern subjectivity remains deeply invested in the way this bundle centers the individual as a locus of autonomous moral agency (127).

Considerable attention has been focused on the cultural contrasts that appear when modern Protestant-inspired ideals of sincerity are juxtaposed with Chinese discourses of moral agency (Reilly 2012). For example, Andrew Kipnis invokes *ganqing*—the "feeling of *qing*"—as a way of identifying the Chinese approach to moral virtue as socialized and formalist rather than individualized and spontaneous. "*Ganqing* is not primarily an individual matter. Rather it is a type of feeling that must be conceived of more socially than psychologically (i.e., that is held to exist between and among people as much as in individual's heads). Furthermore, sincerity—at least a notion of sincerity that requires one's words and facial expressions to accurately represent the 'inner' feelings of one's heart—is usually absent from *ganqing*. To be 'sincere' with one's *ganqing* is to be serious about and to live up to the obligations incurred in [relationships]" (Kipnis 1997, 10).

The discourse of *qing* is part of an idiom of socialized moral agency. This invites engagement with properties of the human will (things like individual character and social solidarity) in ways that reject the presumption that moral agency is founded on an individual's capacity for "free will" (Fingarette 1972). Clearly, as a cultural formation, this is well suited to rationalizing illiberal policing technologies. The forms of authoritarian policing described in this chapter were overtly rationalized as a project of cultivating political will, part of a party-led revolutionary project of "political warfare" conceived as "the management of non-violence in the pursuit of military aims" (Marks 1998, 144). Wang Sheng, lead architect of Taiwan's political warfare system, described its aims as follows: "People say Political Warfare emphasizes brainwashing, controlling peoples' thinking. But you can't wrap paper around fire. We are [principally] educating young people. We try to educate them. We cannot control their thoughts" (quoted in Marks 1998, 168). The point is not thought control but subject formation, a project of the will, not the intellect (Bullard 1997).

To grow up in Taiwan under martial law was to become a political subject in a world with an autocratic political center, without checks and balances or the separation of powers and, most definitively, without any safe institutional avenue for political dissent. Nonetheless, there were ways to exercise agency within this constrained political arena. It was a form of politics that Partha Chatterjee describes, by contrast to the bourgeois-liberal idea of "civil society," as "political society" (Chatterjee 2004; K.-H. Chen 2010). The political arena was organized not as a rational debate over abstract principles, but rather as an embodied struggle for basic resources. Leninist mobilizational authoritarianism allowed ordinary people to pursue collective representation of their interests through interest groups, which were very carefully distinguished from political parties. In 1987, when martial law ended, Taiwan had 11,306 registered civic associations, with 8.3 million members (Tien 1989, 45–46). These were the bread-and-butter associations of local politics: the farmers' associations, irrigation associations, trade unions, and commerce or industry associations, through which resources (like bank loans and procurement contracts) were allocated within the system of party-based clientelism (N.-T. Wu 1987). The KMT's Leninist model of social mobilization encouraged voluntary association, treating the institutional structure of civil society as a "transmission belt" for party ideology (Tien 1989, 45). The pursuit of interests was cultivated as a factional game, to be played within a single ideological arena. Interest groups were "protective associations assisting their individual members [which] made no generalized claims on government" (Pye, quoted in Tien 1989, 45).

This arrangement turned front-line executive bureaus into political arenas. "The implementation of policies and laws can be more important to the interests of associations or the general public than [their] formal content. . . . Individual and group demands usually reach the political system at the enforcement stage" (Tien 1989, 55). In other words, the theater of agentive citizenship—the space in which political performances capable of actually affecting one's political life could be staged—was not the legislative assembly but the police station. Conversely, the most politically consequential aspect of policing was the preparatory work done by local elites prior to their contact with the police. The political arena of local citizenship institutionalized by the Japanese under the sign of *qing* persisted, through the arrangements of KMT factionalism, well into the democratic era. My ethnography shows Taiwan's *paichusuo* still function as arenas for a politics of the will, articulating the qualities of individual character and collective solidarity into the political process that maintained the neighborhood's policed order.

POLICING AND THE POLITICS OF CARE

[This is a] *locality* [*difang*]! We aren't like a government organization. We exist in our own community, in the village where we were born and raised. And we Taiwanese, we have this basic common quality: mutual assistance [*xiangzhu*]. Of course, as agricultural society turned into industrial society, and now into this high-technology society, well the *renqingwei* [compassion—literally the "flavor" of human *qing*] gradually eroded. So, naturally, we need to take this, take this so-called *renqingwei*, and make sure it's preserved, that everyone still mutually assists. The people, before, whenever they had trouble or difficulties, well their neighbors would just mutually assist. We're performing that same mediating role [*qianxian de dongzuo*], just weaving the threads. These days, neighbors have nothing to do with one another. But then, because of some certain element, or when some particular thing happens, then people come out and cooperate. And then the conditions are there, for working together to deal with things.

(member of a volunteer vigilance patrol brigade)

Modern policing is closely associated with patrol. Max Weber's idea of the state as a territorial monopoly on political violence suggests that "control of space is a fundamental aspect of overall police efforts at social control" (Herbert 1997, 10). In 1829, when Robert Peel established the historical prototype of the modern police department, he made its core service "preventative" patrol. This drew on precedents as old as the night watch mentioned in the Old Testament, updated for the modern age by advances in science and technology generated by the likes of Cesare Beccaria, Jeremy Bentham, and Patrick Colquhoun (Reeves and Packer 2013). The police power began to assume its familiar contemporary form as developments in communication technology—the invention of automobiles with wireless radios, for example—afforded state agencies an increasingly advantageous "relationship to the time/space axis" (Reeves and Packer 2013, 371). The generic concern of modern governance with the population as a biopolitical object produced the specific form of a local police department that measures its operational "capacity" by the number of patrol officers out driving around searching for something to do (Moskos 2008, 94).

Any mode of policing that puts patrol at its core is oriented by the goal of controlling space. There are valid reasons for projecting police power through space. But if the relationship between the police and the community lacks a shared purpose, the goal of maintaining police control over space can take on pathological attributes. Indeed, Peter Moskos's ethnography of street patrol in Baltimore is a good example of this. There, the war on drugs has given the police department the "moral perspective [of] an occupying force at odds with the community" (2008, 181). Under these conditions, as Moskos describes it, the work of patrol has become a cynical and hopeless endeavor, oriented to the short-term objective of "clearing corners" in order to "assert [the police] right to control public space" (104). The language of "right" here is a kind of euphemism for terror. Police do not expect the community to respect their commands, leaving violence as the indispensable means of control; compliance, says Moskos, is due to "the simple fact that a previous post officer had beat the crap out of some guy who questioned his authority" (105). Echoing the social dynamics of the French anticrime patrols studied by Didier Fassin, Moskos's colleagues took pride in the fear they inspired throughout their jurisdiction. The police institution itself became defined by a subcultural ethos that combined "an exclusive sense of their moral community with a minimalist interpretation of their moral obligations" (Fassin 2013, 212).

Taiwanese *paichusuo* have a patrol function, but the way it is used embodies an understanding of the utility of patrol somewhat different from that presumed in most patrol-centered police studies. The *paichusuo* where I worked kept a single patrol car in operation twenty-four hours a day, driven by officers in two-hour shifts. Thirty officers worked in the station. Each of them would be assigned lead patrol duty once every other shift, on average. These were twelve-to-fourteen-hour shifts, meaning that the "patrolmen" spent, on average, less than 10 percent of their working time actually patrolling. Patrol is clearly not the core of substation policing, nor is the Taiwanese approach to policing defined by the purpose of controlling space. As the historical materials of chapter 2 made clear, the orientation of the Taiwanese *paichusuo* is defined by population first and geography second. Indeed, four hours of every patrolman's daily shift were dedicated to the work of "registry inspection" (*hukou chacha*), during which time he was expected to physically visit the address of each *hukou* record in his *qinqu*, and confirm that all information in the registry was up to date.

If patrol is tangential to the police mission, why do the police patrol? What do they accomplish by projecting their power through the space of the city, and how does this fit into the larger process of policing (i.e., whatever it is they are doing with the other 90 percent of their working time)? This chapter takes an ethnographic description of patrol as a point of departure for considering the overall police-community relationship in contemporary Taiwan, and begins the process of developing an ethnographically grounded model of the police function in the context of Taiwanese democracy.

Patrol

I sat in the back of a police car, on patrol. The landscape outside was a mixture of cheap apartments and unlicensed factories, punctuated by neon lights advertising restaurants, hostess bars, and betel nut stands. Seven million people live in the mountain basin at Taiwan's northern tip. At the time of my fieldwork, the region's administrative structure had not yet been revised to create New Taipei City. The administrative affairs of this population, nearly a third of the island's total inhabitants, were organized into dozens of distinct cities that had emerged independently during the previous fifty years and fused into a sprawling contiguous urban landscape. These were referred to as the "satellite cities" (*weixing chengshi*) of Taipei City proper, suggesting the pseudonym I use for the single city I studied: Weixing City.

Weixing sat across a river that marked the limit beyond which the orderly grid of the capital's streets gave way to a tangled maze of unplanned construction. It had been a small village until the 1960s. Then Taiwan's "economic miracle" brought a flood of people. They came north on the "Axis Line" of Taiwan's old railroad, the Zongguan Xian. Weixing was the last stop before Taipei. Economic migrants pulled by the opportunities of the capital city, but too poor to live there, got off the train in Weixing village. They made the village into a city of its own, one associated with the virtues required to "*baishou qijia*" (build a house with white hands / establish a family from nothing). This building began, stereotypically, with wage labor in the tiny start-up factories that produced things like shoes, umbrellas, and machine parts during Taiwan's initial transition from the import-substitution to the export-focused phase of its state-managed economic development. As the scale of Taiwan's export economy expanded, so did the city, and so did the ambitions of its residents. "Better to be a chicken's head than a cow's ass" (Ningwei jitou buwei niuhou), they said, and used their wages to strike out as petty capitalists en masse. The city's economy expanded as a proliferating network of subcontracting relationships rather than through the growth of large corporate firms (Rigger 2009).

In this developmental pattern, Weixing exemplified a mode of capitalism associated with the "Asian tiger" economies of the 1970s and '80s, which came to be called *guanxi* capitalism. It took its name from the Chinese idiom of "networking" (*guanxi*), which allows a field of individual entrepreneurs to coordinate collective enterprise in a distinctive way. People would secure orders for goods without any way to produce them, then rely on the social capital of their network connections to assemble an ad hoc production network capable of filling the order. It was a mode of production that could turn on a dime and scale instantaneously to satisfy the flexible demands of the foreign brands that sourced their products from Taiwanese suppliers (products that soon included fully manufactured electronics and computer components in addition to shoes and umbrellas).

The Axis Line figured centrally in this arrangement. The railroad was the material infrastructure for a social network that connected Weixing City to every field and factory on Taiwan's west coast. This network constituted an expansive subcontracting economy secured by particularistic forms of solidarity at most one or two degrees of separation from the primary bonds of kinship and native place. The new city became an especially powerful node of network capital, and Weixing citizenship acquired the brand-like qualities of a corporate identity ("I just bring out the name, and everyone takes three steps back," one proud local told me). The term "Axis Line boss" (*Zongguan Xian jiaotou*) became a mark of prestige, used to refer to a group of entrepreneurial elites characterized by a distinctive kind of network power.

The key to *guanxi* capitalism lay in the informal bases of the trust through which it was organized. What transformed the promise of a contract into actual delivery of a product was not a corporate entity governed by formal bureaucratic rules. It was, rather, a constellation of informal commitments between people who knew one another personally, whose faith in one another's promises rested on kinship, friendship, or other genres of intimacy. The migrant community of Weixing provided an open reservoir of this kind of collective capacity, held (self-consciously) as a kind of mutual property. Network members in good standing could represent themselves to outsiders as the owner of an enterprise, and secure contracts on the basis of this representation, confident they would be able to find others willing to help them deliver on their promises post hoc. Maintaining good standing within the community was crucial to the career of an individual. And the integration of the overall system was carried by the integrity that people invested in their individual reputation. The political life of a city built from *guanxi* capitalism is anchored in the substantive weight of personal reputation. People cultivated their reputational identity—*guanxi* citizenship, one might say—by displaying the virtues that invite social recognition of a trustworthy character (Y. Yan 1996; Kipnis 1997; Osberg 2013). The performance of Weixing citizenship emphasized the fierce virtues of a self-made bourgeoisie—the decisiveness of *ashali*, the integrity of *yiqi*, the generosity of *dafang*—even as it gestured toward a surface discourse of broadly "Confucian" orthodoxy (Martin 2013c).[1]

The Axis Line network acquired mafia overtones in the larger popular culture. Its bosses were understood to be capable of guaranteeing contracts that were not always negotiated under purely voluntary conditions. From the murky field of reputation, rumor, and innuendo arose a determinate institutional formation: the "Weixing Gang" (Weixing Bang). Half *chaebol*-style business conglomerate, half political faction, the Weixing Gang featured prominently in Taiwan's tabloid media. Its public face included political figures at every level, from the national legislature to the city council, as well as some of the country's most prominent capitalists. These connected individuals were understood as part of a larger and less visible network, which, among the many things it did, controlled the city's municipal administration as well as its informal economy. The ubiquitous power of the Weixing Gang circulated through the capillaries of city life as the borough chiefs (*lizhang*) and "pillar feet" (*zhuangjiao*) who cultivated the networked fabric of "vote brokerage" by which Taiwanese democracy operates at its grassroots.

This was the political economy the police kept in order. Our patrol car navigated tangled streets, village pathways transformed into canyon-like boulevards by an unbroken wall of four- and five-story buildings, put up at breakneck speed during the '70s and '80s. We stayed on the larger roads, close to the concrete fortifications that protected the city from its surrounding rivers. No need, yet, to venture into the tiny one-lane (or smaller) alleyways through which most local residents accessed their homes and businesses. Inside the car, Axiong, the lead patrol officer, Acu, his support officer, and I smoked cigarettes and made small talk. It was after midnight in monsoon season. Everything was glazed with rain, amplifying the reflection of the neon lights through the windshield.

The dispatch radio in the dashboard came to life with Axiong's station house number, "402, 402 . . ." We fell silent to listen to the call. The dispatcher relayed that an anonymous person had reported an illegal gambling casino operating inside the headquarters of the All People's Taxi Drivers' Union. We were to go check it out. Axiong burst out laughing and remarked, apropos of our ongoing conversation, that there could be no more perfect illustration of what "patriotism" (*aiguo*, literally "love of the state") meant in Weixing City: gambling at someone else's table, then turning them in to the police if you lose.

Axiong turned the car around and drove back to the police station. The union headquarters and the police station were located within eyeshot of one another, diagonally across a T-shaped intersection next to the levee, sharing the shelter of a large bridge. The union headquarters was a two-story building that marked one edge of a large territory controlled by taxi drivers. Their union was a federation of separate chapters, each of which elected its own leadership and claimed a different segment in a stretch of land that ran from one bridge to the next along the levee. Individual chapters built physical compounds in this space by stacking railroad-boxcar-size shipping containers on top of one another to create a perimeter wall, then cutting doors and windows into the steel to turn the containers into functional space. Inside these walls, they parked their cars and conducted their business. During elections, the sections flew chapter banners from their ersatz ramparts and occasionally lit bonfires at night, which illuminated the flags from behind and created a visual effect that reminded me of a medieval castle. It was widely rumored that the fortresslike space created by the assembled compounds was used for trade in untaxed gasoline, prostitution, and gambling. The police, however, seemed to ignore the existence of the edifice, despite its proximity to their station. I was interested in how this call would be handled.

We parked the patrol car at the police station and walked across the street to a doorway in the perimeter wall adjacent to the headquarters building. A man was standing outside the door. The patrolman told him we were responding to a complaint and wanted to go inside. We stood talking with the doorman for a while, as a flood of people poured out of the doorway and disappeared up and down the street. Once the doorway was clear, the doorman took the three of us in the door, through a muddy space full of vehicles and improvised buildings, to a structure made from two shipping containers welded together. We were met there by a burly man with his hair done up in a permanent wave and a thick gold chain around his neck, evidently a boss in the operation. The doorman left, and the boss showed us inside the room, revealing a collection of green-felt-topped tables of the kind on which people play *majiang* (mah-jongg). But there were no people inside, and no gambling tiles. Axiong walked slowly around the room inspecting the tables. Then he told the boss, "Listen, we're getting complaints. The cars out front are blocking the street." The boss looked stern, but he replied politely, "OK, don't worry. I'll take care of it." "Thanks," said the patrolman. And we were escorted back out to the street.

Later that night we broke for tea at the station house, and I asked about the call. It was the first time I had seen a policeman enter the compound across the street, I began. "Oh, that," Axiong interrupted me. "You need to be careful over there, or you can get your ass kicked [beida]. 'All People' is a powerful group." Oh. Well. What kind of power do they have? I asked. Axiong looked at me blankly. "Tamen you chulai jianghua de quanli," he said: They have the power to come out and speak.

The police station and the union headquarters were uneasy neighbors, brought together by the historical process that built the city. Their shared relation to the bridge above them exemplified their connection. The bridge was huge, more than a kilometer in suspended length. Its final span extended into the city for several blocks before touching ground. The police station itself was adjacent to the span, with one of its parking lots directly underneath. Standing on the station's front porch I could see where the bridge passed over the levee, intersecting with an elevated road. That juncture was a monumental tangle of cement, a conjuncture of different structures, all built at different times, none of them quite fitting into the others. The top of the levee had a footpath that I used to walk to and from the station. At night, reaching the intersection with the bridge, I tiptoed past figures sleeping there. It was one of the places where the city's homeless lived, inhabiting the contingent shelter created by a public architecture designed to protect the property of householding citizens.

The union headquarters sat directly beneath this intersection, backed up to the levee, shadowed by the bridge, spreading the steel walls of its chapter compounds along the embankments to either side. Like the homeless camp on the levee above it, the union compound was a transitory occupation of functionally marginal, ostensibly public space. It held ground that had been requisitioned for a municipal drainage project. Political expropriation endowed the land with a complicated legal status. This complexity was well suited to the union's powers, which combined a reservoir of networked political capital the union had accumulated during the democratic transition with a standing capacity for organized collective violence by its membership (cf. Harms 2013). Indeed, the process by which All People's Taxi came to hold its territory was of a piece with Taiwan's democratic transition. The union itself formed during the unruly election season of 1994, which included the first popular election of Taipei's mayor following the end of martial law. During the campaign, the union provided security for candidates running against the erstwhile party-state. Upon gaining office, these politicians helped build the union compound as quid pro quo.

Cities are built as a human intervention in the conjuncture of various forces and flows. The physical geography of the Taipei Basin is defined by huge rivers that drain from its mountains to the sea. When monsoons come, if the tide is high, those rivers can suddenly overflow. Flooding is a chronic problem. But housing in a floodplain is cheap. And cheap housing is always in short supply. In the 1960s and '70s, a wave of domestic migrants drawn to the economic opportunities of the metropolis transformed the villages surrounding Taipei into an agglomeration of three million people living in cheap-rent districts with population densities as high as forty thousand people per square kilometer. In 1972 an agricultural engineer named Lee Teng-hui launched his political career (as "minister without portfolio" in the central government) by championing a public works project to shift built structures off this floodplain and contain its rivers in a series of dikes and canals. It was a project of a type and scale designed to make economic fortunes and political careers. Lee ("Mr. Half-Democracy" his critics later called him) used the project to cultivate the clientelistic networks through which he became mayor of Taipei in 1978, governor of Taiwan in 1981, vice president in 1984, appointed president in 1988, and, finally, in 1996, the first democratically elected president of the Republic of China.

The authoritarian single-party regime dissolved during Lee's ascent. As mentioned in chapter 2, it ended when the first opposition party, the Democratic Progressive Party (DPP), was born from the "Outside the Party" movement. The process of regime change saw an efflorescence of new party organization, as factional networks cultivated within the erstwhile party-state shattered into a multitude of aspiring proto-parties competing for office on their own accounts (K.-l. Chin 2003). Throughout this tumultuous time, the DPP remained the dominant opposition party. They accumulated seats in the limited slate of elections open to general suffrage prior to full democratization, and continued to agitate for constitutional reform to open more important legislative and executive offices to election. Their victories in this endeavor were intertwined with the career of Chen Shui-bian, a lawyer who entered politics in 1979 trying to keep "Outside the Party" activists out of jail. In 1989 he was elected to the national legislature. In 1994 he became the first elected mayor of Taipei. And in 2000 he became the country's first opposition president.

The years between the formation of the DPP in 1986 and the 1994 election in which it took control of Taipei were tumultuous, a scramble for the spoils of deregulation in a context of dynamic constitutional ambiguity. All People's Taxi was born of the unsettled and sometimes violent politics of this period. Members of the union explained their origins in a sort of Marxist allegory. Taxi drivers share a vocational interest in the way their vehicles—their "means of production"—are regulated. The end of martial law promised to liberalize all forms of regulation. Of immediate concern to taxi drivers was licensing reform to allow individual ownership of cars, breaking the Leninist trade monopoly that had previously allocated licenses as a reward for supporting the party. The founding members of All People's Taxi came together as a syndicate of independent drivers supporting political figures who championed this reform agenda.

The incorporation of the union happened to coincide with a deregulation of telecommunications. The nascent taxi firm acquired a dispatching system that allowed lateral car-to-car communications, a technology formerly restricted to military use. The drivers immediately began to use the new radio system to organize quasi-military action. In the lead-up to the 1994 election, the union began protecting candidates they supported from street violence, their new communications capacity allowing them to function as a vigilante patrol apparatus providing on-call security to political patrons.

The "class" interests of taxi drivers were not united within a single political party, however. There were other taxi unions, allied with other patrons and other parties. This created a volatile situation, connecting the emergent space of democratic political struggle between parties to the enduring economic conflict between taxi drivers over control of physical space (as different firms struggled to enforce permanent claim to lucrative sites for taxi stands outside hotels, etc.). The patrol capacity enabled by a radio-dispatched fleet provided a mechanism for increasingly organized campaigns for control of territory. Taxi firms could now project force in ways similar to the police. Conflicts between individual taxi drivers over access to customers began to scale, almost instantaneously, through networks of radio-linked cars, into battles between opposed armies.

The state police struggled to find a safe position in the taxi driver wars of the early '90s. Some of the most polarized electoral competitions were for seats on local councils. Another post-authoritarian reform, the "Local Autonomy Law," gave those councils considerable influence over budget and personnel arrangements of the police stations located in their districts. Dealing with the taxi wars thus combined the physical danger that police face as a third party in somebody else's fight with the institutional intrigue of a battle for control over the political and economic foundations of police operations. Video footage of the most dramatic encounters show police decked out in riot gear huddling in a defensive position to one side, as hundreds of taxi drivers fight running battles with sticks, knives, cars, and petrol bombs. Those spectacles marked a moment in the process of democratic reform when the political grounds of police power shifted perceptibly. The old order of autocratic command was being replaced by a democratic struggle for power between factional networks of the kind embodied in taxi drivers' unions.

Those battles ended years before my fieldwork. The members of All People's Taxi I came to know included individuals who had already served the five- and six-year sentences handed out (indiscriminately, they claimed) for the injuries and deaths that occurred in the violence of the early 1990s. The city's transitional period of street-fighting politics had been absorbed into the peace of an established balance of territorial and political powers. The ideological intensity of All People's Marxist rhetoric had muted as well. They still explained themselves as "standing completely on the side of labor"—that is, their drivers, whose struggle for control over the means of their economic livelihood mobilized the original movement. But they qualified these principles by cynical observations of a "cyclic process in which unions, formed around collective ideals, degenerate into interest groups . . . everyone is just focused on money now." The tragic self-interested quality of human nature justified the union's current identity as just another corporate player in the city's segmentary political economy. Their solidarity no longer held any utopian hope for reform. It had settled into a conservative commitment to factional alliance necessitated by the struggle to maintain control of an established economic estate.

The history embodied in the union's territorial claim to its compound endowed union members with a citizenship adequate to meet the police on a more or less equal footing. And, thus, the encounter I observed that evening was resolved entirely through reciprocal gestures of "giving face." Superficial politeness was adequate to repair the momentary disequilibrium of a historical balance of powers provoked by an errant complaint. It may have been a coincidence that the powers rebalanced by this ritual formality were headquartered in buildings beneath a bridge, but bridging is certainly an apt metaphor for the cultural dimensions of the situated encounter. Sheltered beneath a physical bridge, the uneventful resolution of the encounter moved across a virtual bridge on which the police and the union met each other halfway, so to speak. This kind of bridgework—opposite sides coming together through a careful consideration of power and propriety—kept the historically conflicted political economy of the city in order.

Everyone has to live somewhere. Not everyone grounds a claim to space on pugnacious factional solidarities of the sort that empowered All People's Taxi. I rented. During my fieldwork I spent several years living in something called *jiagai*, "extra construction." This was an apartment on the sixth floor of a seven-story building. The two top floors of the building had been added surreptitiously, after the building permits had been secured and inspections completed. They were, thus, unregistered. It was a common arrangement. I was told the custom arose during the martial law period, when there was a general ban on buildings taller than five stories. As economic prosperity brought migrants to urban areas, people began to build "extra" structures on top of existing buildings. This remained a common practice after height restrictions were eased, producing an irregular skyline of extra stories, rooms, pigeon houses, and other functional appendages. Such unregistered housing was cheap (and tended to have great views), but it came with a distinctive set of problems. One had to "borrow" (as it were) someone else's legal address for one's ID card, health insurance, voting registration, electric and water services, mail delivery, etc. Living physically off the registry grid channeled one's official business through the bases of informal solidarity by which registry addresses were shared.

While I was living in *jiagai*, my *hukou* registration was filed using the address of a friend's legal apartment several blocks away. At one point, an awkward spell in relations with that friend resulted in my "official" (as it were) channel of communication with the state being temporarily cut off. During that period, I had the strange experience of running into a mutual acquaintance of my registry-address friend, a woman I barely knew. Upon seeing me, she rummaged through her purse and handed me a photograph of myself committing a traffic infraction, exhorting me to take care of this matter quickly, before the fines began to increase exponentially (see Martin 2013).

Traffic violations in Taiwan are documented by hidden cameras, with the photograph and ticket being subsequently mailed to the census address at which the license plate is registered. Receiving a citation by purse is an outcome of the interface between the formal anchor of the registry address and informal networks of neighborly concern. As an event of law enforcement, this experience exemplified the kind of bureaucratized intimacy people use to cultivate the administered life they hold in common. The shared accountability of a registry address served to integrate an ethos of neighborliness and mutual concern within the formal enforcement of a legal penalty. The operative regime of discipline was a hybrid formation that effectively fused intimate compassion with bureaucratic surveillance. Such arrangements are perfectly suited to maintaining the baroque complexity of order in a city that has taken historical shape around and beyond the limits of law.

And so a traffic ticket was issued, delivered, and eventually paid. The circuit of a single policing event was closed, its purpose realized. To speak functionally, what all this work accomplished—what it was *for*—was not (just) adding money to the municipal treasury or altering my driving behavior, but performing neighborliness. The movement of a penalty through a network consolidated the field of care-for-one-another that linked it to its target. The lasting product or effect of this act of police enforcement was a revitalization and intensification of the threads of solidarity that defined me as an element in the nested hierarchies of mutual care which embedded me in the city's social order. A banal and mild example, to be sure, but it resonates with the visit to the taxi union compound. In both cases, the eccentric movement of police attention through the city had the effect of activating and exercising its historically balanced network of powers as a tangible reminder to be careful.

Police have to live somewhere too. The *paichusuo* patrolmen lived in a dormitory on their station's top floor. This was not their formal registry address (which, as far as I knew, was generally at their wife and children's residence if married, parents if not). But it was where most of them got most of their sleep. They didn't get much sleep. The time pressure a busy *paichusuo* placed on its front-line staff was intense. Formal shifts ran twelve to fourteen hours a day. An individual officer's daily shift was arranged to rotate around the clock; every day or two it began two hours later than it had started the previous day. This ensured the police station was fully staffed twenty-four hours a day without separate day/night/swing shifts. It also effectively disrupted any semblance of normal routine for police officers, imposing the temporality of their job over any other chronological pattern.

The internal organization of their shift contained some flexibility. This was not intended for the benefit of police, but rather for the community they served.

Much of the patrolmen's work involved writing reports in coordination with members of the community, whose schedules had to be accommodated by flexibility on the part of the police. This expanded the actual distribution of an individual patrolman's engagement in his work to cover, essentially, twenty-four hours a day, seven days a week. Patrolmen slept in whatever breaks they could find between tasks, often amounting to only four or five hours a day. The physical stress of sleep deprivation was a significant aspect of the police lifestyle, leading to health problems known colloquially as "death by overwork" (*guolaosi*). This was a real syndrome. During my fieldwork one patrolman, at the relatively young age of thirty-five, fell unconscious to the floor while working in the station. He was rushed to hospital, where it was discovered that he had suffered kidney failure caused by high blood pressure, aggravated if not induced by his working routine.

The fact that the patrolmen lived in the station gave it a domestic atmosphere. Whatever else might be going on there, it was home to thirty chronically tired men in their twenties and early thirties. At any given time of night or day some of them would be just waking up. If it happened to be near a mealtime, they would make their way to the dining room in the basement to be fed by the matronly woman who worked as the station cook. If not, there was usually a pile of food on the tea table, leftovers from various midmorning, midafternoon, or late-night snacks brought into the station to be consumed en masse. A waking patrolman would fill his belly and smoke a few cigarettes at the tea table, wander over to his locker to finish putting on his uniform, and, finally, check the duty roster on the wall.

The duty roster was a chart composed of a horizontal axis that represented twenty-four hours broken down into two-hour periods, and a vertical axis that listed categories of shift duty (detailed below). An individual policeman's time on duty was marked by his name appearing in these cells, dispersed throughout the matrix of responsibilities so that his assignment generally changed every two hours. This supplied the basic rhythm of substation life: every two hours the operations center came to life in a flurry of activity, as it filled with men returning from patrol, inspection, or census duty, signing into and out of various record books, and exchanging the car keys, reflective vests, radios, traffic batons, record books, handguns, and bullets that they shared.

Standard daily duties for a patrolman included lead patrol (*xunluo*), patrol assistance, staffing the station desk (*zhiban*), "beat investigation" (*qinqu chacha*), preparatory work (*beiqin*), plus a more eclectic collection of timely or specialized forms of work, like the "inspection" (*linjian*) of street checkpoints or businesses; standing guard (*shouwang*) at recent trouble spots or public events; information processing (*ziliao zhengli*); testifying in court (*fayuan zuozheng*); material requisitions (*huowei jian caimai*); or participating in any one of the multitude of "special projects" (*zhuan'an*) always under way, which ranged from street-clearing initiatives and drunk-driving crackdowns to guarding polling booths or securing the transport of nuclear waste through the city.

The most significant assignment was lead patrol. The policeman with this assignment was, for the two hours he held it, personally responsible for all cases that occurred within the substation's jurisdiction (an area of roughly two square kilometers containing a resident population of about forty thousand people; the city as a whole had ten *paichusuo*). He drove the patrol vehicle (car or motorcycle) and, accompanied by the policeman assigned to assist him, was dispatched as first responder to all calls. He was held personally responsible for the paperwork generated by any case he responded to. The amount of paperwork involved in a single case could be considerable. Given the chronic difficulties of scheduling interviews and gathering supporting documents, the processing time for a complicated case could stretch into weeks or even months. Dealing with the paperwork backlog generated by the caseload gathered during time spent on lead patrol was one of the primary reasons for a patrolman to become sleep deprived. This potentially unmanageable workload was at the core of many of the "complicated" (*fuza*) aspects of policing—particularly the mode of bureaucratic deflection referred to as "eating cases" (*chian*)—that is, not filing them.

Patrol might seem like a universal feature of policing, an elementary technique with little potential for variation across different systems. That is not the case. Mobility in the abstract does not have a single functional purpose. Taiwanese *xunluo* was quite different from the American police patrols I have observed. It was modeled more on the juridical tour of a county magistrate than the belligerent slog of an infantry soldier, which is to say that its aesthetic tended more to visitation than invasion.[2] To be sure, the formal purpose of the practice was defined (in line with Robert Peel's founding conception of municipal policing as a patrol-centered practice) as preventing crime by maintaining a publicly visible police force. To amplify the preventive effect, it was policy to keep the flashing lights of the police car permanently on, and otherwise broadcast police presence as ostentatiously as possible. The "proactive" dimension of patrol, which filled down-time when not engaged in the "reactive" work of answering calls for service, was treated as a more or less passive advertisement that police existed. It consisted of driving slowly through the city's permanent traffic jam, lights flashing but no less stuck in traffic than everyone else, while stopping periodically to get out of the car and sign in to patrol boxes.

The formal organization of patrol consisted of a fixed route defined by small metal boxes hung on the walls of buildings.[3] These boxes contained a paper pad stamped with shift times, on which the responsible patrolman would sign his name as he passed by, documenting his presence in the area. Signing all the boxes on a given route was the definition of completing it. A motivated team could, if not interrupted by calls for service, dispose of their patrol route in about thirty minutes (with advance coordination, a team could take care of several shifts in the same thirty-minute route, by signing multiple cells on the form). The rest of the shift would then be used for socializing, hanging out in back rooms of local businesses, in the back-alley clubhouses of borough chiefs and corner bosses, or in the private rooms of local restaurants and karaoke bars. This kind of socializing was (according to my interlocutors) not malingering: it was the beating heart of their job. Leaving the station house was an opportunity to exercise the circuits of reciprocity that connected them with their institutional "friends" in the neighborhood. This is an interpretation of police patrol not defined by the practice of driving around looking for predefined problems. It invested resources of time and police attention in hanging out in the back rooms of local businesses, where they could participate in the social processes where problems are defined (see Martin 2013a).

Minli, "Civil Force"

The social dimension of policing is, among other things, a space of dialogue about the kinds of problems that police deal with. Elements of this dialogue are consequentially involved in the way problems are dealt with. Mild forms of influence began with the casual banter in the station's reception area, and escalated through the *yingchou* circuits that consolidated the networked circulation of police powers through the wider community. When an especially thorny case was brought back to the *paichusuo* (as I will describe in the next chapter), an ad hoc informal assembly would be convened in the station's back room for the quasi-parliamentary task of developing a politically tractable interpretation of the problem at hand. The more consequential the political discussion, the higher the status of those called up to participate. At the top of the national hierarchy is a class of people I have described as "outlaw legislators" (Martin 2013c). In the humble confines of a neighborhood police substation, the *difang renshi* "local elites" (mentioned in chapter 2) serve as the regular informal parliamentarians of the backroom assembly.

From the origins of modern policing in Taiwan to the present day, the *paichusuo* has functioned as a platform for articulating the countervailing powers of local politics and central administration. Its quasi-parliamentary aspect is the functional core of a dialogical mode of policing. As one policeman described the contemporary version of this practice to me,

> When it's not too serious, a verbal disagreement or some sort of personal dispute, then police are basically there just to mediate. And there

are times when the people, both sides, neither one is willing to give! They don't necessarily always listen to us. So that's when we call the village chief, or some local elites, maybe some of the township councilors, and we ask them to come down [and] stand in an intermediate position, and pacify the two sides. . . . When people see that the village chief himself has come out to deal with it, well then they just improve their posture a bit, you know. The emotions calm down. So, actually, the [local elite's] role and the police role are, like, well when we [police] are dealing with a situation, some sort of dispute, if we already know both sides, then that's pretty easy to deal with. We just communicate directly with both sides and calm things down right away. But when we don't know them, well, then there is no possibility that they are going to give us any face. Each individual is just going to insist they have their own reasons. So, really, then the role of the village chief is just that he knows both sides of the dispute. He is better placed as a bridge, to bridge the difficulties.

This is an interpretation of policing as the labor of keeping peace by negotiating reasonable adjustments to the sentimental fabric of community life against a backdrop of abstract legal institutions (the so-called shadow of the law). Within this endeavor, the capacity of local elites to operate as what might be called "sentiment brokers" makes them a crucial resource. Neighborhood policing in Taiwan is unimaginable without them.

The powers that local elites bring into the police station are anchored somewhere outside it. As my opening anecdote about All People's Taxi illustrated, law enforcement is not the only problem-solving game in town. Local elites come into the process of dialogical policing holding a perspective slightly different from that articulated by the policeman above. A *cunzhang* (village chief) explained the system to me as follows:

[How to respond] really depends on the precise nature of the problem. For example there are some things, like street fighting and such problems between the youngsters, they just go directly to the local gangsters [*hunhun*], you know; the "local head snake" [*ditoushe*], the local big man [*laoda*], is going to come out and solve those problems, those kind of criminal matters. But now, if you're talking about violation of a regulation, like a traffic infraction or something, well then sometimes, sometimes they don't want us to get involved. Because when regulations have been broken, and the police are writing up a citation . . . well, we are the ones who "speak sentiment" [*shuoqing*]. And we local village and borough chiefs, we *minyi daibiao* [representatives of popular will], we see those things, their nature, well, like suppose you are doing something you know is obviously wrong, or you aren't showing people respect. In that case we aren't going to "speak sentiment" on your behalf. . . . Generally speaking, if it's something like a traffic infraction, then the residents here are definitely going to ask the village chief to come down and use a bit of *guanxi* [*guanshuo yixia*] . . . or at home, when a household has a domestic disagreement, then they will get the village chief to come look at the situation. And if there is something troublesome, then we can ask the police to come. Because, when it comes to the judiciary, there is a big difference between the police and the village chief. The judiciary is more inclined to believe the police, because the village chief is embedded in human *qing* [*shou renqing de baowei*].

Both accounts describe police work as sitting in a juncture between two contrasting domains of order. The *difang renshi* represents a sentiment-based order of local politics; the police represent the legal authority of the central administration. The two sides come together through a common understanding of the state-based political system as a hierarchical world. Its bottom is the spontaneous solidarities of *qing*. It moves upward from this concrete ground into higher realms of abstraction, at first through absorption into the broadly representative institutions of local politics (an arena including the formal offices of local *minyi daibiao* and the reputation-based status of local elites). The police come into the picture at the next level, another step in the escalation toward formal mediation and then into the courts. This is precisely the model developed over the *longue durée* history of modern policing in Taiwan described in chapter 2. The *hukou* is the infrastructure substantiating and supporting this idea of the state. Each individual belongs to the administrative apparatus as a "mathematical" unit (*kou*) contained within the politically defined collective of a *hu*, which is, in turn, part of the duty area assigned to an individual policeman. The *hukou*-police nexus, as a taken-for-granted political infrastructure, shapes the political culture of Taiwan. Modern subjects carry an internalized sense of the state within themselves, an "idea of the state . . . (partially) constitutive of 'available' modes of being human" (Corrigan and Sayer 1985, 179–80). The *paichusuo* anchors a world in which the politics of police dialogue—ranging from informal networking over a cup of tea to high-stakes performances in the para-parliamentary arena of the station house back room—effectively police the dialogical politics of democracy.

The basic bureaucratic logic of Taiwanese policing is supplied by the population registry. But patrol is not organized by the *hukou*. The physical projection of police power into the city cross-cuts and exceeds the rationality of the population registry system. The dialogical ethos of policing is carried into the structure of patrol through the category of *minli*, "civil power." This is a bureaucratic category that shows up in the organizational diagram of *paichusuo* operations to denote functions executed by volunteers. Two constituted volunteer systems were left behind from the Leninist mobilizational era: the Civil Defense corps (Minfang) and the Volunteer Police (Yijing). Both of those institutions remained active through the democratic transition and are mobilized every New Year's holiday to spend a month patrolling alongside the police in a ritual known as the Spring Peace Work (Chun An Gongzuo). Supplementing those Leninist legacy organizations is a much more active form of volunteer policing institution that was created during the democratic transition, called "vigilance and mutual assistance patrol teams" (*shouwang xiangzhu xunshoudui*; cf. Martin 2010). Unlike Civil Defense and the Volunteer Police, which are civilian adjuncts organized entirely by the regular police, vigilance patrol teams are organized independently from the police and conduct their own independent patrol operations. A number of different agencies are legally authorized to create them, including the lowest-level political representatives (i.e., the *lizhang* / borough chiefs), the management committees of high-rise apartment buildings, and a kind of semi-NGO called a Community Development Association (Shequ Fazhan Xiehui). After their legal authorization in the 1990s, vigilance patrol teams became ubiquitous. By the early 2000s, there were some sixteen thousand nationwide, an average of ten per *paichusuo* (Martin 2010). The jurisdiction of the *paichusuo* in which I conducted fieldwork had a dozen active vigilance teams, meaning there were two to three times as many people working as vigilance volunteers than there were regular police patrolmen. The *paichusuo*'s commanding officer made a weekly tour in which he visited them all, spending anywhere from a few minutes to half an hour sitting in their clubhouses talking (and drinking) with their staff. Such social visits were an important part of the commanding officer's job, he remarked to me the first time I accompanied him on these rounds, because "these groups are important sources of information. So of course I have to visit them regularly, to cultivate trust and *ganqing*."

I conducted interviews with a few of those teams and went out on patrol with one several times (ending up on the nightly news as a "foreign volunteer"). A few years after my *paichusuo* fieldwork, I spent an entire summer doing participant-observation with a vigilance patrol team in southern Taiwan, as part of a National Police Administration–sponsored evaluation of community policing initiatives (see Martin 2010). One night early in that project, as we made our rounds, I noticed strips of black paper covered with arcane pictographs glued to the doorjambs of the houses we drove past. In some cases, the strips were pasted adjacent to the white plastic patrol boxes that the vigilance team had used to mark out their official route (thus distinguishing their route from that marked by the green metal patrol boxes of the police). The juxtaposition of black paper and white plastic was visually striking, and I asked the driver of the car about it.

> "Those paper strips are charms [*fu*][4] issued by the Court of the Three Kings [Sanwang Gong, a local temple] for their Circuit of the Jurisdiction [Raojing, an annual ritual]. You know, when God goes out on patrol," he said.
>
> "Oh! God also patrols?"
>
> "Yes. Once every year. On his birthday."
>
> "God patrols . . . like you patrol?"
>
> "No, no, no. [*laughter*] That's like [*pause*] there are a lot of people. It's like a parade. It's totally different."
>
> I mulled this over. "OK, it's totally different," I said. "So what is it that makes them both 'patrol' [*xunluo*]?"
>
> He was silent for a moment. Then he replied, "They are both types of *care* [*guanhuai*]."

Defining patrol as an expression of care is a compelling idea. And the fact that the policed landscape was arranged to be read for signs of care, emplaced by a plurality of guardian forces (secular and spiritual), came as an epiphany to me.[5] My work with those volunteers opened up a cultural nexus implicating their policing activities in several different idioms of caretaking. Coming to see the overall field of social control as a division of caretaking labor produced a wholesale shift in my analytic perspective, significant far beyond the lexical coincidence I stumbled across in the term *xunluo*. Individual members of the team proved to be remarkably articulate about the affective dimensions of their practice. Indeed, they took discussion of feelings (*ganqing* and *renqing*) and compassion (*renqingwei*) as the natural discursive frame in which to evaluate policing outcomes.

This made institutional sense because of the way vigilance patrol was organized by a discourse of guardianship as mutual concern. This discourse was crystallized in the preamble to the team's formal charter, which opened,

> In Taiwan's early agricultural era, folk custom was simple and honest. Residents of village and neighborhood were intimately familiar with one another. And, thus, practices of "vigilance and mutual assistance" [*shouwang xiangzhu*] were prevalent. But with the industrial age, social custom was transformed. Interpersonal relations became weak, transforming us into strangers no longer possessed of active mutual concern. Gradually, this led to a degradation of the social order, and qualita-

tive changes in the environment, with such a proliferation of "signs of chaos" [*luanxiang*] that community life was no longer secure.

The term "vigilance and mutual assistance" carries pivotal significance. It is a *chengyu*, an idiomatic set-phrase that invokes the authority of its literary source. Its source is a passage in Mencius describing quality of life in a well-governed polity: "Coming and going in mutual amity, vigilant in mutual assistance, mutually supportive in illness and adversity, the people live in harmony." In the late 1990s, this *chengyu* was deployed by the Lee Teng-hui administration to encourage the formation of a new type of civil police organization, as mentioned above.[6] The team's charter drew on the traditional overtones of its government-issued classification to articulate a mandate for volunteer policing against the specter of anomie. Economic progress, it explained, causes social problems; modern markets disconnect economic survival from personal relationships, and the "mechanical solidarity" of primitive community gives way to a troublesome mixture of instrumental solidarities and normlessness (Durkheim 1893). Founding their mandate in this trope gave the vigilance patrol broad latitude to respond to "signs of chaos" that invoke order as a potential or absent presence. The institutional legitimacy of vigilance patrols asserts traditional social "harmony" as a natural fact, tragically eroded by the artifice of modern alienation. No further details of how this authentic/primitive "folk custom" actually worked (or, perhaps, failed to work) need be provided. Indeed, that such natural harmony has become obscure to the contemporary mind can be taken as evidence of how far that mind has fallen from the pristine clarity of its original intuitions. Thus does policing legitimated by ideological tropes of modern degeneration substitute vague nostalgia for explicit policy.

This interpretive strategy is ubiquitous in "community policing" discourse worldwide. The locus classicus of "broken windows" policing, for example, explicitly defines the "order" at stake in policing as "an inherently ambiguous term, but a condition that people in a given community recognized when they saw it" (Kelling and Wilson 1982). A police mandate founded on such nostalgia empowers its executor to traffic in controlled applications of "moral panic" (Caldeira 2000). This is a strategy that leverages the founding idea of Durkheimian criminology: the contrast that sets criminal law apart from other kinds of law in regard to the underlying modality of "social solidarity" at stake. Crime, in this approach, is constituted by the spontaneous, collective revulsion of shared moral intuitions. Civil, administrative, and constitutional law, by contrast, are founded in the less immediately affective sphere of abstract rational interdependence (Durkheim 1893). In the anomic environment of a late-modern "administered society," images of crime are a useful instrument for generating scarce resources of moral solidarity and collective will (leading to the trend toward "governing through crime" observed in many places around the contemporary world: see Simon 2007; Penglase 2014; Larkins 2015; Comaroff and Comaroff 2016).

Members of the vigilance patrol were cognizant of this technique and placed it consciously at the center of their enterprise. "You only have to say that there is a thief somewhere, and a kind of a solidary psychology arises, a kind of unique power of unity. Everyone comes out searching together. Everyone comes out to surround, to advance, to 'handle the situation,' together. I have learned this, I have *felt* this," one of them said to me:

> For example, there was one time, just before the New Year, oh we were so happy! The factory's burglar alarm went off, the phone call came, and we were all here [at headquarters], so we deployed immediately. And it was not only our team that responded. The villagers too, when they heard the news, well, twenty or thirty people all came out to go and catch those thieves. And that, *that* has really achieved the meaning of "vigilance and mutual assistance." You see something like that, oh, it is the most meaningful thing for us. The people, the villagers, it's like they already have achieved consensus, that all-encompassing "mutual assistance." . . . And *that* is our purpose. Really, patrol is not the responsibility of the patrol team. It is everyone's mutual responsibility. That is the goal we are trying to achieve.

A particularly illuminating feature of the narrative reported above is the connection it establishes between the operational practice of vigilance patrol—its policing "function"—and the ideal of "mutual assistance" (*xiangzhu*) as a normative description of quality of life. Here is a civilian volunteer describing a peak experience through his engagement with policing, identifying this experience *as* "mutual assistance" and qualifying its meaning in terms of an expansive yet inclusive "solidary psychology" that constitutes a collective subject capable of responding effectively to violation of its normative order. It would be possible to argue that this illustrates the functionalist principle associated with Durkheim's "mechanical solidarity"—that is, its normative dimension is functional by virtue of the order-restoring reaction it motivates. But I would argue that the most important theoretical insight to be taken from this native testimony lies in the opposite direction: that is, in its *ontology* rather than its utility. Vigilance patrol objectifies human mutuality as a thing, an object to be pursued, cultivated, policed. The practice is significant to its agents not merely as a functional means to an end but, more significantly, as an example of what Arendt called "*entelecheia* . . . activities which exhaust their full meaning in the performance itself*" (Arendt 1958, 206). In other words, the fact that the normative aspect of the practice may be functional is less significant than the way in which its functional qualities are ethical. People engage in the practice as a way to access the subjective peak experience of realized purposefulness.

The Politics of Care

A literature on the "ethics of care" has taken shape around an expansive definition of care as "everything that we do to maintain, continue and repair 'our world' so that we can live in it as well as possible" (Tronto 1993, 103). This is a useful orientation from which to reflect on the politics evident in the ethnographic materials of this chapter, and think about how they relate to care. I have described an expansive engagement in policing, organized explicitly and intentionally to bring state police, volunteers, and ordinary citizens together in the shared project of "maintaining, continuing, and repairing" the policed order of their common world. It is a system of control organized by an ethos of mutualism, embodying a politics of care as the joint venture through which people co-curate their life together.

Like all police, Taiwanese patrolmen are responsible for maintaining the status quo. This puts violence into their work, because violence is intrinsic to the task of enforcing the asymmetries of an established political hierarchy (Martin 2018). But the historical process that created the *paichusuo* bureaucracy situates its capacity for violence in a place different from that we are led to expect by mainstream literature on policing. Most studies of police conflate violence with its physical instantiation (Martin 2018). This follows Egon Bittner's (1990a, 127) influential argument that the capacity to use physical force is the core of the police role. Taiwanese policing does not follow this model. Its primary engagement with political violence is not expressed as physical force but rather through the processes of social exclusion by which people are disqualified from the "we" who cares for "our world."

The most concentrated leverage police hold over this exclusionary violence, described in the next chapter, comes from their bureaucratic position in negotiations over who "we" are and what "our world" should be. As I have shown in this chapter, in democratic Taiwan, the dialogical process of these negotiations penetrates and encompasses the police institution. Six decades of mobilizational governance, beginning with the fascism of the 1930s, subjected the police bureaucracy to the role of an adjunct in the domestic "political warfare" system, specifically responsible for maintaining the population registry. Into the democratic era, the institutional role of the *paichusuo* within the political field remains that of a mediator, responsible for the registry that maps between the grassroots order of *qing* and the higher powers of law. This intermediary position between two countervailing sources of higher authority puts individual patrolmen in a weak position within their political environment. Their only real source of independent leverage comes in writing registry records. They use this clerical power to generate political leverage through the discretion they have over the processes that create official texts and move them through the legal-bureaucratic hierarchy. This is policing as a form of representational power, created by the human agency that translates *qing* into *fa*. I describe the technical operations of this mode of policing in the next chapter, characterizing it (by opposition to conventional ideas of "law enforcement") as "administrative repair."

The political power of administrative repair is relatively weak. To argue that the police capacity of a functional state can be founded on such a weak power— rather than, say, the exceptional power of physical violence over biological life— flies in the face of the conventional presumption that strong police are necessary to ensure state security. By revealing the inaccuracies of this presumption, Taiwanese police have the potential to help us better understand the way state-based security fits into the politics of care. Security—*se-curitas*, literally "to be without care"—is, of course, integral to the modern politics of care (Hamilton 2013). Indeed, by Hamilton's reading, the politics of security are defined by tensions between care and its absence, especially as these are inflected through "securitizing discourses" that shape political concern by invoking threats to collective existence (cf. Pedersen and Holbraad 2013). In the anthropology of policing, Stuart Hall's analysis of moral panic (Hall et al. 1978) and the Comaroffs' (2016) discussion of the specter of crime are examples of the ways historically specific securitizing discourses have intensified and/or mutated modern police powers. These examples, along with many other ethnographic studies, have cataloged a variety of ways police powers are driven by security. But it remains uncommon to see counterexamples of ways that state-based security can be organized to marginalize and/or disempower the police. The Taiwanese *paichusuo*, designed as a link holding together the politics of care associated with *qing* and the arrangements of state security per se, is one such counterexample.

To understand how modern policing can be institutionalized in a weak position within the field of security politics, it helps to begin with a psychological characterization of security. According to R. D. Laing, the deepest level at which a human being experiences security is the "ontological security" requisite to sanity, which he characterizes as the consistency obtaining between one's reflective concepts of self-and-world and one's actual experience (Laing 1960). Anthony Giddens then borrowed this term to refer to the sociological process of intersubjective assurance that a normal-way-of-the-world is not in collapse, which provides the immediate social ground for individual self-making projects (Giddens

1991). Ian Loader and Neil Walker subsequently brought the term into policing studies per se, using it as a basis for the first half of their distinction between "subjective security feelings" and "objective security situation," both of which are always at stake in debates over the quality of policing (Loader and Walker 2007). Taken together, these three moments in the intellectual genealogy of "ontological security" provide a useful framework for connecting, on the one hand, every-day habits of social care through which people supply one another the worldly grounds for subjective existence to, on the other hand, bureaucratically alienated forms of power through which state agencies perform their promises to guarantee the continued existence of a collective world. It is the emergence of this second domain—the modern state—that turns security into work, and establishes the conditions for policing to take on the attributes of a modern profession (Foucault 2007).

According to Andrew Abbott, modern professions emerge though a process by which different forms of expertise are claimed as the exclusive property of a collective subject (Abbott 1988). "The definition of a problem is an object of struggle between different occupational groups who compete to establish their exclusive control over the supply of expert labor required to solve it. . . . The struggle to define professional expertise in policing is a struggle to distinguish the problems to which policing is the answer from those problems to which something else is the answer" (Liu and Martin 2016, 359). The specific problem over which a profession claims expertise is, in Abbott's terms, its "jurisdiction." The question of how Taiwan's police power has come to occupy a juncture between an inclusive politics of care and exclusionary practices of state-based securitization can be explored through examining the way police rely on claims to exclusive jurisdictional authority over some particular kind of skill or expertise in the course of their work.

The study of such claims-making practices is facilitated by concepts of "boundary work" and "translation": boundary work examines the ways people keep things—"objects, concepts, people, and forms of knowledge"—from moving across contexts (Briggs 2018, 215), while studies of translation focus on the work required to successfully move such things across contexts (Star and Greisemer 1989). Ethnographic studies of the "caring professions" (doctors, nurses, social workers, etc.) use these concepts to analyze the way arguments over the quality of care are adjudicated within the parameters of claims to professional authority, what in Abbott's terms we would call the "jurisdictionalization" of care as an object of professional expertise. This literature becomes directly relevant to questions about policing through a tendency to figure care and violence as opposed categories. The boundary work engaged in establishing the jurisdiction of care often invokes the category of violence to stand for the other side of that boundary.

For example, Akerstrom's study of nursing home workers dealing with aggressive patients showed how careful they were to avoid classifying physical behaviors like punching and biting (not to mention the physical techniques used to control such behaviors) as violence, "to avoid pushing persons outside the boundary of normalcy and of continued acceptance" (2002, 515). Such dynamics led Willem de Haan to conclude, more generally, that caregiving professions are the polar opposite of "police who have a vested interest in ensuring that 'violence' is an issue for which they can claim professional competence and which they can use to preserve the image of their jobs as dramatic and dangerous" (de Haan 2008, 38).

This binary contrast is conventional in studies that frame care work as an occupational sector associated with a feminized "ethic of care" (Gilligan 1982) and thereby defined by opposition to the "masculine authority of the state" (Mulla 2014, 15). This is, of course, an accurate characterization of the ethnographic facts at issue in the empirical basis on which this work has taken shape. But those ethnographic facts have themselves been produced by historical processes that have institutionalized culturally contingent associations between gender and forms of power. At a purely logical level, the dialectic of care and security is mutually constitutive. It is impossible to determine, as a theoretical principle, whether care or indifference is more fundamental, basic, or powerful. Patriarchal associations between masculinity and power could just as easily end up valorizing care as an attribute of masculine power. The determining factor in the emergence of such cultural associations will be the underlying, historically constructed system through which power is actualized. The theoretical model here is Weber's historical sociology, a path-dependent dialectic of cultural values and historical structures. Taiwan offers a counterexample to conventional ideas of policing because of the way its history was shaped by the mobilizational politics of Japanese fascism and Chinese authoritarianism, which conclusively subordinated the indifferent technologies of bureaucratic administration to the care-based logic of political warfare, operationalized through the apparatus of *qing*-control.

The dialectic of care and indifference supplies a neutral principle of strategic utility: either side can be used as a resource toward controlling the other. As mentioned, Taiwanese policing was shaped by a political system in which a Leninist politics of sentiment dominated legal institutions. By contrast, under the normative expectations of the "rule of law," political feelings are discounted as private and subordinated to a public authority represented by abstract legal principles. Both strategies can generate robust political systems, but systems that operate on different principles. Which makes changing from one to the other—replacing a system of mobilizational authoritarianism with liberal democracy, for example—a difficult problem.

Some of the most innovative recent anthropological work on policing has examined police institutions under conditions of political change. Julia Hornberger's work, for example, addresses police reform in South Africa after apartheid. She used a multi-sited ethnography to follow a liberal rule-of-law-based policing ideal, from the authoritative version supplied by the global police reform industry, through the shifting administrative architecture of a democratizing state, into the street-level practices of patrolmen and detectives. The idea of human rights, Hornberger argues, has been translated into the street-level practice of South African policing through a creative process of "forgery" that keeps its contradictions contained within the backstage arenas of struggle over the production of front-stage texts. The ironic result of this is that the relentless application of progressive legalistic pressure to policing's front stage has, paradoxically, intensified the violence involved in its backstage operations (Hornberger 2011). Elif Babül (2017) studied a similar situation in Turkey, where a campaign to subject police (among others) to human rights training produced a similarly illiberal outcome. Babül's focus is slightly different from Hornberger's, concerned less with the street-level consequences of reform than its effects on the bureaucratic field itself. She shows how government bureaucrats respond to the experience of being subjugated to an externally authorized idea of liberal legality by developing a kind of subcultural ethos she calls (following Hertzfeld) "bureaucratic intimacy," binding them together as a community of complicity that shamelessly subverts the intention of the reform project.

Babül and Hornberger each show, in slightly different ways, how the unintended consequences of liberal police reform arise from a troubled interface between law's abstract authority and the substantive bonds of solidarity that bind people together around their common relationship to police power. Hornberger focuses on the way law's putative universalism authorizes experts in the code to ignore the context of application. This leaves the problem of fitting policy to context in the hands of parochial agents, who have no choice but to adapt it to serve the local powers to which they are obligated. Babül, by contrast, looks at the way legalistic reform is depoliticized, marked as foreign, and treated as irrelevant by an entrenched bureaucratic subculture. In both cases the problem for analysis is framed as tensions between the legal-bureaucratic form of expertise and an entrenched domain of political intimacy.

To assume that legal-bureaucratic authority could actually realize its own ideal, if it could only break free from the tenacious interference of local tradition, is an implicit acceptance of the telos of legal modernization. Taiwan's modern bureaucracy took root in a different paradigm. The Japanese architects of Taiwanese police granted the field of intimate politics a sui generis primacy, and focused their modernizing ambitions on hybridization rather than rationalization, "grafting" a bureaucratic superstructure onto the intimate base of *qing* (Ts'ai 2009). Managing the troubled interface between law's abstract authority and the substantive bonds of intimate solidarity has been, explicitly, the primary task of the Taiwanese police from their inception.

Policing as the Curation of Political Will

The world is neither an end nor a means. It is not a telos. It is not *for* anything. It simply is. Put another way, the anthropological concept of worlding, as articulated by Veena Das (2007) and Anna Tsing (2010), uses the concept of "world" to denote the a priori principle that holds a people, or a "we," together as the mutual ground of one another's existence. This draws on the Heideggerian philosophical tradition, in which care is the quality of human experience that grounds being in a sense of world (Hamilton 2013). Arendt developed a political theory on this basis, defining authentic politics as the creativity that emerges from the play of difference-in-unity by which a pluralistic world continually re-creates and renews itself. The metabolism of this process of world (re)production is, in Arendt's (1958) terms, an *entelecheia*, a process that cannot be represented in functionalist terms.

The most tangible manifestation of a world is its presence in the shared presuppositions that calibrate the habits of behavior through which a community stands together as the mutual ground of one another's existence. For example, at the level of language, the existence of a world is inherent in presupposing that other people can hear what you intend to say (Das 1998). To use the terminology of speech act theory: the consequences of speech rest on perlocutionary conditions, and the world inheres in the infrastructural basis of perlocutionary forces. This observation is the point of departure for Justin Richland's (2013, 217) theory of legal jurisdiction. A court's decision manifests a world through the "perlocutionary force [that] persists in the silent authorizing move that backs [its] proceduralism with the generalized sovereign force and legitimacy it presupposes." More specifically, the ongoing creativity of legal activity, along with all the institutional conditions it must maintain to stay active, manifests a world in which modern state sovereignty exists, is powerful, and is structured by the rule of law.

Much of the ongoing metabolic process of world (re)production is done informally, without the kind of formal apparatus associated with law, and without the kind of explicit reflexivity through which legal agents attempt to take conscious responsibility for the world-making consequences of their actions. Ordinary ontological security is generated by instinctive habits, the routine forms of care by which people stand to one another as evidence that the world is indeed as we suppose it to be. It is, in Arendt's (1958, 79–174) terms, labor not work. Only in the modern world, with the rise of the modern state and its proposal to make security a durable condition, does it become possible to treat security as the object of a professional jurisdiction, like law or policing. But where law is the paradigm of a truly successful profession, policing remains mired in chronic problems defining the scope of its exclusive professional jurisdiction.

This chapter described the contemporary practice of a mode of modern policing that was initially created in the historical context of mobilizational authoritarianism. This origin established the *paichusuo* as a street-level institution designed to cultivate political affect. This functional orientation endows street-level policing in Taiwan with a practical logic quite different from that entailed by the conventional idea of police as "a mechanism for the distribution of nonnegotiable coercive force" (Bittner 1990a, 131). The adaptation of the *paichusuo* to Taiwan's democratic regime preserved the practical focus of its street-level operations on the work of cultivating worldly care. Democratization merely shifted the aspirational telos for this kind of work from a vanguardist rhetoric of revolution to a more humble idiom of democratic tolerance. In other words, the neighborhood police of democratic Taiwan curate the political will of a self-determining collective subject to live in peace with itself, despite its chronic failure to live up to its own ideals. This project provides the foundation for the specific "jurisdictional" claims of Taiwanese police power. That is, *paichusuo* police claim an exclusive power to traffic in the forms of bureaucratic representation that mediate between the local politics of *qing* and the central politics of *fa*. The next chapter describes the practical organization of this kind of policing as manifest most clearly in the administrative repair of political problems.

4

ADMINISTRATIVE REPAIR

Policing and social control are so closely related it can be difficult to say where one gives way to the other. Foucault's analysis of the modern world identified care itself as a mode of "pastoral" power, implicating the most intimate aspects of subject formation in the field of governmentality (Donzelot 1979). "Family, community, even society itself are all . . . sites of police and sources of police power" (Garriott 2011, 3). What distinguishes policing, as a distinctively modern institution, from the discipline embedded in all forms of sociality is its aspiration to be something different. The institutions of police are supposed to stand apart from ephemeral bonds that can dissolve as spontaneously as they arise, and uphold an order made durable by its artifice and formality. Care makes worlds it cannot secure, so the work of security must sometimes turn away from care. The commitment to state-based security embodies a patriarchal "ethic of absolutes," an allegiance to abstract principles, which gives police authority a weight and an edge that distinguish it from the maternal "ethic of care" (Gilligan 1982). This opposition gives rise to a paradox because care—*curitas*—and *se-curitas* are mutually implicated: "The concern for security is at bottom a concern to be without concern. In turning the alleviation of worry into a pressing source of worry, security unworks itself" (Hamilton 2013, 10). The practical work of police is never free of this contradiction. Each specific conflict police are called to solve demands an investment of creative will in finding a way to steer the volatile dialectic of care and indifference back into the routines that reproduce the normal social world. In this chapter I explore some of the techniques Taiwanese police use to do this work. My central concern is the nature of the boundary that sets police power apart from the other kinds of power at work in the city's political metabolism. The conventional expectation is that law provides this boundary. I demonstrate how that expectation fails in this environment, and reflect on what unconventional possibilities this might reveal for the idea of a police power grounded in a political ethic of care.

Indifference

Summer, late afternoon. A drunk man, barefoot, betel spit dried down his shirt, walked into the police station. He stood unsteady in front of the receiving counter and stared at Atun doing paperwork on the other side of the glass barrier. "Give me fifty yuan to get something to eat!" the drunk shouted. Atun didn't look up. The drunk repeated his request. Atun continued to ignore him. The drunk wandered past the receiving counter into the case-processing room. The only policeman there was Aliang, sitting at a desk writing a report. The drunk walked up to him and shouted, "Give me fifty yuan to get something to eat!" Aliang ignored him. The drunk stood staring at him for a little while, then repeated himself. Without looking up from his work, in a voice of quiet menace, Aliang said "Fuck off." The drunk wandered over to the tea table where I was sitting. "Give me fifty yuan to get something to eat!" I ignored him as well. He walked over to a full-length mirror on the wall next to the front door and stood looking at himself for a moment. He left.

Autumn, early evening. A disheveled woman rushed into the station, enraged, screaming that someone had beaten her up. She was so agitated that it was hard to understand what she was saying. The receiving officer responded to her incoherence with irritation. Seeing this, Lieutenant Zhang, the station commander, left the group around the tea table and joined the conversation at the front counter. He returned a few minutes later saying, "She won't press charges. This isn't going to go anywhere." Two men arrived to join the woman, and she calmed down. One of the men was bleeding from his head and from a gash in the palm of one hand. Atun brought towels to stop the bleeding and called an ambulance. After helping treat the wounds, Atun led the three outside to wait for the ambulance, which arrived about thirty minutes later. The ambulance took the injured man and his companion away, leaving the woman alone in front of the police station. She became agitated again and began pacing up and down in the street, pausing occasionally in front of the station's open door to scream, "Police! Police! Get over here! They are coming for me!" All the policemen in the station were busy with clerical tasks and paid no attention. The only acknowledgment of her performance came from

Akim, sitting with me at the tea table watching TV. After the third or fourth time she shouted for police assistance, he turned from the television and looked at me, remarking, "Aya! Drunk people can be such a disorderly mess!"

As these anecdotes illustrate, it is possible for a person to walk into and out of a police station without being recognized, without receiving any response. Being drunk or incoherent, having expectations or desires that deviate from the mandate for police service (as the police understand it), can sometimes render a person invisible to the police gaze. This is not supposed to happen. Police are thought of as an absorptive institution. The door to the station is always open, there is always someone there on duty. But the institutional openness of the station house, and the putatively universal responsive competence of the institution, do not translate into an unqualified capacity by citizens to call police into action. Police power is selectively applied.

What is the logic of the selection process? What accounts for the capacity of a person or problem to mobilize police power? As an ethnographic question, this is an issue that implicates both jurisdiction and situation. The situations above are cases in which individuals failed in attempts to mobilize police attention on the basis of informal aspects of their deportment. They performed their pleadings in a manner that failed to trigger the imperative power contained inside the police institution. Practically speaking, this failure to activate police power came down to a decision, made by people institutionally empowered to make it, *not* to engage with another person's problems. This is a common response to trouble. Indeed, in ordinary life, most people ignore each other's problems most of the time, and most of this indifference is figured as a nonevent. To see indifference as an *event*, as something that supports (or demands) further explanation, is evidence that something cultural has already happened: a normative expectation of engagement has come into play. The empirical fact that these unsuccessful appeals were made in the first place (as well as the fact that an observer might find their failure interesting) is evidence that the police role has become associated with an "ethic of care" (Gilligan 1982; cf. Wender 2008). To call the police makes sense only on the basis of an expectation of response to the call.

To approach the police power by walking through the front door of the *paichusuo* where I worked brought one face to face with a portrait of the former dictator, Chiang Kai-shek, looking down from the back wall where it met the ceiling (the highest possible point in the room). Below the generalissimo, this wall held a large red-velvet plaque with raised gold characters bearing the official four-clause mission of the police of the Republic of China (formalized in the 1953 Police Law): "Preserve public order. Protect social safety. Prevent all harm. Promote people's prosperity" (Weihu gonggong zhixu. Baohu shehui anquan. Fangzhi yiqie weihai. Cujin renmin fuli). In front of this plaque, facing the door, was a desk staffed by the *zhiban* officer (see chapter 3 for discussion of categories of duty). On this desk was a telephone that received calls to the substation's direct line as well as dispatches from the countywide emergency response center (the 119 system). To one side was a transmitter for the citywide wireless radio system used for official communication between policemen in the field. On the other side, against the wall, was a collection of alarms connected to local banks, and a computer terminal linked to the police information network (at that time a bureaucracy-specific Intranet system not connected to the World Wide Web). The back of the desk, where the policeman sat, contained not drawers but shelves, holding dozens of loose-leaf binders containing the variety of documents that had to be filled out in the course of routine duties.

The official designation of this desk was the "case-receiving" portal. It supplied the interface between calls to and responses by police power per se. It was the formal point of contact between state and society. The formality attached to police reception was embodied in the binders full of "forms" shelved behind this desk. These forms were the thing-itself of bureaucracy as rule-by-writing— ready-made textual prototypes with blank spaces into which an officer on the scene could specify the particulars of the situation at hand. "Cases" were made by filling out these forms, supplementing them with other documents, authorizing them with signatures and chops, then sending them up through the bureaucratic hierarchy to people with legal power to decide when cases would be opened or closed. Such was the means of producing events within the larger legal-bureaucratic machinery for which the police station served as a street-level outpost. And such was the formal raison d'être for the *paichusuo*: street-level clerical work.

The actual filling out of a form almost never took place at the receiving desk. Paperwork was processed in the adjacent room. There was space there, huge tables with chairs for everyone who might become involved in the production of a given dossier. The legally consequential bureaucratic facts that emerged from the interactions between people and police that played out in this room were elaborate productions, shaped by a multitude of contextual social and political forces. In a Taiwanese *paichusuo*, these contextual forces are personified by the extensive collections of people who involve themselves in the conduct of routine police business. The case-processing room was a sociopolitical arena used to stage the processes by which social life acquired bureaucratic representation.

Sitting at the tea table, in the corner of this case-processing room, as I generally did, focused my attention on the sociopolitical processes at work in the literal (and figurative) arena of a police station's "back room." The most interesting performances came in agonistic struggles between competing forms of authority, staged in the ad hoc political assemblies that spontaneously gathered around some convergence of interests. The stake-holding elite, as they came together in discussion of a given case, constituted a localized "space of appearances" in which policed outcomes were negotiated (G. Feldman 2018). Such assemblies were a primary arena for the production of the neighborhood's policed order. And they were clearly structured, in large part, by powers other than law and bureaucracy. Based on this kind of ethnographic observation, policing appears to be not merely embedded in its sociopolitical context, but in fact *constituted* by the powers operating there. The backstage decisions that steer the course of events through the architecture of police processing use the legal-bureaucratic attributes of the police power as an adjunct or instrument for the work of maintaining an order of mutual complicity in the shadows of the law (cf. Babül 2017).

The maintenance of this complicit solidary was a self-conscious project. The station house tea table was one of the places where it was made explicit. Thus, by virtue of its vantage point, my ethnography illuminates a social world embedded in the circulatory dynamics that connected the informal dynamics of police "reception" (*jieshou*) to the "dispatch" (*paichu*) that gives the "dispatch post" (*paichusuo*) its formal identity. Policed order is constituted in the closure of this circuit.

Paichusuo patrolmen are not the most powerful participants in this dialogue. Their only real point of autonomy, as we saw in the opening anecdotes of this chapter, is in situations where they can refuse to get involved. But decisions by police agents over whether to accept or reject a plea to care about someone else's problem involve a complex blend of concern and indifference, ultimately overdetermined by their position in the political landscape. As an ethnographer, I spent considerable time talking with individual patrolmen about how they made decisions of this sort. It was a conversation that elicited a kind of ideal-type model of police power, as seen from the position of a subaltern agent of that power. This is a good data point for exploring the intrinsically situational issue of how police power is distributed: it tends to be allocated in accordance with the way immediate agents of that power understand themselves and their situation. In this chapter, I give some examples of the spectrum of different ways I observed the police power being mobilized and applied through the *paichusuo*. On this basis, I characterize the unique value that substation police bring to their routine interactions with the public—the content of their professional "jurisdiction," in Andrew Abbott's sense of the term—as the provision of administrative repair.

Processing a Case

Early summer, morning. A couple walked into the station. Their behavior was hesitant. The man sat on a chair by the door while the woman went to the reception desk and began timidly describing to Abao that she was being harassed by someone who fancied himself her suitor. Abao told her to go away; unrequited love is not a police problem. Her companion then joined her at the window and began speaking more assertively on her behalf. Actually, he said apologetically, he was the one who persuaded her to make a police report. The situation was beginning to seem a little dangerous. The stalker had taken to lurking outside the woman's apartment, aggressively harassing her at every opportunity. Together, the couple convinced Abao that the woman had a legitimate fear for the safety of herself and her children. Abao escorted them to a desk in the case-processing room, where they were joined by Aliang to begin the process of transcribing their complaint into an official case-recording form. Among the first pieces of information the policemen requested was the name and address of the accused stalker. The couple provided this. Aliang then went off to call the substation in whose jurisdiction the address was located (who would hold the *hukou* record of the accused) to check if there was any prior record of such behavior.

Here is example of a performance of civic insecurity that successfully recruited police recognition. The couple achieved administrative legibility, persuading the police to open a case. Their successful performance drew on resources not available in the failed attempts with which I opened the chapter. For one thing, there were two of them. The gendered dimension of the status quo is obvious here; it is not for nothing a woman brings a man with her to make a police report of sexual harassment. Clearly they invested some labor in attending to informal sensibilities about politeness and etiquette. They arranged their affairs to visit the police station during daylight business hours, when staffing was at its peak. Once there, they carried off an unblemished performance of clean and sober humility. The implicit reliance of police on such informal cues to evaluate the nature of the situations that demand their attention embeds the operation of police power in the reproduction of existing social hierarchies, reinforcing historically normalized inequalities.

But formal resources also figured significantly in the course of this event. Specifically, the *hukou* registry was of central significance. Among the very first pieces of information required to produce an administrative representation of a complaint was the *hukou* registration of everyone involved—plaintiff and accused alike. The capacity of the complainants to provide this information for the person about whom they were complaining was actually a crucial element in successfully getting police to take the case. Indeed, every flowchart in the substation's manual of standard operating procedure (described below) presumed the capacity to identify the *hukou* identity of the people involved. Knowledge of registry addresses marks a crucial juncture in the process of registering a civil complaint. It constitutes a crucial, in many cases *necessary*, resource of knowledge/power in the project of calling the police.

Helping Out

Winter. Midnight. Mr. and Mrs. Tan, an old couple who owned a restaurant near the station, arrived for an appointment they had made earlier in the day to speak with Atun, the patrolman who held their *hukou* records. Atun received them at the tea table and prepared tea. After ten minutes of cigarettes and small talk, Mr. Tan began to discuss a burglary that had occurred at his restaurant the previous evening. He and his wife suspected it involved one of their employees. They were adamant that they didn't want any formal record made of the crime. They would, however, very much like Atun's help in trying to figure out what happened and, if possible, to recover some of their lost property. Atun listened sympathetically. After they finished the tea, the three of them left together. Ninety minutes later they returned with a collection of written notes and digital photographs. Atun went to the equipment room and got one of the mobile computers used to access police databases. They sat down again at the tea table, where Atun brewed another round of tea, and began checking the license plates of cars in the pictures.

This anecdote illustrates an ideal police response, as evaluated from the perspective of the neighborhood's petty-capitalist elite. Atun's service to the Tans consisted of "helping out" (*bangmang*). No laws were involved, no paperwork, no courts, none of the bureaucratic apparatus of policing was mobilized at all, save a database through which technologies of registration could reveal who was where, when. Aversion to formal legal processes was widespread in the neighborhood. People sought to solve quotidian problems like car accidents, personal conflicts, and minor crimes through informal networks without calling the police in any formal capacity. There was an articulate and hegemonic rationale for this, an ethical discourse that explicitly valorized the informal order of intimate networks (*qing*) over the alienated powers of state-based law (*fa*). From this perspective, the capacity of police to "help out" in an informal capacity prior to the invocation of formal police powers was the most desirable service at stake in the struggle to achieve police recognition.

In other words, Mr. and Mrs. Tan's sophisticated appeal did not simply recruit police services—it secured them as a personal favor kept entirely off the record. Such an outcome marks the pinnacle of civic empowerment in calling the police. The capacity of businesspeople like the Tans to achieve such mastery over the police power drew upon a considerable, ongoing investment of resources in cultivating their relationship with the patrolman holding their *hukou* and business licenses. Although I do not have specific evidence in this case, it is more than likely that Atun ate regularly at the Tans' restaurant and received red envelopes (containing money) from them on appropriate holidays, as this was an established general practice in the station. Indeed, there is real reciprocity here. Atun's service in this case was given at personal cost. Keeping this situation off the books meant erasing any record of his own work in the bureaucratic accounting of his labor time. To shelter a situation from law, a patrolman had to forgo personal credit in the bureaucratic sphere. "Helping out" was a gift in the *guanxi*-based networks of the gift economy. When it came time to convert the generic social capital of gift-mediated obligation into a specific request for service, the tea table provided a stage for the Tans to make a polite ask. The tea table was a pivotal node for articulating the informal gift economy into the formality of bureaucratic routine, and right back out the other side.

"Helping out" was a term of art in police parlance, one of many euphemisms police used to describe their work. I eventually identified three terms that, it seemed to me, marked a significant distinction in the kinds of formality involved in police work: "helping out," "handling a situation," and "processing a case." That is, for example, in talking with my police interlocutors on a cell phone, they would say things like "I can't make it right now, I need to go to Three Harmonies Market and *help out* [*bangmang*]." Then, at another time, they would say, "We will be there as soon as we are done *handling this situation* [*chuli shiqing*]." And, in other circumstances, "I can't come. I am in the middle of *processing a case* [*banan*]." Imposing a layer of theoretical clarity only slightly above the native use of the terms, it is possible to use these three categories to code a systematic difference in the level of formality active in different kinds of police business.

"Helping out" is intimate. It is the mode of policing contained within the sphere of social obligations organized by *qing*, which is to say institutionalized conventions of reciprocity like those described in Mauss's (1966) treatment of gift economies. "Helping out" refers to a sociality defined entirely outside the law, even if law may figure instrumentally into the content of the help. By contrast, "processing a case" happens entirely inside the law. It involves entering the alienated sphere in which the police role loses its sociality and collapses into a conduit for supplying courts with information. The couple that reported the stalker elegantly moved through the station's front door directly into the work of processing a case. And between these two extremes is a space of ambiguity that has to be carefully "handled." The complexity of the police role in Taiwan is exemplified in the delicacy of "handling situations" in which the networked solidarities of "helping out" come into contradiction with the bureaucratic arrangements of "processing a case." Prospective clients of police services may prefer any one of these three different modes of response. For the police, however, handling ambiguous situations is clearly the most labor- and skill-intensive form of work

Handling Situations

One summer afternoon, making my way to the station, I ran into Abao and Acu dealing with the immediate aftermath of an accident. A taxi had broadsided a truck at an intersection in a street market. The truck was knocked into a fence, which then fell on top of two other cars. Nobody had been hurt, but the damage was extensive, and the intersection was completely blocked. Culpability was ambiguous, however, as the (illegal) street market had narrowed the street to a single lane, and the fence was illegally constructed. Abao was interviewing a small crowd of people about what happened, while Acu walked around with a tape measure, taking pictures and sketching a map in his notebook. They sent me to the station for a can of spray paint to mark the location of the cars on the street. When I returned, Abao's interviews had degenerated into a heated argument with the proprietor of a dumpling stall about compensation for the collapsed fence. As soon as the vehicles' positions were marked on the street, Abao and Acu left and went back to the station (leaving the cars where they were). Four people from the accident scene—owners of the involved vehicles—were waiting for them there, and Abao immediately began taking formal statements and filling out documents related to the accident. He was still on lead patrol duty, however, and twenty minutes into this process he was called out to deal with another accident. The group dispersed as he left, making plans to reconvene a few hours later, after Abao's patrol shift ended. When the group reconvened, it had expanded considerably. Each of the four drivers had acquired an entourage, including mechanics, insurance agents, and friends or relatives who had come to give support in the negotiation process. Under Abao's direction, this group verbally negotiated an agreement about who would pay what to whom. Money changed hands, and the group finished filling out the paperwork. Everyone then signed a "document of reconciliation" (*hejieshu*), authenticated it with a chop or fingerprint dipped in red ink, and the case was closed.

The station's handbook of standard operating procedure had a flowchart for handling traffic accidents. This formula began with a patrolman receiving information about damages sustained through a traffic accident. Such knowledge obligated him to immediately assist the involved parties in gathering evidence to create an *anzi* ("report," "file," or "case"). In the process of developing this case file, the first inflection point came in determining whether or not human injury had occurred. If so, the case was to be classified as A2 (A3 in the case of death), and the completed file would be transferred to civil court. If no injury had occurred, however, the case would be classified as A1, and a second decision point would arise as a choice about whether or not the situation could be resolved through mediation. If mediation was prima facie impossible, the file would go directly to the Traffic Accident Investigation Committee (an office outside the police bureaucracy). However, if mediation appeared possible, a final set of decisions arose over how to manage the formal dimensions of the mediation process to successfully generate the legally binding document of reconciliation that completes the case file. There were three levels or contexts in which this document of reconciliation could be produced: at the scene of the accident, in the police station, or in the chambers of the municipal mediation committee. Failure at one level implies escalation to the next. If all three forms of mediation failed to generate reconciliation, the entire packet of evidence gathered over the course of the proceedings must be passed to civil court.

Such standard operating procedures are models of clarity. Indeed, modeling clarity is their existential purpose; procedure is created as a resource to help make the messiness of real-life situations more manageable. Ethnographic observation of police work produces an account of police work categorically different from standard operating procedure. Ethnographic observation foregrounds the emergent messiness of the situations police are called to deal with over the retrospective clarity of the policed outcomes that are, eventually, produced. The experience of dealing with events-in-process is defined by a horizon of uncertainty. The uncertainty intrinsic to real-life experience is radically different from the artificial clarity of an event's retrospective representation in a finished file. Describing how Taiwanese patrolmen deal with traffic accidents, for example, filled my field notebook with arguments over things that appear, from the retrospective vantage point of a completed file, as obvious facts beneath the level of disputability. Had an accident actually occurred? Was there actually any damage or injury? Were these damages in any way connected to the accident?

The relentless pressure of their workload compelled patrolmen to minimize the energy they invested in any individual case. This made it prudent to delay beginning any formal record-keeping until after the involved parties had conclusively agreed that something had occurred that needed policing. For whatever reason, this kind of agreement was relatively rare, and most of the practical labor police invested in handling traffic accidents was directed away from the standard operating procedure flowchart through a generous interpretation of the ambiguity inherent in "receiving information about damages sustained through a traffic accident." If the necessity to initiate formal case making was not triggered, nothing worth writing down had happened. Keeping the formal order of administrative representations in good repair was achieved, in part, by keeping on-the-ground "reality" at one step removed from the textual sphere of police reports.

Autumn, out on a late-night patrol. We received a dispatch call of an accident and rushed to the scene. A motorcycle lay in an alley where it had crashed into a parked car. The motorcycle's driver lay twisted against the curb some twenty feet away. He appeared to be dead. Neither of the patrolmen I was with bothered to check his condition. They called an ambulance and set up cones to direct traffic around the accident. We stood there for a while waiting for the ambulance when, to our surprise, the driver began to writhe and groan. He slowly recovered consciousness and struggled to a standing position against a car, dripping with blood and stinking of alcohol. Acu walked over and, without touching him, began talking to him. "What are you doing? You have been in an accident. You are seriously injured. An ambulance is coming. You need to lie down." The driver tried to respond, but produced nothing but incoherent groans. He began stumbling away from us, leaving a bloody smear along the parked cars he used to keep himself upright. We followed him, keeping a distance, Acu repeating his advice. By the time the driver had reached the intersection with the main road, he could stand unsupported. He flagged a taxi, got in, and disappeared. We walked back to the accident scene, pushed the motorcycle to the side of the road, canceled the ambulance, collected our cones, and left. Without a hospital report, there was no proof of injury, and it was highly unlikely that the man who had just fled the scene would retroactively request an accident report. It the owner of the parked car noticed damage upon return and decided to call the police, it would be up to whichever unlucky colleague was on patrol at the time to deal with it. The record of the call was marked, "Call for service concluded at the scene."

Late summer. Afternoon. Abao came into the station out of uniform and sat down to brew a pot of tea. It was his day off, but he had a meeting scheduled with a group of people involved in a traffic accident from the previous week. As we drank tea, he remarked to me that he had miscalculated. He thought the participants had come to a mutual agreement not to file any paperwork. But it turns out whatever agreement they reached at the scene of the accident failed to hold. If today's mediation was not successfully concluded in the station, Abao confided, he would have a serious problem: there is no way to retroactively create the documents required to transfer the case to the municipal mediation committee. However, he continued, this sort of thing was really his specialty. He was confident he could successfully produce a document of reconciliation in the substation. The threat of ending up in court is usually sufficient to get people to behave reasonably.

We were shortly joined at the tea table by an older couple and a young man, parties to the mediation. Abao took them upstairs to a private conference room. An hour later they come back down to the main case-processing room with a stack of papers, where they finished signing and fingerprinting the reconciliation agreement. The younger man received 3,000 New Taiwan dollars (NT$) from the older man, then left. The older couple stayed on for a while, expressing their gratitude to the policemen around the tea table, and pressing a red envelope into Abao's pocket.

Such are situations "handled" by *paichusuo* police. Their role consists in managing the human conflict that arises from accidents, torts, and crimes, shepherding people through a space of potential adjudication, sometimes guiding them toward the legal machine, other times keeping them away from it. It is a discretionary art, difficult and demanding but relatively straightforward. At least until politics gets involved. Politics is what makes things difficult. Politics enters the process of administration through the inequalities of status attached to the parties in a given negotiation.

Winter. Late night. I stood next to Aliang in the lobby of a cheap hotel watching him try to interrogate a prostitute. She maintained staunch silence as he emptied her purse on the countertop, verbally inventorying its contents. "Your condoms," he said. "Your KY. Your *fu* [protective charms]. Your renminbi [Chinese currency]." Aliang was looking for an ID. He didn't find any, but the Chinese currency was enough: she was *touduke*, an illegal immigrant fresh from the mainland.[1] This status was of much more consequence to the proceedings than the fact that she had arrived at the hotel in response to a phone call from a desk clerk soliciting a prostitute on behalf of a patron who, as it turned out, was secretly working for a detective in the local precinct. Prostitution is a minor vice crime in Taiwan, but illegal immigration is implicated in issues of national security. Everybody involved in making the arrangements leading to the present situation was exposed to serious prosecution—not just the taciturn woman carrying condoms, but the taxi driver who brought her to the hotel, and the desk clerk who made the call. This desk clerk was an older woman who, along with her husband, in fact owned the hotel. As befits businesspeople in that sector of the economy, the hotel owners maintained a roster of political "connections" (*guanxi*) for smoothing over rough patches in their operations, such as a potential charge of procuring an undocumented sex worker. Thus, even as Aliang continued his attempt to determine the prostitute's identity, the hotel lobby was gradually filling up with people. "The locals" had been called out: one group arriving to support the hotel owners, a complementary collection to support the police on the opposite side of the impending formalities. It was a strange crowd assembling at the hotel at 2 a.m. Some arrived in chauffeured Mercedes-Benzes wearing expensive suits. Others drove up on motor scooters still wearing their pajamas. Before long the lobby overflowed into the street with little clusters of people standing around talking in low tones, warming up the social mechanisms that would determine how the formal record of this case would eventually be recorded. The prostitute, however, remained silent. Aliang finally gave up. The processing of this case was clearly not going to be concluded at the hotel. It was time to move the proceedings to the *paichusuo*, in a long convoy of police cars, motorbikes, taxicabs, and Mercedes-Benzes.

The rationale for this spectacle was bureaucratic. The detective who set this particular arrest into motion worked in the city's central precinct. His motivation for staging the event was gaining "merit points" (*jixiao*) attached to successfully capturing an illegal immigrant, toward meeting his annual quota, perhaps even contributing to an eventual promotion. The unexpected implication of the hotel owners, however, had transformed certification of the prostitute's identity/provenance into an issue of political delicacy. The administrative repair of such political problems is central to the function of the *paichusuo*.

To be sure, this political function of the substation is formally invisible. It is a historical legacy of the way the administrative policing function has been practically defined by the work of registration. The enterprise of maintaining the state registration system includes both individuals' household registers and business licenses. The work of maintaining these records involves substation patrolmen in personal relationships with the people holding these licenses and registrations. The way these relationships are organized through the territorial police beats, which assign jurisdiction over all records of a specific area to an individual patrolman on a fixed basis, creates a formally documented relationship of mutual accountability between the constable covering the hotel's census jurisdiction and the owners of the hotel. This kind of particularistic relationship—and the mode of political intimacy it generates between police and policed around the project of keeping state records in order—is fundamental to the character of the Taiwanese police as an institution.

In the situation at the hotel, this facet of administrative design provided the precinct detective a conventional response to the political resistance gathering in the lobby. As things became complicated, he simply called a subordinate in the substation (in this case, Aliang) with the request/command/offer to share the quota points credited to the arrest in exchange for Aliang taking responsibility for completing the paperwork necessary to transfer the case to the prosecutor's office. Aliang immediately notified his colleague responsible for the hotel's registration—for he too would suffer if they were found guilty (for his failure to discern the criminal character of the hotel, evidenced by his signature on its hitherto unblemished record). The case was thus passed from the criminal to the political side of the division of social control labor.

A change in personnel was apparent in the movement from the hotel to the substation. The company that arrived at the *paichusuo* was not identical to that which departed the hotel. The detective, the original agent of legal mobilization, was absent. The principals of the assembly were now a conglomerate of grassroots political figures aligned with the hotel owners, the hotel owners themselves, and the unhappy Aliang and coworkers saddled with the responsibility of ensuring that their bureaucratic superior would acquire his expected quota points without besmirching the record of the substation. As we arrived at the substation, the silent prostitute was placed in a holding cell, and the taxi driver taken into the padded interrogation room for his formal statement, while the rest of the party retired to a large conference room for tea and polite discussion of how to find a solution to their awkward situation. I sat in the reception area along with the drivers, bodyguards, and other bit players, waiting for the meeting to conclude. An hour later the big shots emerged from the conference room in an effusive cloud of salutations and camaraderie, characteristic of the banquets at which this particular group of people more routinely crossed one another's paths. They moved through the lobby led by the substation's commanding officer, who politely escorted the hotel owners to their car and saw them off with a conventional display of traditional hospitality (see Martin 2013c, 626–28).

I remember the departure of the hotel owners from the police substation that evening most vividly for a comment it evoked from Akim, sitting next to me on the tea table bench. As the hoteliers walked past us on their way back home, surrounded by an entourage of well-wishers that included the chief of the substation, Akim put his arm around me and whispered mirthfully into my ear with whiskey breath, "Taiwan de falu, zhende heian"—Taiwan's law is truly a darkness. This is a fitting ethnographic commentary on the role of law in that situation. Mobilized by the police quota system, it became entirely submerged within the reactionary machinations of municipal politics. The meaning of legal and bureaucratic procedure collapsed into a political instrumentality, a mechanism through which a political problem was administratively repaired at the cost of its politically weakest figures—the illegal migrant sex worker and a taxi driver charged with human trafficking. The ethnographic commentary on law in that situation, by Akim, depicted it as a source not of justice but of "darkness," providing the shadow arena in which the constituent powers that hold the city together could reestablish their harmonious complicity in the extralegal "consensus" of policed order (Rancière 2010).

Such is "law enforcement" in a substation. Trouble is absorbed into a status quo balance-of-powers arrangement by street patrolmen steering events through a complex landscape where different locations implicate them in different regimes of superordinate accountability. Their bureaucratic superiors demand merit points. The neighborhood's bosses demand security for their economic operations. The particulars of the situation that evening, in which a contradiction between these two demands became acute, propelled a case from the street (or hotel lobby) to the substation. The substation is police home base, a place where the shadow of law looms contextually larger to improve the leverage of the patrolman's mediating position. The trajectory of the event after it reached the substation, however, reveals something essential about the nature of Taiwanese policing. The heart of the neighborhood police station as a venue for police work—the aspect of the institution most significant for structuring the character of "policed" outcomes—is not the holding cell through which the objects of police processing are eventually delivered to the courts. It is, rather, the back room in which ad hoc assemblies of local elites (the subjects of policing) convene to parley, to stage informal parliaments negotiating the meaning of the unfolding event.

The quasi-parliamentary representational capacity of the Taiwanese *paichusuo* was at the center of its original Japanese design. From the moment it arrived on the island, the modern state has articulated its powers into Taiwanese society through this specific institutional interface: bodies of local elites assembled in the neighborhood police station, working in the face (or jaws) of central authority to represent the interests of their clients in developing a solution that respects superordinate demands (Ts'ai 2009). This history remains tangibly present in the ethnographic anecdotes of this chapter, organized by the way the registry-police nexus specifies who is "on the hook" for records of legal culpability. The census-based police function constitutes the police-citizen nexus as a distinct modality of modern citizenship (Von Senger 2009). Democratic policing in Taiwan operationalizes a form of citizenship substantiated not through the abstract rights and responsibilities of legal process, but in the concrete solidarities of particularistic patron-client networks willing to mobilize for backroom negotiations at the drop of a hat. Anyone without such connections (in this case, the hapless prostitute and the taxi driver) has no political representation. They become the objects rather than the subjects of politics, the means of adjustment through which a problem is fitted with an administrative solution that repairs the political status quo.

Such midnight conferences are regular events in the course of substation operations. Nonetheless, they are events, exceptional by contrast to the drone of nonevents that compose the bulk of everyday working routines. The status quo order of sociality in Taiwan is well established; most substation policing reproduces it automatically through conventional processing techniques. In these routines, the police function is displayed as a smoothly operating machine, well lubricated by conventional ideas of legitimacy.

Measured by time spent, for example, the primary occupation of a substation patrolman is processing traffic accidents. The conventions of this work exemplify established understandings of what police are, and what they do in Taiwanese society. Qualities of particularistic representation are fundamental to these conventions. The art of policing traffic accidents in Taiwan is founded on two principles: popular aversion to legal institutions and a presumption of bureaucratic overload. To begin with the latter, filing the paperwork for a typical traffic accident—taking statements and collecting various affidavits—requires about six hours. Given the frequency of accidents, it is imperative to operate more efficiently whenever possible. As mentioned above, accidents are classified in grades of severity, and the police role in dealing with them moves from on-site mediation through a series of increasingly legalistic venues to the courts. This trajectory—unresolved conflict moving through an institutional landscape of escalating formality from street to police station to municipal mediation chamber—defines commonsense expectations. The defining ethos of police practice sees social problems as better resolved by organized give-and-take between the involved parties (and their political patrons) than by any forceful imposition of extrinsic legal principle. This understanding of the police role in society reaches beyond the sphere of traffic problems. Police intervention in any type of civil conflict—fistfights, noise complaints, divorce proceedings—is approached in identical fashion, moving into and through the same institutional landscape of street, *paichusuo*, and mediation committee. Moreover, Taiwan's criminal code allows for victim-offender mediation in selected cases, and minor criminal prosecutions are contingent on the initiative of the victim in pressing charges (Berti 2011; Hsu et al. 2004). An understanding of police work as the facilitation of mediation is general to every form of social intervention that the neighborhood *paichusuo* are routinely asked to provide.

Even as the guiding ethos is mediation, there is nonetheless an established trajectory of escalation, each step of which introduces qualitatively more abstract, distant, and powerful forms of mediating authority. The movement from on-site mediation to the police substation, for example, introduces an entourage of supporters. As in the case of the hotel prostitute, the unresolved individual dispute in the street escalates into an argument between opposed groups composed of family, friends, patrons, and the local elites. If this proves inconclusive, the affair ends up in a formal mediation committee. This institution induces voluntary agreements by bringing aggrieved parties together, in closed-door proceedings, under the aegis of politically appointed local elites (Jung 2007). Here culminates the conventional trajectory of most police intervention. What begins by calling police in response to a street-level problem ends in a political institution designed to generate moral suasion. Sociologically speaking, this is the scaling process by which local conflict is absorbed into Taiwan's state institutions. Culturally speaking, this is the logic of justice by which trouble is absorbed into the cosmological order of a Taiwanese society-in-police. Politically speaking, this is Taiwanese democracy. The active principle—socially, culturally, and politically—is the power of networked particularistic connections. The significance of local elites in policing—in police parlance "the locals" (*difang renshi*)—is iconic of this network-based power. Caroline Ts'ai (2009) argues that the field of governance anchored to the *paichusuo* made "the local" the vernacular concept through which the idea of modern self-governance in Taiwan took root. A century later, democracy has taken root in the *paichusuo* through the same discursive formation.

Democracy, as an ideal, has been described as "the possibility that the governed and the governing might be one and the same" (Balbus 2010, xiii). Taiwanese policing has found a way to approximate this ideal. The local elites vocationally involved in police mediation deal in a particular kind of "political representation" for the process of objectifying police problems. Their role in policing embodies and empowers a governing subjectivity that is simultaneously particularistic and democratic. The *paichusuo* is used as a mechanism for political process, not law enforcement. It functions as a node within the local arrangements of democratic government. Substation police manage instances of crisis or conflict by moving things away from their original site of manifestation, projecting them into other contexts where they can be more effectively controlled or resolved. This is policing as a recontextualizing function: mapping events from one framing "space" to another. The mechanism of this recontextualizing policing function in contemporary Taiwan is an apparatus of democratic representation. This is to say that contemporary Taiwanese policing—from the mundane routines of processing traffic accidents to the exceptional moments of criminal arrest—is not just vaguely political, but specifically democratic. How it is democratic is an exemplary manifestation of what democracy means under Taiwan's present historical circumstances.

Standard Operating Procedure

One uneventful afternoon, alone at the station's tea table, I passed time reading magazines stored on a bookshelf by the TV. There, buried under back issues of *Police Torch* (the official magazine of the National Police Administration), I found a paperback book titled *Compiled Protocols for Common Duties Implemented by Local Police Substations*. I opened it to find a set of instructions for conducting the routine aspects of substation business, "structured from the user's perspective on case management" (NPA 2001, ii). This perspective produced a kind of procedural portrait of substation police work. It depicted the job as seventy-six flowcharts in four categories: (1) Consultation and assistance with civil affairs (five items); (2) Administrative actions (nineteen items); (3) Criminal cases (forty items); and (4) Traffic problems (eleven items). Each individual protocol was diagrammed as a decision-making tree. These began at the point when police made contact with something warranting their attention. And they ended with the spectrum of ways the issue could be either resolved under substation authority or passed to an authority outside the substation. Next to the boxes and branches of the flow diagrams were columns of notes, annotating every juncture with a list of practical considerations. Each procedural chart was headed by a list of relevant laws, judicial interpretations, and bureaucratic regulations. Footnotes were used to give encouragement like, "When receiving a consultative request from the public, render service with an attitude of amity and enthusiasm."

The handbook had been published in June 2001, about six months before I found it. I deduced it had been shipped to the substations along with their regular delivery of state propaganda, thus ending up in a pile of official magazines gathering dust next to the television. In ironic contrast to this undistinguished reception, the book's preface announced its publication as an event of historical significance. "Traditionally," it stated, "police relied on the communication of personal experience or self-study to learn their working routines. However, given the diversity of personal experience and self-acquired knowledge, this method has generated disagreement, inefficiency, fragmentation, and disparity in the quality of law enforcement" (NPA 2001, i). Moreover, the democratic transition had "reconstructed the service environment of front-line police organizations," which greatly aggravated these problems. Thus, toward the goal of simultaneously "satisfying the legal requirements of the police mission and the expectations of the public," the Executive Yuan commissioned researchers from Central Police University to create a new manual of operational procedure for front-line institutions. These researchers developed the content of the book through "field interviews recording actual working procedures of active substation policemen, integrated with reference to current laws, regulations, and plans, and reviewed in consultation with all the police departments in the country" (NPA 2001, ii).

I was thrilled by my discovery. I did not lack for written descriptions of Taiwan's police system, but the para-ethnographic ambitions of this particular text promised something closer to the ground-level reality I was observing than the materials I had already collected. Police knowledge in Taiwan is organized as an academic discipline. Every commissioned officer in the Taiwanese police begins his or her career with a four-year degree at Central Police University, and every member of the rank-and-file works through a two-year curriculum at the Police College. The textbooks used in those classes provide an authoritative, detailed description of the legal and bureaucratic organization of policing. Moreover, Central Police University is a research university. It produces PhDs and publishes academic journals (*Police Science Quarterly*, *Law Enforcement Review*) that sustain an active, creative sphere of policing discourse connected to global, interdisciplinary intellectual concerns. This is an unclassified sphere of publication, making Taiwan one of the richest environments for policing studies I have ever seen. However, little of this knowledge is informed by ethnographic sensibilities.

I sat engrossed in the handbook until the next shift change, when Atun returned from patrol and sat down next to me to make tea. After getting things ready he glanced over at me. "Doing your homework, hey, Brother Ma?" I handed him the manual, saying, "Now I can finally understand what you guys are doing." "What the fuck is that?" he said. He took the book and thumbed through it for a few seconds, then threw it down on the table. "Fucking useless!" he scoffed, returning his attention to the teapot. I remained interested. Over the next few weeks, I read the manual every chance I got, and managed to transcribe most of it into my field notes. During this process of sitting in the reception area "doing my homework," I had a similar interaction with a half dozen other patrolmen besides Atun. None of them appeared to have seen the manual before. And all of them, after figuring out what the book was, remarked in one way or another that, regardless of its advertised significance, "What we do in here has nothing to do with that," "Nobody in here knows any of that stuff," "That's just bullshit," etc. Eventually, I had such an exchange with the station's commanding officer, and he gave me the book as a gift. A few weeks later he found a companion volume while cleaning out a drawer: *Compiled Protocols for Specialized Duties Implemented by Local Police Substations*, and he gave me that as well.

Administrative Repair

The contrast between my interest in the standard operating procedure book and the scornful uninterest displayed by my police interlocutors is significant. It reflects a tension between text and context that is central to the concerns of ethnographic theory. Attention to context is a signature move of ethnographic critique. One thickens textual description by considering the significance of the table onto which a manual of standard operating procedure was tossed, the scratch paper on which a traffic accident was sketched, the bottle of wine across which a friendship was forged, etc. All of those examples figure consequentially in the stories I tell about how policing worked in Weixing City. Ethnographic theory aims to account for how such contextual things matter to the concept of policing itself. But the concept of policing cannot be reduced to contextual contingency "all the way down." Texts still matter, even when (as in this case) their significance is disavowed by those who ostensibly enact them. To ignore or disavow standard operating procedure is a way of relating to it.

Modern police power is founded on an idea of state authority as relatively autonomous from the kinds of intimate, particularistic, factional social dynamics that could tear a polity apart. Codified texts are the mechanism through which the state is lifted up out of its context and made to stand for an inclusive general interest, and to thereby serve as a check on the centrifugal forces of localized particularism. Law is part of policing even in situations where policing clearly cannot be described as "law enforcement." The role of police power emerges from the distinction between law on the books and law in action. The abstractions in law books are constitutive as a condition of possibility for specifically *legal* action, in supplying an institutional anchor for the ideal of formal autonomy that distinguishes legality per se from other bases of authoritative judgment. Policing operates in the shadows or margins of the law, but those are spaces nonetheless connected to—and through that connection, *determined* by—the legality from which they deviate. At the same time, policing is not strictly legal. It occupies a space between law and law's relational other (Tomlins 2007). This position defines the orientation involved in the work. The art of policing comes from an attunement to text that privileges the dynamics of context over those of the text.

Michelangelo famously described sculpture by opposing it to painting. Where a painter creates an illusion by layering paint onto a blank canvas, "the sculptor arrives at his end by taking away what is superfluous" (Duppa and Quincy 1876, 151). A similar aesthetic applies to the creation of police records. Like carving away pieces of stone to reveal the figure trapped in a block of marble, drafting a police report is an act of clarifying erasure: cutting through a contextual field of political forces and historical contingencies to allow the Platonic form of an administrative procedure immanent within the unfolding event to stand out against a blurred backdrop of irrelevant detail. The formal integrity of a police report is an effect created by the artist's skill in disguising the artifice involved in its production. It is a fabrication, connected to reality the same way a finished statue is connected to a block of uncarved stone.

Of course, police work is not a fine art. Police reports are representations created for the purpose of changing the trajectory of events represented. Their clarification is a mode of intervention. Trouble tends to come to police attention as situations of indeterminacy saturated with conflict. In response—*if* they respond (for it is a political achievement to get the police to pay attention)—police carve out a determinate bureaucratic "object," which they can use for the purpose of dispelling the forces that compel them to respond. They do this, in part, by erasing context and masking various political powers active in that context. Patrolmen at the front line of the Taiwanese police apparatus experience their job primarily in these terms. For them, policing is a kind of repair. Problems compel police attention because something in the political field that stabilizes the status quo has broken. From the police point of view, a problem can be considered as solved when the normal political inertia has been restored to a degree that the issue at hand no longer demands their attention. Police treat their job as the administrative repair of political problems.

The tools of this work are mechanisms for converting social action into bureaucratic representation: police reports, registry records, documents of reconciliation, etc. *Paichusuo* policing involves police powers located primarily in *inscription*, rather than in physical violence or legal decision. The technical task of administrative representation is further qualified as "policing" by its engagement with a political ethic of *repair*. The idiom of repair is the trope through which Taiwanese police engage with democratic values. The aesthetics of a good police report is one that allows a self-governing collective subject to solve its own problems.

Under the mobilizational regime, Taiwan's police system served the revolutionary mission of the Chinese Nationalist Party. The primary responsibility of administrative police in that system was maintaining the population-registry-cum-political-intelligence system. Democratic reform released Taiwan's political society from tutelary subjugation to Leninist control, empowering citizens of the ROC to become "the subjects of [their] own story" (Rigger 2011, 34). The formal role of police shifted from implementing party imperatives to servicing a self-organizing political society. And the ethos of service embedded in the routines of substation policing shifted from Leninist political warfare to the task of helping a self-governing subject tell its own story. This abstract ideal is converted into the grunt-work of administrative inscription as a process of distinguishing the political subjects (like the hotel owners) whose story is at stake from administrative objects (like the prostitute and taxi driver) who can be manipulated to create a narrative that effectively relieves the political imperative for police to act.

The common euphemism for policing as "law enforcement" expresses a functionalist ideal: police are a means to legal ends. In a democracy, under the division of powers, the content of legal ends is defined by legislative process, a separate arena from the executive sphere in which police act. The medical model of police professionalism embraces this analogy. Justice is likened to the health of the social body, and the professional jurisdiction of police over the coercive aspects of legal intervention appears similar to the privileges a medical doctor enjoys over extraordinary medical interventions like surgery.

David Thacher has pointed out a basic flaw in this analogy. Legislative enactment is nothing like medicine. Legislators may say whatever they want, but their pronouncements do not change the way human communities are constituted by pluralism and diversity. Statutory law is not health, and the work of policing is nothing like delivering medicine to a sick patient. Where doctors deal with the integrity of an organic body, police deal with the pluralism of human worlds. They manage this pluralism by making decisions that should, in theory, "take everything relevant into account" (Thacher 2001, 391). Unfortunately, taking everything into account is impossible. The best approximation of this impossible task depends on skills in identifying the different values at stake in a given situation, and distinguishing how each of them might be relevant to the outcome of the event. Such skill in disentangling clarification is completely distinct from the instrumental question of what to do given the unquestioned primacy of a given end; "policing is not a treatment" (Thacher 2001).

When a police institution establishes a strong professional perimeter around its authority, it insulates its decisions from outside interference. And responsibility for disentangling the complexities of value pluralism, a fundamentally dialogical undertaking, becomes contained within the bureaucratic environment of the police institution. Democracy is replaced by autocratic command.

The Taiwanese *paichusuo* turns this mode of containment inside out. It serves as an absorptive arena for convening collective deliberation over the divergent political interests brought into direct contradiction within the scope of a police intervention. This function of the *paichusuo* is attributable to the low degree of professional autonomy enjoyed by Taiwanese police. Their claim to speak for the common interest is weak. The decision-making bureaucracy of their institution is vulnerable to figures with stronger claims to represent the public values at stake in police action, such as the "representatives of popular will" (*minyi daibiao*) and the "local elites." This extra-bureaucratic aspect of police process changes the *paichusuo* from a mechanism for enforcing the law into an arena for curating a common world. Assembled representatives of the different interests at stake decide together (albeit agonistically) what to keep and what to cut away, what to put into the police report and what to leave out.

This is a curatorial project driven by will, not reason; the interests at stake determine the arguments that are made. By organizing this kind of curation collectively, the *paichusuo* functions as an institutional site for the production of a collective will attached to each of the potentially contentious policed outcomes it manufactures. The liberal fetish of sovereign reason generally neglects the significance that will has to legal order (P. Kahn 2011). But, as Hannah Arendt (1962, 179) reminds us, the original meaning of *lex* (the Roman term for statutory law) referred to a constitutive act of will. Roman ideology framed the founding of the Republic as an intimate achievement, a union of tribes. This union was achieved through war, the war ended in a treaty, and it was this treaty—this *lex*—that constituted the legal order of the Republic as the instrument through which "former enemies became 'friends' and allies" (180). The binding nature of legality, Arendt argues, does not come from the abstract order represented by a legal code, but rather from the sociality of shared allegiance to that code. Law is a *relationship*—a relationship of collectively willed subjection to a common authority—before it is a rational model of order. The Taiwanese *paichusuo* draws on the primacy of will over code to reverse the means-ends logic of "law enforcement." In the work of administrative repair, police do not enact force as a means to the end of law. Rather, they use textual resources supplied by code and procedure as a means to the end of recomposing the force of will holding a group of stakeholders together in common subjection to a policed repair of their momentary contradiction.

HOLDING THINGS TOGETHER

"The most important single characteristic of the state is that it constitutes the illusory common interest of a society" (Abrams 1988, 64). Police power is often seen as a means by which agents of the state uphold this illusory common interest, imposing it by force when need be. But the police work described in the previous chapters does not follow that logic. For Taiwan's neighborhood policemen, democracy brought an end to their responsibilities for imposing a preconstituted idea of order. Taiwan's authoritarian period shaped policing as an element in the Leninist project of curating an explicitly defined general will; the end of authoritarianism left the police without an explicit motive ideology. In the democratic era, police use their curatorial powers for administrative repair: suturing ruptures of the grassroots' collective will to live together. This collective will does not valorize any particular order or telos. Rather, it embodies a tolerant accommodation of disorder and contradiction.

My ethnographic account of this mode of policing shows its democratic efficacy. Such policing can accommodate pluralism. It serves the interests of everyone with a seat at the negotiating table, while ensuring that the opinions of those who lack the political capital to participate are made irrelevant. It is clearly a functional mechanism for reproducing the neighborhood's political economy. But it remains unclear how such policing can uphold the state's claim to represent the common interest of society as a whole. When the police power is thrown open to dialogue about how to manipulate law and procedure to accommodate disorder, what keeps the state from collapsing into factional disagreement? How can police generate a relative autonomy from their immediate context adequate to stand apart from the contrary interests they are supposed to mediate and reconcile?

This chapter explores police involvement in "order maintenance" work (Thacher 2014), looking at how they engage these issues through an idiom of a balance among sentiment, reason, and law. I show how patrolmen rely on this idiom to do their job, and how it provides a scaling logic for reconciling the localized concerns of *paichusuo* policing with more abstract ideas about state-based order. One of the most important aspects of this idiom is the way it relies on the category of *qing* to provide a rationale for bringing things of the will into the processes that produce policed outcomes. These "things of the will" include all the elements bundled into the category of *qing*, as described in chapter 2, things like character, virtue, and solidarity. Virtue and social solidarity are crucial elements of policed order, but, as things of the will, they cannot be "represented," only enacted (Pitkin 1969). "Membership in a free community must be perpetually willed by each of its members. From such a perspective . . . representation is a giant fraud" (6). The dialogical dimension of *paichusuo* policing instantiates a microcosmic arena for direct participatory democracy, generating the collective willing subjection of small groups to the policed order at stake in their lives. In other words, the role of *qing* in Taiwanese policing allows a measured adjustment of collective will, harmonizing it case by case in a way that supports the overall processes of world reproduction.

Keeping Space in Order

Abao's beat contained one of the most *renao* ("hot and noisy") areas of the station's jurisdiction. This was a street entirely lined with restaurant and market stalls set up illegally on the sidewalks. Under the bureaucratic arrangements of the *qinqu* system, whenever illegal or unlicensed operations are "discovered" by higher authorities, the patrolman in whose beat they are found is penalized for his failure to have previously detected and reported them. Thus the entire street market was operating through Abao's official liability. It was an intractable situation for him. The market was a historically established, iconic feature of the local landscape, and a source of livelihood to hundreds of people. Money from the market flowed through the political circuits of the city's regulatory apparatus, ensuring they remained comfortably aligned with its continued operations. There is no way Abao could have single-handedly done anything to reconcile the existence of the market with the licensing and registration codes it violated. Abao was simply, unavoidably, "on the hook" to make sure that the arrangements securing the market's continued existence did not become an irritation to people in parts of the bureaucracy disconnected from its informal quid pro quo.

Unfortunately for Abao, the market had become an irritation to a new resident of the street. This was the anonymous author of a concerted campaign of daily e-mails sent to the city government, complaining that when he arrived home from work in the evening he could not get in the front door of his apartment building because it was blocked by crowded restaurant tables. Thus, one afternoon, during the four-hour period of each shift dedicated to maintaining the *hukou* records for his beat, Abao stuffed a button-down flannel shirt into his bag, put me on the back of his 125 cc police scooter, and drove us over to the market. He parked down an alley, put the shirt on over his uniform,[1] and we walked over to one of the restaurant stalls. As we sat down, the proprietor came over and made us comfortable, and Abao ordered two bowls of noodles. The food arrived, then beer, and soon the table was crowded with unsolicited dishes pressed upon us by the zealously friendly management. We ate and chatted with the husband and wife who ran the operation.

After Abao paid a nominal bill, his informal banter with the management turned substantive. "There have been complaints," he began apologetically, "about your use of the sidewalk here. Some guy that lives in one of these apartment buildings can't get in his front door when he comes home from work." "Who is it?" the proprietor immediately asked. Abao replied that he didn't know, but "*you* guys must know; this kind of situation doesn't just happen overnight." He went on,

> Now, you know that I am not the kind of cop that writes tickets. Hell, I don't write more than thirty tickets a year, and I take a lot of heat for that from the guys with the hats. But these aren't just the kind of complaints that I can "harmonize" [*xietiao*]. Somebody is doing a whole *chenqing*[2] campaign, writing daily e-mails to the city police station. So this time it's got to be "strict enforcement" [*yifazhifa*, literally "enforce the law according to the law"]. I came over here to try to help you guys out. The way it works is that I am going to have to come over here tomorrow at three in the afternoon and take a picture of your operation for evidence, then I am going to have to take another picture after the situation has been cleaned up. So if you can wait until after three to set up your stall, I can take the after picture before and the before picture after. Plus, and I'm sorry about this, but I am going to have to give you a 300 yuan ticket.[3] And I am going to have to keep doing this until the complaints stop. So if I was you, I would try to figure out who it is that you are pissing off. . . . You need to come to some kind of an agreement with that person.

The proprietors agreed to the plan. We then walked all the way down the street, having essentially the same conversation with the other half dozen restaurant owners on the sidewalk in front of the apartment building. In every case the result was the same, a rather stilted acquiescence on the part of the disciplined to a rather convoluted invocation of the law.

As we drove back to the station, Abao volunteered that I had just witnessed a prime example of good policing. The "sentimental feeling," the *ganqing*, of the relationship between the substation and the population in its jurisdiction was very good, he said. And it was techniques like the one I had just witnessed that kept it in such good repair. From Abao's perspective, the objectives of policing— maintaining the peace and tranquility of the community, and discharging his immediate orders without generating "a lot of yelling in the street"—were being successfully achieved. I was impressed by his casual ad hoc orchestration of a street-wide performance of order for the benefit of the state's camera. However, Abao was dismissive of the creativity involved in this technique. He was simply killing two birds with one stone, combining the inconvenience of performing order with the issuance of formal sanctions to apply a focused and relatively gentle pressure to targets of civil outrage, motivating them to find the source of the complaint and settle the matter privately. In his narrative to me, he expressed clear personal sympathies with the businessmen who had just fed us: Taiwan is a crowded country, and people selling goods in the streets and sidewalks are working hard to survive, he said. How can you try to keep people from making a living just because they inconvenience you? Nonetheless, he went on, when the order comes down to clear the street, you can't tell the commanding officers at the county police department, "We've got good *ganqing* here, so I didn't do anything. You have to enforce the law. Dealing with conflicts in the street is simple," he said. Then he added, "The problems always come in how to write the official reports [*gongwen*]."

A dissatisfied resident of Taiwan hoping to enlist state agency to do something about the use of space has a choice between two broadly distinguishable political strategies: either staging a public *chenqing*, "complaint" (literally, "to display the situation"), or mobilizing a particularistic network by "going through the back door" (*zou houmen*) of personal connections. These two channels are by no means exclusive; in fact, it is generally understood that successful invocation of higher authority will likely require some degree of involvement in both. Nonetheless, even as both avenues may simultaneously be at work in a given situation, they remain superficially antithetical, and their prima facie contradiction exemplifies the tensions that characterize police action in contemporary Taiwan.

To begin with, the "back door" is wide. Mobilizational authoritarianism organized society into dense overlapping networks of political clientage, and relics of this remain embedded in the habits of social solidarity. Even as the democratic transition shifted the defining mission of the state from revolution to "service" (*fuwu*), it remains de rigueur for politicians within the category of "popular representative" (*minyi daibiao*, a category that includes borough chiefs, city and county councilors, and national legislators) to maintain outreach offices through which their constituency can bring matters to their attention in a quasi-informal capacity. These offices function as campaign headquarters during elections, and the gathering of electoral support is self-consciously understood as the formation of a patronage network, with campaign materials stressing the responsiveness of the aspiring representative to his or her clients.

At the same time, however, by virtue of the competitive aspect of the democratic process and the complexity of the administrative bureaucracy, back channels are not universally accessible and/or effective. And so it also frequently becomes strategic in the pursuit of a particular goal to deploy the forces of public attention. Public complaint shows up in a variety of media, from graffiti or the "white cloth / black letter" banners hung in protests, through the entire spectrum of advertising, and right into the content of the news itself. There is an art to framing effective complaints, and the conventions of this genre impose a structure on the content of public statements of dissatisfaction. As illustration, consider the following complaints taken from the Taipei County ombudsman's Internet message board. These two complaints, concerned with an incident of illegal construction, provide an example of the general voicing and conventional scripts used for the public expression of dissatisfaction in contemporary Taiwan, and are especially revealing of the slippery boundaries between public legitimacy and particularistic efficacy.

Complaint 1:
In Weixing City, at Popular Sovereignty Road No. 232, the emergency exit and the front sidewalk have been used by the first-floor property owner for illegal construction! He has also built a metal-skinned garage in legally stipulated empty space. This guy could be called a local bully! He even challenged us to try to report him, with the threat, "You go make a report! If you have the ability to get this thing taken down, then I will 'join your lineage' [*gen ni xing*]!" Is that flagrant enough? And not only this, he has got the "Black Way" [i.e., gangsters] making irregular patrols around the area 24 hours a day (this is real, I am not exaggerating)!!! We have already been appealing to the authorities [*chenqing*] for a long time (starting June 1), most recently we took our appeal to the [national] presidential office. And with both the presidential office and the county government, the speed with which the situation was handled was initially quite quick. They immediately dispatched the appropriate units to take up the matter. However, as soon as the case was transferred

to the Weixing City government and its related offices, it disappeared like a stone sinking into the sea. Afterward, I understood: this landowner has some powerful forces behind him. It's because there are some Blue Party [KMT] legislators and [county or city] council members behind him propping him up, powerfully suppressing this entire case, so the demolition team from the public works department doesn't dare to take action. Originally I had not thought that such a small borough chief could have such a large influence, but it was just the Blue Party all along.

O great official, the lives of your county-subjects have been cut off from heaven by a few pairs of mean hands. They have covered over the safety of our lives and property. Could you grant this some importance? Don't wait until a disaster has occurred, then send a few grief-faced officials to kneel and light incense. Then it will be too late. Save us!! Get to the bottom of who it is that has eaten our case. Otherwise, truly I cannot believe in the king's law [*wangfa*]; I can only believe that those with power and those with connections are the king and the law. County government, express your courage!! Thank you.

Complaint 2:
About two weeks ago . . . the demolition team came, and they had checked everything out and were prepared to demolish the construction, when suddenly a person showed up claiming to be from the city government. As soon as he arrived he said, "OK, go ahead and demolish a little something, that's fine, but don't cause too much loss to the owner." He only spoke a few words to the demolition team, and then left. The strange thing was, the demolition team left with him!! What on earth kind of a thing is that?? The city government man came out to the site and openly "peddled influence." Is this reasonable? Just because that property owner has power and influence, has legislators and councilors as patrons, so we the people should just go die? Because we have no patrons, are we simply doomed to suffer our own anger and swallow our own voice?

These kinds of things will never reach the ears of the County Executive's officers, because the Weixing City government, and the demolition team, and the public works department within your jurisdiction are all deceiving you. Just because of the influence peddling of a few powerful figures, the demolition team doesn't dare to take the thing down! Today, by this letter, we who are under this miserable situation would like to notify the great County Executive. We hope that the great County Executive can uphold justice and fairness on behalf of his small subjects, and thereby show the true law! And if, County Executive, you also do not dare to handle this or only superficially gloss over the affair, then we can only sigh that we were blind to have given our vote to Su Zhengchang!!

The basic form of these complaints derives from the complainants' attempt to align their position as closely as possible with foundational values in Taiwan's contemporary political mythology, most particularly "the people's" entitlement to effective enforcement of "true/impartial law" (*zhengfa*). Motivated by irritation with the illegal construction of a garage, they present a plea to legitimate authority in the abstract, calling for disaster-averting intervention on behalf of a humble and hapless subject population threatened by the "mean hands" of a local bully. The undifferentiated category of "the people" is held up as the definitive legitimate political subject, specifically opposed to the unjust manipulation of political power through a factional patronage network. The illegal building is made to signify a "flagrantly" unjust world, animated by individual selfishness and produced through the machinations of a political system that operates effectively only when manipulated by the hidden networks of personal connection lurking within the representative bodies of the local and national government. In this case, the complainant exposes the network behind the garage to be the political machine of the "Blue Party" (i.e., the KMT; it is relevant that the county executive was at the time of this complaint a member of the "Green Party"—i.e., the DPP—while the mayor of Weixing City was a KMT member).

The crux of these particular complaints is the "eating of a case" (*chian*), the disappearance of a case midstream in its bureaucratic processing. "Eating cases" is a chronic dimension of government operations in Taiwan, a technique used for diverse purposes, including easing overwork, manipulating crime statistics, and integrating the demands of personal networks with the bureaucratic process. It is, accordingly, one of the most common concrete concerns expressed by Taiwanese citizens frustrated with the incapacity of the government to do what they want it to do.

Finally, despite the centrality of the accusation of "influence peddling" to the complaint, it is not, however, an appeal to rule of law in the abstract. The positive aspect of the appeal is framed by reference to the vote as a personal transaction between subject and elected official, and directed to the personal virtue of the officeholder, suggesting that the official's "courage" in the specific action at issue will be decisive in restoring a just world ordered by the "king's law" in place of the existing situation ruled by power and connections.[4] This is key: even as the machinations of backdoor connections are scandalous from the perspective of a public *chenqing* plea, politics remains nonetheless understood in personal terms.

As a successful *chenqing* is accepted as legitimate by its addressee, it is publicly validated by a response,[5] whereupon it disappears into the bureaucratic machinery to be converted into the procedural requirements of the formal division of administrative labor. Complaints like those described above, concerned with illegal construction in public space, regardless of the channels through which they were received and acknowledged, generated their first practical response within two offices of the county government: the department of public works (responsible for demolition of illegally built permanent structures) and the department of environmental protection (responsible for dealing with temporary constructions, debris, and pollution). Those departments were responsible for evaluating the actual situation on the ground, and then making or recommending remedies according to relevant legal codes (potentially including mobilization of a demolition team to clear the space). The implementation of these responsibilities generally takes place through subordinate bureaus of the county-level departments, housed within city government offices.

Police involvement in street-clearing operations is standard on the pretext that forcing people to relinquish their control of space tends to cause conflict, and managing conflict is the police mission. It is uncommon to see demolition of "permanent" structures of the kind mentioned in the above complaints, probably because few people are foolish enough to invest resources in building them without first "smoothing the way" (*baiping*, i.e., marshaling the connections required for a given project); when buildings are torn down, this takes place in the context of pitched political battles that are qualitatively distinct from the routine invocation of police authority at issue in this chapter. However, throughout 2002, the environmental protection department sponsored a large-scale street-clearing campaign aimed at nonpermanent structures, and under these auspices the city government kept a forklift and dump truck in continuous circulation throughout the city, cooperating with individual police substations on a weekly basis. Under this initiative, I was able to observe many instances of police action in clearing public space.

These events would begin with an employee of the city's environmental protection office (the forklift driver) arriving at a substation with a stack of books filled with thousands of official reports of "street occupation" (*luba*). Covering several months of investigative activity by his office, these books were filled with entries recording the sites of such things as "motorcycle repair operation causing sidewalk blockage," "discarded vehicle," "flowerpots." Under each heading was a list of dates of observation, each followed by the notation "Checked. No improvement." This documentation was carried into the field as an immediately accessible formal justification for a raid on the day's targeted street. The actual work of clearing the street was executed by the forklift and a dump truck, augmented by a troop of a half dozen or so older women who volunteered at the city environmental protection bureau and were thus called "environmental protection mamas." Working together, this team was capable of indiscriminately scraping the sidewalks and streets clear of all nonpermanent structures, loading everything from restaurant operations to piles of garbage to potted trees to boards covering potholes into the truck to be taken off to the dump. While doing this, they were accompanied by two policemen in their official "guardian" function, who observed the goings-on, wrote tickets to selected violators, and documented the results of the cleanup effort.

A typical outing is described here. After a half hour gearing up at the substation, we drove over to the day's target, a narrow and heavily trafficked road leading to the Central Bridge. When the police and I arrived, the city team was already assembled and waiting for us there. The first target was a restaurant on the corner, busy with the breakfast crowd. Like many restaurants in the city, its operations centered on a small ground-floor room open to the sidewalk; at night the room was used for secure storage of equipment; when open for business it spread its tables and chairs out on the sidewalk and used the room as a kitchen. We approached, Patrolman Wang took a few pictures of the restaurant's illegal breakfast service, and then the forklift driver inaugurated the raid by cutting down a huge banner advertisement hanging from their awning. The crew of city workers then set to work dragging some of the restaurant's more peripheral accoutrements (potted plants, garbage cans) to the dump truck, while Sergeant Yang walked over to the owner with his ticket pad open to a fresh page. After a few moments of confusion, the restaurant's crew began dragging their tables and chairs back into their storage space, working in what seemed a strangely slow and detached fashion. One young man stood holding on to an expensive steel sink chained to a tree, while another went to look for the key to the lock. The city workers ignored him and the sink, concentrating their efforts on uncontested objects. Within about ten minutes, the city workers managed to convey to the dump truck a number of storage bins, all the restaurant's free-standing signage, and one food-preparation table, while the rest of the material infrastructure of the operation had been successfully stuffed back into its overnight storage facility. Throughout this process there was no sign of acknowledgment between the two sides, certainly no appearance of hostility or overt conflict. Sergeant Yang spent the entire time writing up a NT$1,200 (about US$40) ticket for the owner, a middle-aged man who remained a picture of apologetic subservience throughout the process. As we finished up, Patrolman Wang took the all-important digital pictures of the cleared street corner, to be filed as official evidence of a successful mission. And we went up the street to the adjoining address, cutting the chain attaching a collection of steel drums to a pillar.

In this manner we moved very slowly up the road, ripping out and sweeping up everything that was not removed from our path. In many places the sidewalks were filled with commerce, but the merchants in attendance were lackadaisical about dragging their wares back into their overnight storage facilities before confiscation became imminent. This meant we remained constantly in the situation of two opposed projects being carried on simultaneously with a mutual lack of acknowledgment. Some of the operations for which the sidewalk had been appropriated were unstaffed at this early hour (about 9 a.m.), and these were simply trashed. The environmental mamas worked hard, moving piles of garbage off the sidewalk in a wheelbarrow, lifting chunks of rubble onto the forklift, and sweeping the newly opened spaces clean. Parked motorcycles and professionally built structures were left alone—though they were illegally located, the bureaucratic processes involved in enforcing the law on them were beyond the scope of the environmental protection department.

It soon became obvious that the practical goal of our team was not to dispose of material, but rather to provoke the owners to move it (temporarily) back into officially private space so that a picture of a clean street could be produced. About halfway down the block we reached one of the city's official public marketplaces, a covered structure filled with licensed stalls. The market had long ago spilled out of its official confines onto the surrounding sidewalks, and as we drew near, the proprietors of illegally located stalls began to drag their equipment into the walkways of the permanent market. One operation, however, a tiny stand with a handwritten sign advertising Buddhist cuisine, was unattended. The policemen involved in this street-clearing operation were, of course, intimately familiar with the people on whom the policy was being enforced: as the official intermediaries between the state and the populace of their jurisdiction, substation patrolmen are responsible for maintaining *hukou* records and business licenses. This market was a major institution within the substation's jurisdiction, and the policemen knew the little food stand not simply as a piece of random detritus but as the livelihood of an unfortunate old woman. Our progress down the street halted. We rested, exhorting the surrounding shopkeepers to summon the owner to come move her business off the street so we could take our picture and move on. People were dispatched to find her, but they returned without success. After ten or fifteen minutes, the neighboring shop owners made a show of moving the gear themselves (although in fact it simply ended up in the recently cleared space behind our team). We took our picture and moved on.

After two hours the dump truck was full. We had not come very far (we could still see the corner where we had begun), and the sense of empty formality was profound. Somewhere between the proprietors making a show of getting their stuff off the street, and the city officials making a show of throwing it away, the street was momentarily clear enough for Patrolman Wang to take the picture that would be passed up the bureaucratic channels as proof the day's mission had been accomplished. As the dump truck made a trip to the dump, we stood around chatting. "This kind of work is the worst," said Wang. "It does nothing but cause conflict. Half the time, people don't even think that what they are doing is illegal. They think, just because we only come by here once every six months or once every year, it is legal. They don't know it's just that we don't have enough personnel." He gestured down the block to the restaurant where we had started. It was serving the early lunch crowd, set up on the sidewalk exactly as it had been before we arrived. "It's impossible to make any difference," he sighed. "All you do is get into arguments with people. And then they go get their *minyi daibiao* [popular representatives], and it's nothing but trouble."

Again, as with Abao's intervention, the practical logic of the operation focused on the production of a photograph of a clean street, a situation that lasted at most a few hours and generally only minutes. This exemplifies a practical approach to law enforcement in which the "thinnest" procedural requirements are used to establish a de facto common goal between the enforcer and the targets of enforcement, which then allows larger contradictions between the higher-level intentions driving the street-cleaning team and the ground-level interests of the street merchants to be bracketed within a space of mutual nonacknowledgment, allowing the two sides to cooperate in production of photographic proof that the mission has been "accomplished." The flexibility with which "thin" procedural requirements can be manipulated to avoid implication in contested dimensions of the contradictory thicker interpretations held by various participants in the event provides a crucial resource for police management of public-order problems in contemporary Taiwan. The messy and potentially volatile street-level conflicts are thus converted into the more abstract and tractable problem of, as Abao put it, "how to write the official reports."

Given some poetic license with translation, the term Abao used for "official reports" (*gongwen*) could be rendered as "public text."[6] And we can take these examples of good police work to be exemplary by virtue of their successful management of the tensions that emerge where "public texts" composed in the language of the law intersect with the fabric of particularistic "sentimental feelings" that define the political textures of local community life. This does indeed appear to be an accurate evocation of the conventional orientation Taiwanese patrolmen adopt in evaluating the quality of their own work. They frequently invoke the trichotomy of law, reason, and sentiment we first saw in chapter 2's discussion of Goto Shimpei's reliance on Qing dynasty jurisprudence in his design of the *paichusuo*. As a practical principle, this frame was invoked by patrolmen to describe their work as oriented by pursuit of a balance between law (*fa*) and sentiment (*qing*), as mediated by reason (*li*).

Beyond its historical role in the policing apparatus, this trichotomy is an established trope in the wider culture, understood as carrying a venerable philosophical pedigree while remaining relevant to a range of modern and contemporary problems. In popular discourse, the most prevalent invocation of the trope was in the form of a contrast between two hierarchical sequences of precedence: "sentiment-reason-law" (*qing-li-fa*) vis-à-vis "law-reason-sentiment" (*fa-li-qing*). In the *qing-li-fa* sequence (which was often identified as traditional, Chinese, or the "rule of man"), sentiment precedes law. That is, sentiment overdetermines law, and so the thick webs of *guanxi*—individualistic relations between kin, patrons, friends, or other varieties of non-bureaucratized solidarity and/or patronage—undermine the systemic integrity of formal organizations such as labor unions, professional associations, or state bureaucracies. The reverse sequence, *fa-li-qing* (which, by contrast to the above was associated with modernity, the West, or the "rule of law"), indicates a cultural milieu in which proper procedure always takes precedence over personalistic ties, and efficient bureaucratic machines assemble almost spontaneously in the aggregation of social individuals like those William Whyte (1956) called "organization man." Thus, editorials in the popular press contain statements like, "In order to improve the contemporary degeneration of Taiwan's political environment and its pervasive political culture of influence-brokering, the Chinese must change this enduring valorization of 'sentiment-reason-law,' which forms the ideal of the 'rule of man,' in order to develop the valorization of 'law-reason-sentiment,' which forms the ideal of the 'rule of law.'"[7] Within this reasoning, there is a sense of zero-sum opposition, where the imposition of law indicates the rupture of sentiment—for example, "Where sentiments are thick, the law retreats. When sentiments are broken, the law advances." This enables as counterpoint to arguments for the rule of law a romantic valorization of the idealized harmony of sentimental community over the impersonal mechanisms of legal authority. Thus, where law sees sentiment as partiality, sentiment sees law as arbitrary. And the debate goes on.

A primary institutional determinant of Taiwanese police culture arises from the nature of the patrolmen's position as state-authorized agents of conflict management; that is, patrolmen spend their time answering summons to situations where something needs to be done and state agency has been invoked to do it (Bittner [1974] 1990b). Accordingly, Taiwanese patrolmen arrive at the scenes of their professional performance as formal representatives of state authority, and the most common self-identification by the patrolmen of their social role is as a "law executor" (*zhifazhe*). This is a difficult role to play; to a Taiwanese neighborhood patrolman, the law is a dangerous thing. As one patrolman put it, the law is a knife, and a policeman must be a skillful surgeon if he himself is not to lose control of the blade:

> The edge that points outward is law enforcement, the edge that points inward will cut you. So how do you really "grasp" it? That is what I am saying; you are standing on the edge of a knife, so you need to take a certain care, because if you slip you will get cut. Protect others, yes, but also protect yourself. I am saying, sure, go ahead and do everything, but you still need to use some thought. In fact, you need to think a lot. When you are enforcing the law, you cannot disregard the other people's power. You have to attend to your own safety, don't let them harm you. Even if you don't understand anything at all, you still need to protect yourself. Just being filled with the courage to write a bunch of citations is completely useless.

Several significant themes appear in this comment. First, it is a "thin" invocation of the principle of legality; it frames law as purely instrumental. From the patrolman's perspective, law is simply a thing used to create a link between misdeed and punishment. "If you aren't wearing your motorcycle helmet, you get a ticket, there is nothing else to say"—that is, that's *just* the law (quotes taken from the same interview). The mechanics of this connection are understood to be "rigid and harsh ... violation of the law is just a fact." Such seemingly arbitrary authority is, on its own, understood by the patrolman to be *unreasonably* absolute; the law carries no connotation of anything inherently legitimate. Indeed, the kinds of logical or sympathetic qualities involved in legitimating legal action are understood to exist as explicitly distinct categories: the harmfulness or helpfulness of a given invocation of law is dependent on "external" criteria, the qualities of reason and sentiment most significant among them. This rationale is consistent with its origins in Imperial jurisprudence, and would be familiar to police from the logic of their work during the martial law era. Under the dictatorship, when lawmaking took the form of executive orders (Cooney 2004, 422), policing was crucially involved with various forms of *qing*-control (*qingzhi*) directed to the task of cultivating popular allegiance to the dictator's "sacred mission."

A second theme in the patrolman's comment is the necessity of consciously appreciating the fact that law, as the formal bureaucratic power of the state, is *not* the only game in town. Self-preservation demands street-level law enforcers be highly sensitive to all forms of power capable of structuring the course of events in their working environment. As Axiong warned me in regard to All People's Taxi, it is imperative to *be careful*. Police must take care because their work is, as they say, "complicated." Complication (*fuza*) is a sort of all-purpose euphemism for anything from routine happenstance to deep political-economic intrigue.

The form of care that complication makes imperative is articulated through *qing*. Post-authoritarian Taiwan is understood to have come under sway of a "Black Gold" regime, a phrasing indicating the pursuit of financial interest ("gold") through hidden ("black") networks of collusion, and referring to a ubiquitous, even structural, intersection of organized crime with the political infrastructure (K.-l. Chin 2003). At the face-to-face level of ethnographic reality, this kind of political economy involves a sort of covert parallel universe of patronage, collusion, and conspiracy submerged within the conventional routines of everyday interaction. As cultural forms, those relationships take the shape of particularistic bonds, more or less euphemistically described and performed in the terms of sentimental attachment, notably kinship terms of address and the motif of brotherhood. It is worth noting here that the use of forms of real and fictive kinship as a basis for economic organization is a human universal, and social anthropologists have long been impressed by the capacity of southern Chinese idioms of kinship to function as the basis of highly elaborate economic formations (e.g., Freedman 1979; Winn 1994a). It is not surprising that the "sentimental" dimensions of life in the substation would serve as the arena in which the shady side of the job is taken into account.

In this respect, we should consider that the average patrolman's middle-class salary of about US$1,500 a month is potentially augmented by an undocumentable but by all estimates roughly equivalent amount in various informal "regulatory fees" (*guifei*), "grease water" (*youshui*), or "A-money" (*A-qian*, or sometimes "A-food," *A-cai*), which flow in through the substation and up through circuits of administrative oversight into the wider regulatory bureaucracy. An organizing principle for the practical integration of the formal regulatory apparatus with the informal neighborhood economy is provided by the fixed responsibility assigned to individual policemen for managing the affairs of their beat—in particular the way their individual accountability for illegal enterprises discovered to be operating there creates an interest in these enterprises (which constitute a significant proportion of the local economy) remaining "undiscovered" (i.e., unremarked upon). The prototypical situation is an unlicensed establishment—paradigmatically the so-called special industries involved in the minor vices of drinking, gambling, and prostitution—passing a "red envelope"[8] containing the equivalent of several hundred US dollars to the local beat officer each month, a sum that is split between the patrolman and certain other cooperating figures. As this money flows into the substation it is accumulated by the working personnel not simply as personal profit, but also (even primarily) as a repository from which to supply the funds that must be passed up the regulatory food chain during periods of administrative review and consideration for promotion.

The operation of this financial system (which exists as an objective social fact generating the conditions under which individual officers navigate their careers) has the effect of maintaining an alignment between the interests of the local regulatory apparatus and those of the local unlicensed economy, ensuring that discretionary slack in the bureaucratic machine is oriented toward the continued smooth operation of the total system. Not every unlicensed enterprise chooses to participate in this system, only those that understand their own financial interests as served by making a long-term investment in the regulation of their local neighborhood—the good citizens of the informal economic order. And since the economic health of the neighborhood is, like that of the island as a whole, inseparable from its informal dimension, such contributions are locally understood (by those involved at least) as ultimately no less legitimate than the formal donations made to the police by the local chamber of commerce, Lions Club, or "Friends of Police."

What chiefly distinguishes these informal economic relationships from more formal taxation is the regime of social relations in which they exist, and which their operations maintain as institutionalized relations of solidarity. That is to say, the day-to-day management of informal economic cooperation is conducted within the idiom of *qing*, as "sentimental" and particularistic relationships defining a space of intimacy explicitly insulated from the formalized distances of public interaction, and generally marked by the strategic inversion of selected "public" values (Herzfeld 2005). Unlike Babül's (2017) Turkish bureaucrats, however, the ostensible "intimacy" of this regime does not make it subversive of the order that police authority is deployed to maintain. Quite the opposite, in fact; when talking about the quality of life in their substation's jurisdiction or their personal beat, patrolmen exhibit their strongest primary orientation to *ganqing*, the "sentimental" dimension. Indeed, most of the routines of working life in the substation take place nestled in metaphors of brotherhood and friendship (or vitriolic *personal* conflict), operating on a rationale that takes "mutual assistance" as the highest human social ideal. This accords with a valorization of social relations based on "compassion" (*renqingwei*), which is one of the most widespread affirmations of what is distinctively good about Taiwanese society. The order of *qing* is, in other words, a rational moral universe defining a normative ideal of the good society, in which the amalgamation of formal and informal money and power makes sense. Grounded in the sentimental values of righteousness and loyalty, patrolmen are just average guys, good family men striving to do right by their intimates as they collectively struggle to survive in a treacherously complicated environment. *Qing* is an ethical field; pursuit of *eudaimonia* on its terms is a fundamentally moral project.

No small part of the complication in police life arises from the fact that, when framed by the expectations of bureaucratic rationality, the intimate circuits of *qing*-based exchange of money and favor are often, quite simply, illegal. To be sure, the tension between "cooperation" and "corruption" always contains a degree of ambivalence (itself a crucial element in the routine operations of any criminal justice system). But there are occasions when the ambiguity must be resolved into a definite value judgment. And when this time comes, the choice of which epithet or euphemism is applied to a particular case depends, ultimately, on the standpoint of evaluation. Public discussion of police corruption in Taiwan is generally unforgiving. The process of political liberalization has fostered public sensibility that the progressive future lies squarely on the side of "rule of law" in opposition to the retrograde past of "rule by man," and, accordingly, public sphere discussion increasingly invokes liberal-democratic discourse about the ultimate value of legality as the defining factor in evaluations of illegitimacy. This is a positive factor in consolidating support for rule of law within state institutions. But at the local level, where the lines between state and non-state authority are hazier, this shift in the terms of public culture exerts a destabilizing effect on the established balance between sentimental community and local public order. In other words, from the perspective of the average policeman on the street, democratization has *intensified* the political tensions saturating the arena of their discretionary practice, making their practical reliance on intimate networks more crucial than ever.

These tensions are described by patrolmen in terms of an acute confrontation between *fa* and *qing*. To understand this discourse, we must recognize that the moral bonds of sentimental alliance are not always valorized as good. People who perceive their social position as exploited through entrenched and inaccessible networks of other people's solidarity interpret the order of sentiment as a tragic element of Taiwanese culture. The "free and easy" qualities of community in which problems are worked out through the deployment of informal social resources is to them an insidious mythology from which the "true law" (to use the rhetoric from the complaint about the illegal garage) should properly rescue them.

There is a broad contradiction in social values here, and police, as professional managers of social conflict, cannot comfortably take a firm stand on either side. Thus, for them, a delicate balancing act arises in every direct confrontation of the mobilized authority of the state's *fa* with the institutionalized political economy of the local "sentimental society" ordered by *qing*. Consider, in this respect, that when a citizen "calls the police," the emergency 119 system automatically routes the call to the county police station, where it becomes a matter of formal record. It is then relayed to the appropriate substation's front-desk telephone line, from which it is radioed to the policeman on patrol duty at the time. Receiving such a dispatch, the patrolman knows that the county station's record of the complaint, combined with substation duty roster, has created a paper trail identifying him *personally* as legally accountable for the management of the problematic situation.

The policeman thus arrives at the scene to which state authority has been called as an individual embodiment of that authority. In this situation, the image of "standing on the edge of a knife" becomes compelling. Whenever called into a situation where informal privilege is being challenged by an outraged citizenry holding formally valid expectations that illegal activities will be disciplined by the state, a policeman finds himself at the cutting edge of an intersection between two distinct regimes of power and authority, to both of which he is beholden. In the course of their confrontation, both forms of power—the formal legal system and the informal political-economic system—threaten to become further mobilized. And escalation in either of these realms will immediately go over the head of the lowly patrolman, circumscribing his discretionary command of the situation while leaving him to account for the actions of his superiors across the awkward disjuncture between two forms of power that mutually recognize one another as illegitimate.

The personal interests and, hence, discretionary resources of the policeman are therefore primarily invested in ensuring that the conflict does not escalate beyond his control so long as he remains implicated in its outcome. In this balancing act, *reason* serves as the decisive fulcrum. This is obvious to an observer of police-mediated negotiation: the policeman's constant refrain is an exhortation to the involved parties to "be reasonable." It is also central to the way policemen reflect on the skills required for their work. By contrast to the harsh cutting edge of law, reason is described as a circular, rounding and smoothing quality that fits the law to context, a "soft" consensus with which everyone (at least, all reasonable people) will "self-identify." And where sentiment is understood in terms of inherently particularizing allegiances, reason is the basis for a universalism in which all reasonable people can be expected to participate (the words in quotes are taken from my interviews with patrolmen).

In some ways, the patrolman's valorization of *li*—taking a natural human capacity for reason as the foundation on which to understand the practical possibility of finding harmony in social relations—resonates with classical liberal political philosophy. This similarity ends, however, at the patrolman's understanding of inherent contextual limitations to the effective authority of reason. That is, the discretionary form of reason used by Taiwanese policemen to mediate the disjoint orders of law and sentiment is not a properly "public" quality. It is provisional, ad hoc, and radically situated in its immediate context. The appeal to reason made by a patrolman in the course of managing conflict takes the form of a call to reflection on the part of the involved parties concerning their shared interest in resolving the specific conflict at issue. This is a definitively *particular* conjuncture of interests, and the appeal to reason focuses on this particularity rather than any ideal of behavior imagined as if it contained a logical principle that might "become through your will a *universal* law of nature" (Kant [1785] 1993, 421).

This form of situated reason, as a mode of reflecting on the possibilities of a collective will within a contextual conjuncture of conflicting interests, is on its own inadequate to challenge or resist the compelling forces attached to state law and/or sentimental allegiance. To be sure, in the routine situation of a standoff between the powers of *fa* and *qing* (that is, the chronic "complications" of local political economy), a mediator can effectively orchestrate resolution of conflict from the detached standpoint of a fair broker. But the slightest shift in the underlying dimensions of the conflict will quickly efface the practical standpoint for this kind of intervention. Thus, from the patrolman's vantage point, there is an antipathy between reason and publicity. Contrary to Kant's formula for political enlightenment ([1784] 2012), the public use of reason just makes things worse. Any mediation that broadcasts conflict into wider spaces of attention expands the number of different interests that must be taken into account in achieving a resolution, attenuating the space of their common conjunction. Compromise is possible behind closed doors, but handling conflict in the public eye utterly transforms the kinds of stakes that are attached to the act of relinquishing one's position; once an event has been pulled into the realm of unbounded public spectacle, there is little likelihood of a reasonable resolution. In other words, keeping contradictions in order *requires* obscurity, a space in which conflicted "principles" can be compromised without causing further repercussion.

When describing to me the skills of good policing, Taiwanese patrolmen occasionally invoked the ideal of *touming*, "transparency." However, in the context of their engagement with the sentimental fabric of local order, they used this term to indicate a relationship of *intimacy*, a relationship of trusting openness between a patrolman and the individual inhabitants of his beat. Implicitly framed by the normative order of *qing*, this idiom of intimate transparency is entirely contrary to the standard association of (public) transparency with the rule of law. Intimate transparency is not a transitive relationship: if A is intimately transparent to B, and B is intimately transparent to C, this does not then imply that A is transparent to C. Quite the opposite, in fact. As intermediary, B finds himself in a delicate position where the slightest indiscretion on his part can have potentially dramatic consequences for the relationship between A and C. Indeed, the fact that A and C rely on B to keep a mediated distance between themselves is less often an accident of circumstance than an intentional and integral aspect of their relationship: for example, B is the patrolman, A is a local businessman, and C is a district prosecutor. The patrolman's crucial function in maintaining a harmoniously integrated balance of powers rests on his skills in strategic translation of the meaningful connections (also known as "information") shared within the intimate order of *ganqing* into those demanded by the operations of the legal system, concealing and revealing information in such a way that none of the involved parties feels their reasonable expectations of orderly give-and-take have been egregiously violated. This space of mediated distances—differences within unity—*is* the political "world" that the *paichusuo* serves to keep in order.

Holding Things Together

Democracy, as a politics of "agonistic pluralism," can be difficult to reconcile with the autocratic powers implicit in the liberal ideal of rule of law (Mouffe 2009). In chapter 2 I mentioned Balbus's (2010, xiii) gloss on democracy as a hope for "the possibility that the governed and the governing might be one and the same." This ideal is hard to realize, especially at a scale where direct democracy is impossible. As a political community of twenty-three million people, Taiwan has to rely on forms of abstract representation to mediate the decision-making processes that structure its common life. But there are limits to how much of a community's political life can be effectively processed through abstraction. "Some activities are of value only if every man does them for himself" (Pitkin 1969, 6). Maintaining a political will to live together in peace despite chronic conflicts and irreconcilable differences is one such activity. Taiwan's *paichusuo* are arenas for this. They enable the practice of a localized form of direct democracy designed to reconstitute the will to tolerate the contradictions and disorder people invoke the police to repair.

This is not politically neutral law enforcement; it is overtly *political* policing, in an Arendtian sense where politics involves the creation of new (or renewed) beginnings (Arendt 1958). This is a fundamentally dialogical form of politics; citizenship is defined by participation in dialogue through which collective decisions are made. Not everybody in a police station achieves such citizenship. As we saw in chapter 4, people without adequate social capital are relegated to the position of mute objects for administrative manipulation. The exclusionary quality of power means that such marginalized people are not necessary to the success of the overall enterprise of keeping the democratic world at peace. All that is necessary is that the space of power itself remains a sphere of dialogue. "The public realm in a republic [is] constituted by an exchange of opinion between equals, and that this realm would disappear the very moment an exchange became superfluous" (Arendt 1963, 83).

The productive qualities of political life—its capacity for creativity or "natality"—arise from its pluralism, not from any abstract principle. Authentic politics becomes something else when dialogue is replaced by enforcement of a rule; democracy ends at the point where politics become "law enforcement." The democratization of Taiwan's police has led to a mode of policing organized by an ethos that keeps politics at a certain distance from law, and organizes policing through an ethic of care. Care, in Tronto and Fisher's definition, is "a species activity that includes everything that we do to maintain, continue, and repair our 'world' so that we can live in it as well as possible" (Tronto 1993, 103). Taiwanese police keep the peace and repair the social by using a balance of sentiment, reason, and law to continually renew attunement to the potentialities of worldhood emergent from the natality intrinsic in human togetherness. It is a mode of policing engaged directly in the political metabolism of the collective will that holds the world together.

STRONG DEMOCRACY, WEAK POLICE

What are police for? I have described Taiwan's police institutions as participants in the curation of a political world. The neighborhood *paichusuo* functions as an arena for staging some of the work required for people to live together in peace. The patrolmen working in that institution are responsible for cultivating a collective will to tolerate the diverse forms of disorder and contradiction that provoke people in the neighborhood to invoke police authority. To fulfill their responsibilities, these police rely on the inscriptive power they have to shape the content of official documents (ranging from the population registry to police reports), which is the only form of power they can effectively claim as their exclusive "jurisdictional" authority. Based on my ethnographic characterization of this overall situation, I describe these police as agents for the administrative repair of a certain class of political problems. This class of problems consists of things that degrade the "in between" from which collective human potential arises (Arendt 1958, 183).

The *paichusuo* is a definitively local institution. It is engaged in a "worlding" process where the world is the neighborhood. It cultivates relationships at the most mundane and specific level. Most of its work is organized as informal mediation, aimed at recalibrating people's tolerance for disorder rather than putting things into order. This is a form of police work that belongs "backstage" and emphasizes affect and/or will over abstract reason. How people feel about the policed order in their lives is a separate issue from what they think about political order in general. When the immediate goal of a policing intervention is to maintain or renew the complacent will to accept inconvenient contradictions, it is helpful to stay focused on qualities of the will rather than abstractions of order. Accordingly, *paichusuo* policing emphasizes *qing* over law.

The *paichusuo* I studied was located in a city whose political economy was only marginally organized by law. There were deep contradictions in the legal foundations of the historical order that police worked to maintain. They managed these contradictions behind closed doors, where it was possible to forge a collective will to move forward without addressing the underlying contradictions of the status quo. Any time this tacit accommodation of illegality became public, it would be attributed to individual corruption rather than institutional conditions. This created a strong antipathy between this form of policing and "public reason." Thus, where the explicit rationale of *paichusuo* policing was conventionally described as maintaining an equal balance among sentiment, reason, and law, the practical imperatives of the situation I observed compelled policemen to rely on *qing* as their best hope for avoiding the nightmare of being held personally accountable by the courts or general public for the historical order they were asked to maintain.

Taiwanese police work in a democratic state. In that sense, everything I have described here is done "for" democracy. However, the shady backstage compromises at the center of my description of police work don't line up well with the conventional idea that democracy is a system where the ultimate foundation of the political world is *public* will. How can a form of policing that protects localized lawbreaking remain aligned with a sovereign authority vested in the will of the people as a whole?

The answer to this question was clarified in 2014 when a unique set of circumstances compelled Taiwan's police to come out into public and, for a period of several weeks, take a stand in direct support of democracy itself. The circumstances at issue involved a constitutional crisis, which erupted in the middle of Ma Yingjiu's second term as president. Ma took office in 2008, returning the KMT to power in the second rotation of political parties after the end of martial law. His electoral platform was based on the promise of economic revival through détente with China. By 2014, his administration had become unpopular. His version of opening to China seemed constraining rather than empowering, and his proposals to radically deregulate Chinese capital investment in Taiwan alarmed the general public. His insistence on implementing his agenda against public resistance provoked a procedural battle in the legislature, which escalated into mass civil disobedience. On March 18, a group of students opposed to the president's initiatives physically seized the parliamentary assembly hall and shut down the government. The protesters held their position in parliament for three weeks, during which time Taiwan's entire police force was mobilized to stand guard around the occupied building (Rowen 2015; Martin 2015; Ho 2015).

This was not ordinary policing. When police are mobilized in response to a violation of the constitutional order, politics is the overt object of their intervention, and any putative "political neutrality" attached to democratic police power disappears. Unfortunately, the institutional contours of this particular political crisis placed Taiwan's police in a difficult spot. Physically, they formed a cordon around the cadre of dissident students inside parliament, separating them from a crowd of some twenty-five thousand people camped outside in support. The purpose of holding this police line was not entirely clear, however. Ultimate authority to command police operations inside Taiwan's legislative chamber is vested in the speaker of parliament. Outside parliament, this authority is vested in the president. The speaker of parliament supported the students in their opposition to the president, fracturing the police chain of command along the same political polarity that animated the crisis in the streets.

Thus divided, the total police mobilization, called up in response to an unprecedented seizure of a central government office, itself seized up. The police coalesced into an inert line just outside the parliamentary chambers, immobilized by the contradiction in their chain of command. This frozen police line then effectively held the opposed forces of an acute political contradiction apart for three weeks, allowing a successful resolution of the situation through an excruciatingly tense political negotiation. After three weeks of negotiations, the speaker of parliament guaranteed a review of the president's proposed policy (sure to fail), and the protesters walked out of parliament of their own volition. The eruption of insurgent energy the protesters represented was then channeled, through the formation of new political parties, into a wholesale reconfiguration of the government in the next round of elections. Thus, even as politics erupted into a police problem, the political weakness of the police power ensured that democracy, not police, provided the solution to the crisis. This event clarified how the strength of Taiwan's democracy rests, in part, on the *weakness* of its police—that is, on their *lack* of relative autonomy from the political dimensions of their environment.

This is exactly contrary to the conventional wisdom that identifies democratic policing with the "rule of law" (Reiner 2010). It shows how politically entangled police action can be staged in a way that allows democracy to reproduce itself through the "margins" of its law. Strictly speaking, the process that resolved the crisis of the Sunflower Movement, as it was called, was just as extra-procedural as the process that provoked it; at no point did the political process collapse into an autocratic act of "law enforcement." As a modality of police action, the response to this crisis was analogous to the way a body responds to an injured joint by flooding it with inert fluid, creating a swelling to stabilize the area during the healing process. The police functioned as an instrument of pure administrative inertia, an immobilizing agent lacking any politically significant "healing" powers. Their indispensable contribution to the management of an acute pathogenic episode was to interrupt the immediate street-level dynamics that produced the crisis, stabilizing the situation and holding it open to remedy by higher-level political agents. They could do no more than this because their institutional capacity for coherent political action was itself overwhelmed by the crisis. This lack of autonomy from political contestation is, I argue, an institutional feature of Taiwan's post-reform police apparatus. Indeed, the delegation of police command authority inside parliament to the speaker of parliament was a victory won during the democratic transition, which relied on leveraging the legally "exceptional" space inside the legislative assembly to push back against dictatorial executive powers (cf. Martin 2013c). With police powers rendered politically impotent by their institutional entanglement in the political crisis, resolution of the event could not come through executive action. It had to be negotiated.

Democracy is predicated on dialogue; the sovereign will of the general public is dialogical before it is legal (Arendt 1963, 83). Dialogue ends where force begins, so when dialogue is necessary, force must be deferred. The Taiwanese police spent three weeks facilitating democratic politics by stabilizing the arena for extralegal negotiations. They did this not because they wanted to, but because they had no other choice. Their lack of professional autonomy left them with no place to stand except in the middle of the political contradiction.

The contrast between the democratic potentials of this kind of extralegal policing and the undemocratic potentials of "law enforcement" per se was further clarified by a similar event that occurred six months later on the other side of the Taiwan Straits: Hong Kong's "Umbrella Movement." The underlying politics of this event were as different from the Sunflower Movement as Hong Kong is different from Taiwan (Ho 2019). But the surface contours of the initial crisis were similar. In both cases, frustration with autocratic behavior sheltered by executive proceduralism brought youth activists into the streets, where they found mass support adequate to disrupt normal politics and create a situation of constitutional crisis. In both case, the political problem erupted initially as a police "public order" problem. However, Hong Kong has a much more robust system insulating the police command structure from political interference. Where the institutional dimensions of Taiwan's crisis rendered the police politically helpless, simply standing by as others negotiated, Hong Kong's police were actively involved in the resolution of the crisis.

The resolution of the Umbrella Movement involved a creative use of "rule of law" ideology to avoid the appearance of overt political policing. After three months of political stasis, during which time major sections of the city remained occupied, Hong Kong's courts issued civil injunctions on behalf of plaintiffs who had sued the protesters under a claim that the occupied streets negatively affected their ability to make a living. The police then "assisted" court bailiffs to enforce the injunction, clearing the streets in a putatively "nonpolitical" act of civil law enforcement. This procedurally neutral act of law enforcement coincidentally secured the political dominance of an undemocratic central authority over the political aspirations of the governed. Subsequently, under the shelter of Hong Kong's then relatively robust civil rights laws, the street movement transitioned into the formal organization of new political parties, and made inroads to Hong Kong's constrained arena of electoral politics in the 2016 Legislative Council elections. However, the antidemocratic potentials of law were once again deployed to prevent these electoral victories from empowering dissenting voices within the government apparatus. A poignant example of this came in the government's use of the procedural guidelines for the legislative swearing-in ceremony to permanently disqualify six opposition party members from taking the positions to which they had been duly elected.

Hong Kong is not a democracy. However, its police powers are organized in conformity with a British ideal of democratic policing, in which the capacity of police action to effectively represent the general interest is predicated on the political autonomy afforded police power by the rule of law (Brown 2016). The events set in motion by the Umbrella Movement demonstrate how such a legalistic form of policing can serve as an efficient vector for active political suppression. By contrast, Taiwan has managed to achieve a substantive democracy, on the basis of weak police and marginal law.

The theoretical goal of this book is to present an argument against the "medical model" of police professionalism, which gives police a jurisdiction over the violence necessary for law to be possible. The empirical basis of my argument is not evidence of how the medical model can fail, but rather evidence for how an alternative ideal can succeed. The materials of this book reveal what Taiwanese police "make available . . . that, all things being equal, would not be otherwise available" (Bittner [1974] 1990b, 234): a productive route through which to channel forms of political conflict corrosive to the status quo. The *paichusuo* is the front line of this system: an arena for mediating antagonism between local forms of political authority. The police use their administrative powers to help mediate specific conflicts, creating a space in which consensus can be found, and articulating this consensus with the demands of central power. The local arena of the *paichusuo* is a capillary tip for the larger policing bureaucracy. When this larger bureaucracy was pushed to its limit in 2014, it revealed the ultimate value toward which all its powers are oriented: immobility (not violence). In Taiwan, the police role in a crisis is to shut things down and close the door, giving the political metabolism space and time to recompose its will to move beyond the crisis. Activated in response to a constitutional crisis, the police held the entire state in temporary cardiac arrest until backstage processes could find a way to recompose a collective will adequate to return to normal politics. This modality of politically implicated, institutionally obstructionist democratic policing stands in poignant contrast to the ostensibly "liberal" version of policing practiced across the Straits. Hong Kong's police responded to a structurally similar situation by deploying the iron fist of sovereign violence behind a velvet glove of legal logic to crush the dissensus inherent in authentic popular sovereignty.

Throughout this book, I have relied on Arendt to characterize politics as an *entelecheia*—something realized in the ontological fact of human flourishing rather than validated by its contribution toward some abstract end; in Balbus's pithy phrase, democracy is the realized unity of the "governed and the governing." The significance of this ideal in the context of policing was described most poignantly by the vigilance team patrolman narrating his experience catalyzing collective solidarity through a hunt for thieves (in chapter 3). According to the analytic framework I have developed in this book, the quality of that experience can be explained by the way individual will and collective solidarity were aligned along the axis of an imagined cosmic principle. The superlative quality of the experience arose when the cosmic principle was actually realized by the success of the collective venture (they did, in the end, catch the thieves). Richland's semiotic analysis of jurisdiction, as a variety of authorizing discourse, explains the mechanics and practical significance of this "cosmic" dimension. The ultimate meaning of the world can be experienced only as a kind of theological revelation (as Paul Kahn, following Carl Schmitt, argues). Richland shows how the routine enactment of sovereignty through the courts is achieved when the unspoken (indeed, unspeakable) presupposition of sovereign power is successfully entailed in the enactment of a legal decision. This analysis can be applied by analogy to the vigilance patrol. The patrols upheld a cosmic ideal of local community rather than state law. The act of catching a thief entailed the presupposition that their idealization of a *qing*-based political order ideal was, in actual fact, the living foundation of their world.

This kind of alignment—between individual will, collective solidarity, and ultimate principle—was also achieved in the Sunflower Movement. Participants often describe their experience in the movement using the glowing terms of realized purposefulness. The Sunflowers dared, together, and in so daring revealed Taiwan to be what it is today.

Participants in Hong Kong's Umbrella Movement also describe their experience as thrilling. But, in retrospect, where the Sunflowers made history as they intended, the Umbrellas failed. To dare together is not enough. For the governed and governing to be one and the same, the intention of the collective venture must be realized in the world itself. When an action fails to uphold the imagined basis of a world, it reveals a world that is not as the actor imagined it to be.

Comparing the vigilance patrol to the Sunflowers illustrates a vast difference in scale and ambition. The vigilance patrol dared to catch a thief; the Sunflowers dared to censure the president of the republic. Both were actions undertaken in uncertainty. But in trying to catch a thief, it is easy to assume that god is on your side. Deciding to stand against the president involves a bit more risk. Nonetheless, the Sunflowers dared, and they succeeded. And by their success it was confirmed that the cosmic principle of popular sovereignty really is the living foundation of Taiwan's political worldhood.

Comparing the Sunflowers to the Umbrellas illustrates a difference between conservative and progressive ventures. The demands presented by the Sunflowers were obstructionist and conservative; they shut down the legislative assembly to prevent enactment of a new law. The demands of Umbrella Movement, by contrast, were creative and progressive; they shut down the city streets to provoke an unprecedented change in their electoral mechanism. Contrasting the success of the Sunflowers with the failure of the Umbrellas reveals something about the limits of democracy-as-*entelecheia* to qualify the specific enterprise of "policing." Policing, as I describe it here, is an inherently *conservative* undertaking. The will to keep a world in police is a will to *be* rather than a will to *become*. The politics of becoming are those of *dissensus*, not consensus (Rancière 2010), the natality of a revolutionary new beginning rather than a renewal of the will to tolerate the world as given (Arendt 1963).

Taiwan is a democracy, and it had been for decades before the Sunflowers came along. The origins of Taiwan's democratic institutions lie in a mixture of circumstances and will that drove a process of regime change through forms of power entirely outside its constituted police institutions. To be sure, the fact that the dictatorship had been organized through an idiom of revolutionary "political warfare" was helpful in conditioning the institutional basis of police powers to accept its subordination to the forms of political will that can change the structure of a state's operations. But it was only *after* the institutional parameters of democratic governance had been created and solidified that it became possible to conserve them through policing practices like those described here.

Policing, Virtue, and Sovereignty

Ethnographic method is a conventional way of studying police power. This convention began with the "discovery of discretion" in the 1950s—that is, the finding that policing, as a point of contact between law and society, is organized as much by the latter as the former (Nickels 2007; Ohlin and Remington 1993; Goldstein 1960). The term "discretion" is used in domains of legal or administrative practice to refer to the creative labor involved in adapting constituted authority to exigent circumstances (Bernstein 2017; Lipsky 1980). From the perspective of constituted authority, discretion is something to be controlled (P. Kahn 2011, 43). If, however, we understand discretion socioculturally, as a mode of "improvisational performance" (Silverstein 1998), then there are compelling institutional and logical reasons to believe that discretion can never be subjected to the ultimate authority of formal rules (Bittner [1970] 1990a; Skolnick 1966). *Pace* the bureaucratic dream of a completely rationalized human world, "discretionary" activity remains a sui generis sphere of creativity and, moreover, a creative activity upon which the very idea of rules is fundamentally dependent.[1]

The centrality of discretion in police work has made ethnography the methodological core of an interdisciplinary "policing studies" literature (Manning 2010; Brodeur 2010). This turn to ethnographic field methods was mirrored by a historical turn in the theoretical understanding of what "policing" actually *is* (Foucault 2007; Liang 1992; Silver 1967). The practical dynamics that keep discretion from collapsing entirely into formal rules do not insulate it from power per se. Quite the contrary: the overall effects of a given police system reproduce the historically established patterns of structural domination that constitute a given social order (Fassin 2013; Ericson 1982). Which is to say, the "order" police keep is defined not by law but by history. Thus, even as the discretionary dimension of law enforcement exceeds institutional oversight and escapes functionalist rationalization, it retains a historical quality. This quality is found in the necessity, experienced by every actor in a policing assemblage, of finding the *fitness* of their particular quotient of power within the historically given circumstances of their contextual environment.

Maximizing this fitness often involves dissimulation. In many states, the formal dimensions of law are used primarily for ideological purposes (Balbus 1977; Pashukanis 1951). Representations of police power based on "law and order" tropes are misrepresentations wherever institutionalized inequalities (those anchored in race, class, and gender, for example) are secured by the dynamics of police discretion in ways that remain formally consistent with the equality guaranteed by law (Amar 2011). Under such circumstances, the critical objective for an anthropology of policing is not closing the gap between ideological representations of policing and actual police practice, but rather theorizing the way in which forms of misrepresentation are reproduced *as* the logic of police practice. Such a project aspires to three things. First, it aims to produce ethnographic descriptions that situate processes of real-time improvisation in the larger flow of historical time. Second, it assembles these ethnographic materials into a broader historical account of how the personal violence of overt coercion is situated within the structural violence of normative order. And, finally, it contributes to a theoretical understanding of the way the visible aspects of actualized power arise from and depend on invisible foundations (Martin 2018; Comaroff and Comaroff 2016).

All three of these ambitions share a similar methodological formula: reasoning backward from empirical observation of police behavior to the empirically inaccessible conditions of possibility for that behavior to exist. This analytic formula reflects a common presumption about the relationship between the concrete actuality of police power and the elusive abstraction of state sovereignty: the revealed behavior of police can be read as a sign of the occult powers of the sovereign. Sovereignty matters to policing, and it matters to the story I tell in this book. However, I approach it as something that matters more at the level of culture than it does at the level of institutions. Here I follow Paul Kahn's approach to sovereignty as a mode of power best understood through the theological logic of revelation (P. Kahn 2011; Schmitt [1922] 2005). According to Kahn, sovereignty *acts* theologically, generating a kind of revelatory politics that exceeds the strictly rational empiricism of scientific reasoning.

Taiwan has an ambiguous sovereign status. Its political future remains an open question, fought over as an issue of theological faith between competing churches. As an issue of international relations, the ROC's lack of sovereign recognition is a result of the PRC's insistence that Taiwan is an integral element in the PRC's own territorial integrity. The PRC has never actually ruled Taiwan, of course. Indeed, that fact is, perhaps counterintuitively, the foundation of the PRC's resolve to "recover" it. In the eyes of the CCP, Taiwan's separation from China marks it as an unrecovered colonial concession. It is the last one, the final missing piece in the project of making modern China historically whole. China's claim to Taiwan thus carries the full weight of the CCP's revolutionary historical mission.

That ideology, backed by China's rising regional hegemony, makes for a powerful argument. But it remains (as of this writing) an aspiration rather than a fact, opposed to the status quo and actively contending with other perspectives on the issue. People living in Taiwan tend to see things from a very different point of view. To be sure, Taiwanese public opinion is far from united. Citizens of the ROC hold a diverse range of ideas about the historical sources and desirable future for their shared political life. These opinions are rehearsed and debated in the course of the electoral processes that presently determine who governs Taiwan. The capacity of Taiwan's population to disagree over matters of substance, while remaining united as a political community through shared deference to the outcomes of a formal political mechanism, is an important attribute of Taiwanese political culture.

The trajectory of the Sunflower Movement showed how police power can fit into a political process ultimately founded on nothing more than a collective commitment to remain united-in-disagreement long enough to recompose a mutual will to coexist. This is a mode of policing calibrated to a sovereignty founded on a historically precarious *xianzhuang* (status quo). This kind of prior commitment to the process of working through conflict is also evident at the ethnographic level, in the qualities of individual character—the virtues—that allow backstage negotiations over police business to succeed (Jauregui 2016). Virtue has been a central theme in Taiwanese policing since it began. It was a defining ideal in the civilizing rhetoric of Japanese colonialism, was equally valorized by the Sunnist ideology of the dictatorship, and remains a framing category in the democratic era through the idea of *gongde*, often translated as "civility" but more literally glossed as "public virtue" (Y. Yan 2017; Shak 2009; Weller 1999). Taiwanese popular discourse is explicitly and vociferously concerned with *gongde*. Debates over the ethical qualities of political action often appeal to this ideal as a consensus basis for moral evaluation of public behavior. The hegemony of the *gongde* ideal embeds Taiwan's contemporary police powers in the historically distinctive cultural poetics that I have placed at the center of my analysis.

The institutional significance of *gongde* for Taiwanese policing can be illuminated by its parallels to the ideal of republicanism developed by Hannah Arendt (1963). She makes a distinction between the values of republicanism and those of democracy. The core value of modern democracy is equality. This, in Arendt's analysis, connects it to "social" concern with the biological qualities of life and thereby sets it apart from the properly "political" value of human flourishing. Republicanism, by contrast, is a fully political ideal. It is an ideal of excellence (thus intrinsically *inegalitarian*), anchored in the value of human "freedom" as something we attain by realizing the specifically human potentials that distinguish us from other biological beings. Republican virtue is logically distinct from democratic equality. Arendt (1963) uses this distinction as a normative basis for evaluating the successes and failures of various historical events of regime change.

All human communities contain tensions between the inclusive-egalitarian qualities of commonality, and the exclusive-hierarchical dimensions of power. Modern democratic republicanism, according to Charles Taylor, reconciles this contradiction through the idea of a general will: "Under the aegis of the General Will, all the virtuous citizens are to be equally honored. The age of dignity is born" (Taylor 1992, 99). In other words, in a republican democracy, citizenship is an elite status defined by qualities of virtue, but as these elite qualities are supposed to be shared equally by all citizens, society can be defined as a condition of equal esteem. This formula is put to a test whenever civic life becomes conflicted enough to summon police power. Calling the police indicates a failure of the presumption of equal virtue; "whoever refuses to obey the General Will shall be compelled to do so by the whole body. This means nothing less than he will be forced to be free" (Rousseau [1762] 2012, 46). The capacity of a nominally democratic government to pass this test without tearing open the fundamental antinomy between freedom and force depends on the strength of the cultural hegemony maintaining a consensus commitment to the specific qualities of virtue that define citizenship. In other words, understanding the cultural processes that reproduce the ideal of republican virtue in the context of police action is a key to understanding the paradox by which the egalitarian order of liberal democracy is secured through the exercise of hierarchical powers.

The qualities of "public" or "republican" virtue at the core of Taiwanese policing are embodied in their purest form by "local elites" (*difang renshi*). These are the leading citizens of the neighborhood, their excellence manifest as the capacity to facilitate the processes that recompose their community's practical will to coexist. By "helping out" in the backroom work of policing, and "speaking sentiment" on behalf of their clients, these figures perform public virtue as a service on behalf of others. In their capacity to enact public virtue in a manner with direct consequence for the quality of community life, they embody the democratic ideal of "representing popular will" (*minyi daibiao*).

Embedded in the political world of these local elites, Taiwanese police work in a compromised situation. They serve a world of political and economic tensions. The peace in this world is not legislated but emergent, a contingent stasis within a historical balance of powers. The job of police is to stabilize as much of this arrangement as they can, provide inertia adequate to keep things from collapsing. They rely heavily on republican virtue to accomplish this. Recall the encounter between Axiong and the All People's Taxi Union, described in chapter 3. That was real boundary work. Axiong had to cross a physical barrier defining the spatial jurisdiction of one of the city's more significant counterpowers. He crossed this border not as the agent of a unitary sovereignty, but as a vulnerable individual navigating a complex plurality of powers. The order of the world he was expected to maintain held no pretension of any singular locus of ultimate control. Axiong had to move carefully and speak politely. The union bosses responded politely as well, "giving face" (as they would say) to their police guests by clearing the room and putting the games away. In the staging of the encounter, the compound's physical walls were a decisive element. They kept the actors apart until the scene was set for them to successfully carry off their roles. When the stage was set, the actors met and delivered their lines—banal formal pleasantries—in a manner that concluded the scene as a nonevent: a polite interaction preserving the peace of a settled balance of powers. As police action, this was order maintenance performed through the contrived dissimulation of polite exchange. That it was a transaction between police and outlaws concerning a report of illegal activity was made irrelevant enough not to interfere with the work of producing a record of an unfounded call. The ritual fiction of order supplied an inertia adequate to shut down further questions about the foundational basis of the situation.

Such policing by ritual inverts the liberal value of authenticity in favor of the Confucian value of harmony. The power specific to ritual form is located in its *inauthenticity*. The autonomy that ritual incongruence achieves from its substantive context is what gives it the capacity to invoke an otherwise nonexistent order. Ritual formality is something that "[allows] actual conduct to be counted unambiguously as successful performance . . . independent of the attribution of particular propositional meanings to the acts" (Seligman et al. 2008, 5). In this case, a ritualized performance of police call-and-response was used to create a formal record that the original complaint was unfounded, a completely inauthentic "propositional meaning" necessary to maintain a fiction of legal order against its materially obvious contradictions.

Talking explicitly about sovereignty in Taiwan leads to nothing but trouble. Taiwan was cast out of the system of interstate sovereignty in 1971, when the UN General Assembly voted to allow the People's Republic of China to take Taiwan's seat in the United Nations. Even before this, however, Taiwanese politics was only superficially organized by pretensions of monolithic sovereignty. The UN seat Taiwan gave up had been held under the fiction that the Chinese Nationalist Party still ruled a country they fled in 1949. And Taiwan itself had barely participated in the civil war that brought the Nationalist rump state to the island, having been a Japanese colony until the end of World War II. Exile from the UN was more a recognition than a cause of Taiwan's chronic incapacity to achieve conventional Westphalian sovereignty.

Given the frequency with which Taiwan's ruling powers have changed, writing a long-term political history that takes Taiwan as its subject involves adopting the standpoint of life rooted in the physical island. This genre of "maritime" history frames the institutions of Taiwan's modern state as artifacts aggregated through an ebb and flow of "externally derived political powers" (*wailai zhengquan*) that have washed over the island throughout its modern history (Su 1986; K.-H. Chen 2010). The political culture incubated by this historical process figures political agency in a distinctive way. Made explicit as a theory of "subjectivity" (*zhutixing*) within the historiographic project of conceptualizing Taiwan as the subject of its own history, this is a conception of political agency as a nodal formation that must be skillfully composed in a field of multiple competing powers (Zhuang 2003). The adaptation of this ethno-theory of political agency to the work of democratic policing is evident in Liu Shengzuo's textbook techniques for "seizing agency" (*bawo zhuti*) described in chapter 2, as well as my own experience with "host power" (*zhuquan*) described in chapter 1.

This model of political agency is consistent with Taiwan's dominant religion. Known as "folk belief" (*minjian xinyang*), this is an absorptive polytheism that figures piety as respect, and recognizes a formless power inherent in things ranging from rocks and trees to policemen and politicians as the proper addressee for gestures of spiritual respect (Shahar and Weller 1996; Nadeau and Hsun 2003). Describing the complexity of Taiwanese religious history and practice is beyond the scope of this book. Nonetheless, I would argue that it is an important source of founding metaphysical principles for the practical logic that integrates strong democracy with weak police. These ideas figure among the oldest sources of "Chinese culture," having as one canonical statement the first line of the *Daodejing*—"Dao kedao fei changdao" (Perkins 2016). The phrase itself is a masterpiece of polysemy. For the purposes of my argument, it can be accurately translated as, "Rules that can be formalized are not constitutive rules." Which is to say it announces a political philosophy that begins by turning away from Kantian hope for a metaphysical "legislation" in which formal rationality bridges the gap between the constitutive and the regulatory dimensions of the world (Perkins 2016).

Taiwan's historical experience resonates powerfully with this ideal. As disjoint "externally derived" powers have multiplied there in polytheistic profusion, one basic theological truth has become ever more self-evident: the formless (*wuxing*) constitutive power of the cosmos is fundamentally incommensurable to the constituted forms of regulatory power. Framed by such historical common sense, the role of police is to cultivate the form-having (*youxing*) order of the human world, primarily by trafficking in more or less vacuous formalism—such as speaking politely with gangsters and writing up administrative reports designed to help solve political problems. Policing, in this environment, is the task of using the intrinsically unfounded power of appearances to maintain the network of substantive connections that articulate relationships between diverse nodes of regulatory power, embedded in a wider ocean of formless cosmic energy. The mode of policing described in this book is ultimately legitimated by this metaphysical principle.

"Ultimate" legitimation is a problematic phrasing, however. It invokes a monolithic rationality. The legitimating process involved in this policing does not depend on any singular authority. It does not depend on the law or the courts. It requires no explicit intervention by any grand tradition at all; Taiwanese police quote Laozi about as infrequently as American police cite Plato. The ultimate, or "theological," dimensions of legitimation operate implicitly, through the "doxic" dimension of practice (Bourdieu 1977; P. Kahn 2011). Police work is centrally concerned with making sense of the world (Manning 2013; Loader and Mulcahy 2003). Police agents rely on the vernacular metaphysics of their cultural environment to supply the meaningful resources required to do this work. The culturally distinctive elements, which distinguish different historical traditions of legitimate force, exist in the unspoken hegemony of cosmological common-sense (Eisenstadt 2000). Thus do the historical institutions of Anglo-European policing carry, as self-evident truth, the objectively reasonable Platonic proposition that law is to force as form is to substance. History has made a different truth self-evident to the Taiwanese police. The institutions in which they live make it objectively reasonable that ritual is to order as appropriateness is to effectiveness, just as Confucius argued (Finagrette 1972).

Policing without Control

> There are others out there on whom my life depends, people I do not know and may never know. This fundamental dependency on anony-mous others is not a condition I can will away. No security measure will foreclose this dependency; no violent act of sovereignty will rid the world of this fact. . . . Final control is not, cannot be, an ultimate value.
>
> (Butler 2004, xii–xiii)

Judith Butler (2004) has described the modern idea of sovereignty as a kind of control fetish. She borrows Lacan's concept of "foreclosure" for this. Any self-conscious subject that understands its self as *independent* from the world on which it actually depends is living a fantasy. Such subjects (whether individual or collective), constituted by a misrecognition of their own dependent-arising, tend to fetishize control as an existential necessity. They look to practices of relative domination for worldly evidence of transcendent/absolute control by some final uncaused cause. Sufficient evidence can never be produced, of course, for the subject is not, in fact, ultimately independent from its surroundings. Foreclosure—repressing the fact of this dependence—can lead to a pathological escalation of desires for control.

Analyzing governance through the concept of foreclosure illuminates moti-vations for disproportionate repression embedded in the deepest constitutive fictions of sovereign independence. This suggests that pathological qualities of police violence may be encouraged by any ideological form that looks to the state as a locus of "ultimate" control. Butler's theoretical approach is aligned with well-established critical positions on totalitarian reason, as old as the "counter-enlightenment" (Adorno and Horkheimer 1992; Taylor 1979). This position has been foundational for the anthropology of the state (Sharma and Gupta 2006). Ethnographic attention to situated practices and local knowledge involved in the practice of administration consistently reinforces an argument laid out by James Scott (1999): the actual order of social worlds consists of patterns reproduced by intrinsically collaborative processes; state actors who misrecognize this order as something they unilaterally create or control are condemned to reap nothing but unintended consequences from all their order-making efforts.

Ethnographic studies of police practice make this macro- and meso-institutional critique of the state relevant to the micro-institutional dynamics of communicative encounter. Police impose a dramatically immediate limit on spontaneous patterns of social action. The act of "calling the police" interrupts the implicit felicity conditions of an informal interactional order by invoking the explicit, formal representation of order on which the idea of the Leviathan state is founded. Police intervention thus sets up a stark contrast between a spontaneous problem and an artificial solution, bringing the two different modalities of "order" in Scott's argument into direct juxtaposition. The legitimacy of modern police force is then predicated on denying the difference between them and pretending that police power can somehow restore a broken world to a fictive, unbroken status quo ante. Following Butler, we can identify this legitimating fiction with the work of foreclosure. It is a denial of the fact that police power is itself part of an intrinsically troublesome, insecure, and disordered world. The police cannot create order, provide security, or force the world to conform to legislative reason. Asking them to do these things will only cause further problems. Granting them a professional monopoly on the use of violence and asking them to control the world is a recipe for disaster.

The Taiwanese patrolmen I knew treated legitimating fantasies of order with disdain. They never claimed to be able to provide order, or even fix the individual problems people called them to deal with. The best they could do for someone who came to them with a problem was help them figure out how to live with that problem. And the only thing they could do for the neighborhood as a whole was help its residents find ways to renew a collective will to continue living in the fundamental disorder of their historical predicament. They offered their public nothing but the ceaseless work of renewing the will to remain together, in the world, as it is. But in this humble offering they held out a promise that such work was worth one's while. It was an undertaking adequate to realize the potential of a human life to align individual virtue, social solidarity, and cosmic principles (of one kind or another).

Institutionally speaking, one of the more interesting features of registry-based policing is the way it mediates between ideas of collective purpose and the concrete qualities of individual character. Where most liberal policing systems operate explicitly in terms of abstractions, and implicitly in terms of stereotypes, the *hukou* is a technology for focusing the police gaze onto specific individuals. The functional purpose of the registry is to make explicit the categories of difference in which the state takes interest, and thereby render them bureaucratically actionable as criteria by which people can be judged. At the height of Taiwan's martial law regime, civil policing was organized as a political intelligence operation. Neighborhood patrolmen were responsible for maintaining political dossiers on the individual residents of their jurisdiction. It was an administrative system rationalized by a conception of policing as a project of manipulating qualities of character. The political intelligence apparatus was designed to activate each individual's civic virtue and cultivate the population's collective commitment to the nationalist revolution.

Political dossiers were thrown out with the end of martial law, along with the erstwhile party-state's grand agenda for revolution. But the *hukou* remained as the jurisdictional infrastructure through which police powers are articulated into social life. The *qinqu* system still assigns every individual resident of Taiwan to the jurisdiction of an individual police officer, configuring the police-society relationship as something personal, and keeping the cultivation of virtue at the center of the police agenda. This is an important legacy the authoritarian period left to democratic policing: a hierarchical ideal of cultivated citizenship, which enables a mode of democratic power based on civic virtue rather than civil rights. Power in the arena of policing is inegalitarian. It is dominated by local elites who use their skill in the symbolic performance of political virtue to legitimate the extralegal dimensions of their dominance in local society. The persistence of this virtue-centric concept of legitimate authority provides a conservative counterweight to the egalitarian leveling often associated with democratic transitions. This conservative dimension, although inegalitarian, has helped keep Taiwan's newly democratic world in peace. Thus has the security of a liberal new beginning been enabled, in part, by the conservative continuation of institutional precedents baked into the policing infrastructure.

Notes

1. BACKSTAGE PASSAGE

1. At this time, I had been in Taiwan for two years conducting research on a project focused on martial arts. It involved police tangentially but did not focus on everyday policing routines.

2. It was coined in 1864 by an American missionary commissioned to translate Wheaton's *Elements of International Law* (Tok 2013, 40). The commission came from the Qing "Ministry of Rites" (Li Bu), the supreme bureaucratic locus under which formal state ritual was administered in the Chinese Empire (Tok 2013, 40). *Li* ("ritual" or "rites") was, at that time, an expansive category covering a set of civilizing practices that ranged from the administration of the domestic civil service examination to the management of foreign relations (Seligman and Weller 2012, 135). This expansive category was integrated around a Confucian theory of social action that identified *li* as any technology used for harmonious mediation of distinctions, such as those between the political center and its peripheral tributaries, or those between the governing self and the governed other (Fingarette 1972). *Li,* "ritual," was the formal keystone of Confucian cosmopolitics, anchoring the milieu of a governmentality oriented to the productive harmonization of cosmic distinctions (Fingarette 1972). The idiom of *zhuquan* "host power" I document in Taiwanese policing, and its connection to *limao* "ritual appearances," resonates with these precedents.

3. The market for tea in Taiwan is similar to the market for fine wines in European societies. A half-pound bag of tea from a notably good year at a famous plantation retails for hundreds of US dollars. The gift economy attached to tea-drinking ritual carries pronounced class overtones.

4. One of the most dramatic experiences I had of having my references checked in this manner occurred one night when I ran into Brother Chin, a pig butcher and mid-ranking gangster whom I knew through a friend of Ahe. While out on other business, I happened across Brother Chin sitting in a restaurant drinking with some of his associates, and, at his invitation, I joined them. It soon emerged that one of the other men at the table, Brother Ke, was Chin's *laoda,* "old big" (i.e., his boss), and in fact was the *jiaotou* or "corner head" of the turf where we were sitting. Although I had actually been at a banquet with Ke once before, I had not been formally introduced. Nonetheless, as we clearly moved in the same circles (based on our previous encounter and Chin's familiarity), and furthermore as our chance encounter that evening revealed us to have *yuanfen,* it was natural for Ke to incorporate me into the banquet in progress. Chin's introductions progressed to toasting around the table, and the party resumed until my presence faded into the background of a passionately tipsy conversation. The conversation turned to sensitive topics, and a moment came where a threshold of confidence was crossed. There was a sudden break in the conversation, and the table full of gangsters turned to look at me. Changing the subject, Brother Chin politely inquired of me as to the health of our mutual acquaintance's (that is, Ahe's friend's) grandfather. I could not speak authoritatively on the matter, so it was suggested that I immediately contact Ahe's friend on my cell phone (it was about two in the morning) so that Brother Chin could ask him directly. The next time I saw Ahe's friend, he made it clear that he was being held responsible for the integrity of Brother Ke's confidences in me.

5. An estimated 30 percent of Taiwan's GDP is produced by the "informal" or "underground" aspects of its economy (Yan 2014). This activity is concentrated in the suburban periphery of large urban agglomerations, of which Taipei County (now New Taipei City) was the largest. Vast areas of the city in which I conducted fieldwork were given over to unlicensed temporary factories, and it was notorious for its red-light districts.

6. For example, I once spent the day with a group of patrolmen dispatched to guard a polling place during a local election, sitting outside in the freezing courtyard of a primary school from dawn to dusk. We spent the afternoon drinking tea and cognac brought in by visiting friends. We drank the liquor "secretly"—that is, we would hold up our glasses to one another and make toasts like, "Secret! Secret! This is forbidden! [Mimide! Mimide! Zhe shi bu keyide!]"

7. It should be noted here that prostitution is legal in Taiwan, although most of it is conducted without the necessary licenses. This does not mean that the women working in the hostess bar were exercising agency of a degree adequate to cross the threshold of affirmative consent, but it does mean that the situation of police-enforced sexual contact was not as ethically intractable as it could have been.

8. Ideals of democracy valorize the human capacity for self-determination above forms of compulsion imposed by external powers. Philosophical discussion of this commonly invokes Kantian terminology, juxtaposing the "autonomy" of self-determination against the "heteronomy" of other-determination. However, as Judith Butler (2004) argues, the apparent clarity of this contrast between opposed categories misrepresents the messy interdependencies of the human condition, and the political pursuit of sovereign autonomy often leads to a violent fetishization of control. S. M. Eisenstadt (2000) describes an irreconcilable antinomy of autonomy and heteronomy as one of the engines driving the dynamism and pluralism of modern culture around the world. And Markus Dubber (2005) puts the dynamic tension between autonomy and heteronomy at the historical heart of modern police institutions.

2. THE *PAICHUSUO* AND THE JURISDICTION OF *QING*

1. In Japan, the term *koban* remained the conventional way to refer to local police stations even after the shift to *hashutsjo*. *Hashutsjo* (Chinese *paichusuo*) is no longer used as an organizational category in the Japanese police system, even as the *koban* has become iconic.

2. The administrative system that emerged from Goto's reform was spectacularly successful. It allowed Taiwan's colonial government to complete a full population census in 1905, fifteen years before the first one was completed in metropolitan Japan (Yao 2006). "By the turn of the 1920s, the *hoko* system had [become] indispensable for the implementation of nearly all aspects of colonial policy" (Ts'ai 2013, 78). In 1925, the Taipei Police Department organized an exhibition to celebrate the "police kingdom" (*jingcha wangguo*) Japan had created in Taiwan. This was organized in three different sites. The main site was divided into nine halls, showcasing the police role in improving social control (*baoan*), crime prevention (*fangfan*), fire prevention (*xiaofang*), electrification (*dianqi*), haute police (*gaodeng jingcha*, i.e., propaganda and political control), police affairs (*jingwu*), weights and measures (*duliangheng*), recreational activities (*yule*), and youth education (*ertong*) (77). The second site was dedicated to aboriginal governance, and the third showcased police achievements in hygiene, such as building modern water-treatment and garbage-processing facilities (82).

3. The history of modern police in Taiwan is told in different ways as it is inflected through different positions staked out in the debate over Taiwan's contemporary political identity. Chinese Nationalist historiography, for example, frames Japanese colonization as the momentary interruption of an otherwise continuous China-centered history.

For them, Taiwan's "retrocession" to the Republic of China in 1945 was simultaneously a renewal and new beginning: police institutions developed in mainland China replaced those established by the Japanese, and the history of contemporary Taiwanese policing can be written without any consideration of what the Japanese did (Charles Chang 2013; Huang Y. 1971).

4. The second-largest scandal broke one month later, with eighty-nine policemen indicted in an unrelated case of a gambling syndicate with the local police on the payroll.

3. POLICING AND THE POLITICS OF CARE

1. These are canonical values in the vernacular politics of everyday life in Weixing City, and, as such, the terms resist simple translation. *Ashali* is a Japanese loan word for "simplicity" that the Taiwanese have invested with ethical qualities of sincerity and transparency; it is the quality of character that makes someone simultaneously decisive and reliable. *Yiqi* is the "righteousness" that solidifies the intimate solidarity of voluntary association, most iconically in the martial solidarities of fictive brotherhood. *Dafang* is a spirit of magnanimity performed through easygoing generosity.

2. Douglas Harper (2014) traces the genealogy of the English word "patrol" to French military slang for "tramping through the mud." I do not know the etymology of the Chinese term *xunluo*, but in contemporary Taiwan it is commonly used to describe the annual circuit made by a local tutelary deity around the territory under his or her protection, a practice that is explicitly modeled on the juridical tours of imperial magistrates.

3. There were actually three different routes in operation at any given time, mapped out confidentially by the *paichusuo* command and rotated through the various shifts, toward the goal of injecting a certain amount of unpredictability into the "proactive" police presence.

4. Taiwanese folk religion is polytheistic and organized into a bureaucracy modeled on the Imperial Chinese state. The paper charms at issue here are symbolic warrants, issued under authority of a god in the role of a spiritual bureaucrat.

5. This vigilance patrol team hung their patrol boxes in exchange for financial support, and their neutrality within the conflicted politics of the larger community was questionable. In other words, hanging a patrol box and pasting a charm indicating allegiance to a particular guardian deity were both politically significant gestures.

6. The full story behind this is beyond the scope of the present discussion, but it was connected to Lee's struggles to prevail in factional disputes within the KMT by creating the Social Development Association system as a clientage network distinct from the entrenched system through which the party had controlled local politics under martial law. See Martin 2010.

4. ADMINISTRATIVE REPAIR

1. At this time in Taiwan's history, there were very few legal channels for ordinary citizens to travel between China and Taiwan.

5. HOLDING THINGS TOGETHER

1. He stated it would be "embarrassing" to be seen in uniform eating at the restaurants on this street.

2. This term is discussed in detail below.

3. About US$10.

4. The paired contrast between *wang*, "king," and *ba*, "bully," invokes classical philosophical discussions of the role of moral force (*de*) in political affairs: the "king" is one whose government relies on the efficacy of moral example, in contrast to a "hegemon,"

who relies on brute material coercion. The word *ba*, translatable as "bully" (as in the "local bully" of the complaint) or "hegemon," is also a verb for the illegitimate occupation of space (for example, getting cut off in traffic is sometimes noted by muttering "*badao*" under one's breath), as we will see in the following discussion of "*luba*" as the legal category of illegitimate occupation of public space.

5. In this case the public works department responded, "In regard to your complaint of illegal construction, the investigators have assigned Northern Demolition Case No. ——. The determination of illegal construction is in process, and demolition will be conducted according to the county's illegal construction priority roster."

6. That is, breaking the word into its components, *gong* as "public" and *wen* as "text." In fact, the two-character word in this context actually means paperwork done by officials, and, somewhat ironically, official paperwork internal to police operations is not open to general public evaluation.

7. This particular statement was written by a supporter of Chen Shui-bian on an Internet message board during the Taipei mayoral election of 1998.

8. "Red envelopes" (*hongbao*) mark the use of cash as a gift, a conventional practice at weddings, baptisms, and on all major holidays.

6. STRONG DEMOCRACY, WEAK POLICE

1. This line of thinking links discretion to the idea of "constituent power" first proposed by the Abbé Seiyès and subsequently developed in a body of scholarship characterized by Beatrice Hanssen (2000) as the "critique of violence," which has produced many of the central themes in the anthropology of policing, including Benjamin's ([1921] 1996) distinction between law-giving and law-keeping violence, and Agamben's "state of exception" (2004).

Bibliography

Abbott, Andrew. 1988. *The System of Professions: An Essay on the Division of Expert Labor*. Chicago: University of Chicago Press.

Abe Yurika. 2003. "Rizhi shiqi Taiwan huji zhidu zhi chutan" [An introduction to Taiwan's household registry system during the Japanese era]. *Taiwan Lishi Xuehui Huixun* 16: 43–52.

Abrams, Philip. 1988. "Notes on the Difficulty of Studying the State." *Journal of Historical Sociology* 1 (1): 58–89.

Adorno, Theodor, and Max Horkheimer. 1992. *Dialectic of Enlightenment*. London: Allen Lane.

Agamben, Giorgio. 2004. *State of Exception*. Translated by Kevin Attell. Chicago: University of Chicago Press.

Akerstrom, Malin. 2002. "Slaps, Punches, Pinches—but Not Violence: Boundary-Work in Nursing Homes for the Elderly." *Symbolic Interaction* 25 (4): 515–36.

Aldous, Christopher, and Frank Leishman. 2000. "Enigma Variations: Reassessing the Koban." Oxford: Nissan Occasional Papers no. 31.

Amar, Paul, ed. 2011. *New Racial Missions of Policing: International Perspectives on Evolving Law-Enforcement Politics*. New York: Routledge.

Anscombe, G. E. M. 1958. "Modern Moral Philosophy." *Philosophy* 33 (124): 1–19.

Arendt, Hannah. 1958. *The Human Condition*. Chicago: University of Chicago Press.

———. (1962) 2006. *On Revolution*. New York: Penguin.

Asad, Talal. 1993. *Genealogies of Religion: Disciplines and Reasons of Power in Christianity and Islam*. Baltimore: Johns Hopkins University Press.

Austin, J. L. 1962. *How to Do Things with Words*. London: Oxford University Press.

Babül, Elif. 2017. *Bureaucratic Intimacies: Translating Human Rights in Turkey*. Stanford, CA: Stanford University Press.

Balbus, Isaac. 1977. "Commodity Form and Legal Form: An Essay on the 'Relative Autonomy' of the Law." *Law & Society Review* 11 (3): 571–88.

———. 2010. *Governing Subjects: An Introduction to the Study of Politics*. New York: Routledge

Banton, Michael. 1973. "The Sociology of Police, II." *Police Journal* 46 (3): 341–62.

Barclay, Paul. 2018. *Outcasts of Empire: Japan's Rule on Taiwan's "Savage Border," 1874–1945*. Oakland: University of California Press.

Benjamin, Walter. (1921) 1996. "Critique of Violence." In *Selected Writings*, vol. 1, *1913–1926*. London: Belknap.

Bernstein, Anya. 2017. "Agency in State Agencies." In *Distributed Agency: The Sharing of Intention, Cause, and Accountability*, edited by N. J. Enfield and Paul Kockelman, 41–48. New York: Oxford University Press.

Berti, Ricardo. 2011. "The *Xingshi Hejie*: Criminal Conciliation in People's Republic of China and Taiwan." Paper presented to the Asian Criminological Society, December 17–19, in Taipei, Taiwan.

Bittner, Egon. [1970] 1990a. "The Functions of the Police in Modern Society." In *Aspects of Police Work*, 89–232. Boston: Northeastern University Press.

——. [1974] 1990b. "Florence Nightingale in Pursuit of Willie Sutton: Towards a Theory of Police." In *Aspects of Police Work*, 233–68. Boston: Northeastern University Press.

——. 1990c. *Aspects of Police Work*. Boston: Northeastern University Press.

Bourdieu, Pierre. 1977. *Outline of a Theory of Practice*. Cambridge: Cambridge University Press.

Briggs, Charles. 2018. "Indexical Disorders and Ritual (De)Centers of Semiosis." *Signs and Society* 6 (1): 205–24.

Brodeur, Jean-Paul. 2010. *The Policing Web*. New York: Oxford.

Brown, Gavin A. 2016. "Prayers, Press, Protests, and Practice: Police Praxis in Hong Kong." PhD thesis, University of Hong Kong.

Brucato, Ben. 2014. "Fabricating the Color Line in a White Democracy: From Slave Catchers to Petty Sovereigns." *Theoria* 61 (4): 30–54.

Bullard, Monte. 1997. *The Soldier and the Citizen: The Role of the Military in Taiwan's Development*. Armonk, NY: M. E. Sharpe.

Butler, Judith. 2004. *Precarious Life: The Powers of Mourning and Violence*. New York: Verso.

Caldeira, Teresa P. R. 2000. *City of Walls: Crime, Segregation, and Citizenship in São Paulo*. Berkeley: University of California Press, 2000.

Canoy, Jose Raymund. 2007. *The Discreet Charm of the Police State: The Landpolizei and the Transformation of Bavaria, 1945–1965*. Boston: Brill.

Cao, Liqun, Lanying Huang, and Ivan Y. Sun. 2014. *Policing in Taiwan: From Authoritarianism to Democracy*. New York: Routledge.

Carse, Ashly. 2014. "The Year 2013 in Sociocultural Anthropology: Cultures of Circulation and Anthropological Facts." *American Anthropologist* 116 (2): 390–403.

Caton, Steven C. 2006. "What Is an 'Authorizing Discourse'?" In *Powers of the Secular Modern: Talal Asad and His Interlocutors*, edited by David Scott and Charles Hirschkind, 31–56. Stanford, CA: Stanford University Press.

Chang, Charles (Zhang Guangming), ed. 2013. *Taiwan jingzheng fazhan shi* [The historical development of police administration in Taiwan]. Taoyuan: Central Police University.

Chang, Chung-li. 1955. *The Chinese Gentry: Studies on Their Role in Nineteenth-Century Chinese Society*. Seattle: University of Washington Press.

Chang, Han-Yu, and Ramon Myers. 1963. "Japanese Colonial Development Policy in Taiwan, 1895–1906: A Case of Bureaucratic Entrepreneurship." *Journal of Asian Studies* 22 (4): 433–49.

Chang, Wen-chen. 2007. "Constrained Justice: Judicial Roles in Transitional Justice and Democratization in Taiwan." Paper presented to Conference on Law and Democratization in Taiwan and South Korea. Madison: University of Wisconsin, School of Law.

Chao, Linda, and Raymon Myers. 1998. *The First Chinese Democracy: Political Life in the Republic of China on Taiwan*. Baltimore: Johns Hopkins University Press.

Chapman, David. 2008 "Tama Chan and Sealing Japanese Identity." *Critical Asian Studies* 40 (3): 423–43.

Chatterjee, Partha. 2004. *The Politics of the Governed: Reflections on Popular Politics in Most of the World*. New York: Columbia University Press.

Chen, C. 1999. "From Landlords to Local Strongmen: The Transformation of Local Elites in Mid-Ch'ing Taiwan, 1780–1862." In *Taiwan: A New History*, edited by M. Rubenstein, 133–62. Armonk, NY: M. E. Sharpe.

Chen, Ching-Chih. 1975. "The Japanese Adaptation of the Pao-Chia System in Taiwan, 1895–1945." *Journal of Asian Studies* 34: 391–416.

——. 1984. "Police and Community Control Systems in Empire." In *The Japanese Colonial Empire, 1895–1945*, edited by Ramon Myers and Mark Peattie, 213–39. Princeton, NJ: Princeton University Press.

——. 1988. "Impact of Japanese Colonial Rule on Taiwanese Elites." *Journal of Asian History* 22: 25–51.

Chen Chunying. 2007. "Woguo weiquan tixi jiangou chuqi zhi jingzheng (1949–1958)" [The police administration in the early stage of structuring of the authoritarian regime in Taiwan (1949–1958)]. *Renwen Shehui Xuebao* 3 (1): 45–72.

——. 2012. *Zouguo da shidai de shenyong: Taiwan jingzheng shi shang de "Tai Gan ban" (1945–1995)* [The figure walking through the great age: Tai Gan class in Taiwan's police history (1945–1994)]. National Science Council Research Project Final Report, no. NSC100-2410-H-011-014.

Chen, Edward I-Te. 1972. "Formosan Political Movements under Japanese Rule, 1914–1937." *Journal of Asian Studies* 31: 477–97.

——. 1977. "Japan's Decision to Annex Taiwan: A Study of Ito-Mutsu Diplomacy, 1894–95." *Journal of Asian Studies* 37 (1): 61–72.

Chen, Ketty. 2008. "Disciplining Taiwan: The Kuomintang's Methods of Control during the White Terror Era (1947–1987)." *Taiwan International Studies Quarterly* 4 (4): 185–210.

Chen, Kuan-Hsing. 2010. *Asia as Method: Toward Deimperialization*. Durham, NC: Duke University Press.

Cheng, Tun-Jen. 1989. "Democratizing the Quasi-Leninist Regime in Taiwan." *World Politics* 41 (4): 471–99.

Chin, Hsien-Yu. 1998. "Colonial Medical Police and Postcolonial Medical Surveillance Systems in Taiwan, 1895–1950s." *Osiris* 13 (2): 326–38.

Chin, Ko-lin. 2003. *Heijin: Organized Crime, Business, and Politics in Taiwan*. Armonk, NY: M. E. Sharpe.

Choi, Kyong Jun. 2015. "Politics of Law Enforcement: Policing and Reform in New Democracies." PhD thesis, University of Washington, Seattle.

Ch'u T'ung-tsu. 1962. *Local Government in China under the Ch'ing*. Cambridge, MA: Harvard University Press.

Chuang, Ya-Chung. 2013. *Democracy on Trial: Social Movements and Cultural Politics in Postauthoritarian Taiwan*. Hong Kong: Chinese University Press.

Cohen, Jerome A., and Margaret K. Lewis. 2013. *Challenge to China: How Taiwan Abolished Its Version of Re-education through Labor*. Great Barrington, MA: Berkshire.

Comaroff, Jean, and John Comaroff. 2016. *The Truth about Crime: Sovereignty, Knowledge, Social Order*. Chicago: University of Chicago Press.

Cooney, Sean. 2004. "The Effect of Rule of Law Principles in Taiwan." In *Asian Discourses of Rule of Law*, edited by Randall Peerenboom, 417–45. New York: Routledge.

Cornell, L. L., and Akira Hayami. 1986. "The *Shumon Aratame Cho*: Japan's Population Registers." *Journal of Family History* 11: 311–28.

Corrigan, Philip, and Derek Sayer. 1985. *The Great Arch: English State Formation as Cultural Revolution*. Oxford: Basil Blackwell.

Croissant, Aurel, David Kuehn, Phillip Lorenz, and Paul Chambers. 2013. "Taiwan: From Martial Law to Civilian Control." In *Democratization and Civilian Control in Asia*. New York: Palgrave Macmillan.

Das, Veena. 1998. "Wittgenstein and Anthropology." *Annual Review of Anthropology* (27): 171–95.

——. 2007. *Life and Words: Violence and the Descent into the Ordinary*. Berkeley: University of California Press.

Davis, Kathy. 1992. "Towards a Feminist Rhetoric: The Gilligan Debate Revisited." *Women's Studies International Forum* 15 (2): 219–31.

De Genova, Nicholas. 2002. "Migrant 'Illegality' and Deportability in Everyday Life." *Annual Review of Anthropology* 31: 419–47.

De Haan, Willem. 2008. "Violence as an Essentially Contested Concept." In *Violence in Europe: Historical and Contemporary Perspectives*, edited by S. Body-Gendrot and P. Spierenburg, 27–41. New York: Springer.

Delattre, Edwin J. 1989. *Character and Cops: Ethics in Policing*. Washington, DC: American Enterprise Institute for Public Policy Research.

Diamond, Stanley. 1971. "The Rule of Law versus the Order of Custom." In *The Rule of Law*, edited by R. P. Wolff, 115–44. New York: Simon & Schuster.

Djang, Chu, ed. 1984. *A Complete Book concerning Happiness and Benevolence: A Manual for Local Magistrates in Seventeenth-Century China*, by Huang Liu-Hung. Tucson: University of Arizona Press.

Dodsworth, F. M. 2008. "The Idea of Police in Eighteenth-Century England: Discipline, Reformation, Superintendence, c. 1780–1800." *Journal of the History of Ideas* 69 (4): 583–604.

Donzelot, Jacques. 1979. *The Policing of Families*. New York: Random House.

Duara, Prasenjit. 1988. *Culture, Power, and the State: Rural North China, 1900–1942*. Stanford, CA: Stanford University Press.

Dubber, Markus. 2005. *The Police Power: Patriarchy and the Foundations of American Government*. New York: Columbia University Press

Duppa, Richard, and M. Quatremère de Quincy. 1876. *The Lives and Works of Michael Angelo and Raphael*. London: G. Bell and Sons.

Durkheim, Émile. (1893) 1997. *The Division of Labor in Society*. Translated by W. D. Halls. New York: Free Press.

——. (1914) 1973. "The Dualism of Human Nature and Its Social Conditions." In *Émile Durkheim on Morality and Society*, edited by Robert Bellah, 149–66. Chicago: University of Chicago Press.

Edmondson, Robert. 2002. "The February 28 Incident and National Identity." In *Memories of the Future: National Identity Issues and the Search for a New Taiwan*, edited by Stephane Corcuff, 25–46. Armonk, NY: M. E. Sharpe.

Eisenstadt, S. N. 2000. "Multiple Modernities." *Daedalus* 129 (1): 1–29.

Elias, Norbert. (1939) 2012. *On the Process of Civilization*. Dublin: University College Dublin Press.

Epstein, Maram. 2001. *Competing Discourses: Orthodoxy, Authenticity, and Engendered Meanings in Late Imperial Chinese Fiction*. Cambridge, MA: Harvard University Press.

Ericson, Richard V. 1982. *Reproducing Order: A Study of Police Patrol Work*. Toronto: University of Toronto Press.

Farquhar, Judith, and Qicheng Zhang. 2012. *Ten Thousand Things: Nurturing Life in Contemporary Beijing*. New York: Zone Books.

Fassin, Didier. 2011. "Policing Borders, Producing Boundaries: The Governmentality of Immigration in Dark Times." *Annual Review of Anthropology* 40: 213–26.

——, ed. 2012. *A Companion to Moral Anthropology*. Malden, MA: Wiley-Blackwell.

——. 2013. *Enforcing Order: An Ethnography of Urban Policing*. Malden, MA: Polity.

Fei Xiaotong. (1947) 1992. *From the Soil: The Foundations of Chinese Society*. Berkeley: University of California Press.

Feldman, Gregory. 2016. "With My Head on the Pillow: Sovereignty, Ethics, and Evil among Undercover Police Investigators." *Comparative Studies in Society and History* 58 (2): 491–518.

——. 2018. *The Gray Zone: Sovereignty, Human Smuggling, and Undercover Police Investigation in Europe.* Stanford, CA: Stanford University Press.

Feldman, Ilana. 2008. *Governing Gaza: Bureaucracy, Authority, and the Work of Rule, 1917–1967.* Durham, NC: Duke University Press.

Fell, Dafydd. 2012. *Government and Politics in Taiwan.* New York: Routledge.

Feuchtwang, Stephan. 2007. "Public Emotion in a Colonial Context: A Case of Spirit-Writing in Taiwan under Japanese Occupation." In *Public Emotions,* edited by Perri Six, Susannah Radstone, Corienne Squaire, and Amal Treacher, 85–101. New York: Springer.

Fingarette, Herbert. 1972. *Confucius: The Secular as Sacred.* Long Grove, IL: Waveland.

Foucault, Michel. 2007. *Security, Territory, Population: Lectures at the Collège de France, 1977–78.* New York: Palgrave Macmillan.

Freedman, Maurice. 1979. *The Study of Chinese Society.* Stanford, CA: Stanford University Press.

Garriott, William. 2011. *Policing Methamphetamine: Narcopolitics in Rural America.* New York: NYU Press.

Giddens, Anthony. 1991. *Modernity and Self-Identity.* Stanford, CA: Stanford University Press.

Gilligan, Carol. 1982. *In a Different Voice: Psychological Theory and Women's Development.* Cambridge, MA: Harvard University Press.

Gold, Thomas B. 1986. *State and Society in the Taiwan Miracle.* New York: Routledge.

Goldsmith, Andrew John. 2010. "Policing's New Visibility." *British Journal of Criminology* 50 (5): 914–34.

Goldstein, Joseph. 1960. "Police Discretion Not to Invoke the Criminal Process: Low-Visibility Decisions in the Administration of Justice." *Yale Law Journal* 69 (4): 543–94.

Greitens, Sheena Chestnut. 2016. *Dictators and Their Secret Police: Coercive Institutions and State Violence.* New York: Cambridge University Press.

Habermas, Jürgen. 1991. *The Structural Transformation of the Public Sphere: An Inquiry into a Category of Bourgeois Society.* Cambridge, MA: MIT Press.

Hadot, Pierre. 1995. *Philosophy as a Way of Life.* Malden, MA: Blackwell.

Haeri, Niloofar. 2017. "Unbundling Sincerity." *Hau* 7 (1): 123–38.

Hall, Stuart, Chas Critcher, Tony Jefferson, John Clarke, and Brian Roberts. 1978. *Policing the Crisis: Mugging, the State, and Law and Order.* London: Macmillan.

Hamilton, John. T. 2013. *Security: Politics, Humanity, and the Philology of Care.* Princeton, NJ: Princeton University Press.

Han, Dong. 2010. "Policing and Racialization of Rural Migrant Workers in Chinese Cities." *Ethnic and Racial Studies* 33 (4): 596–610.

Hanssen, Beatrice. 2000. *Critique of Violence: Between Poststructuralism and Critical Theory.* London: Routledge.

Harms, Erik. 2013. "Eviction Time in the New Saigon: Temporalities of Displacement in the Rubble of Development." *Cultural Anthropology* 28 (2): 344–68.

Harper, Douglas. 2014. "Patrol." Online Etymology Dictionary. http://www.etymonline.com/index.php?term=patrol&allowed_in_frame=0, accessed January 4, 2014.

Herbert, Steve. 1997. *Policing Space: Territoriality and the Los Angeles Police Department.* Minneapolis: University of Minnesota Press.

Herzfeld, Michael. 2005. *Cultural Intimacy: Social Poetics in the Nation-State.* New York: Routledge.

Hevia, James. 1995. *Cherishing Men from Afar: Qing Guest Ritual and the Macartney Embassy of 1793.* Durham, NC: Duke University Press.

Hinton, Mercedes. 2006. *The State on the Streets: Police and Politics in Argentina and Brazil.* Boulder, CO: Lynne Rienner.

Ho, Ming-sho. 2015. "Occupy Congress in Taiwan: Political Opportunity, Threat, and the Sunflower Movement in Taiwan." *Journal of East Asian Studies* 15: 69–97.

——. 2019. *Challenging Beijing's Mandate of Heaven: Taiwan's Sunflower Movement and Hong Kong's Umbrella Movement*. Philadelphia: Temple University Press.

Holbraad, Martin, and Morten Axel Pedersen. 2012. "Revolutionary Securitization: An Anthropological Extension of Securitization Theory." *International Theory* 4 (2): 165–97.

Hood, Steven. 1997. *The Kuomintang and the Democratization of Taiwan*. Boulder, CO: Westview.

Hornberger, Julia. 2011. *Policing and Human Rights: The Meaning of Violence and Justice in the Everyday Policing of Johannesburg*. New York: Routledge.

Howland, Douglas. 2016. *International Law and Japanese Sovereignty: The Emerging Global Order in the 19th Century*. New York: Palgrave.

Hsiao, Winston. 1995. "The Development of Human Rights in the Republic of China on Taiwan: Ramifications of Recent Democratic Reforms and Problems of Enforcement." *Pacific Rim Law & Policy Journal* 5 (1): 161–204.

Hsu Chun-jin et al. 2004. *Jingcha jiguan zai xiufushi zhengyi lilun zhong jiaose banyan zhi yanjiu* [Role of police organizations within a theory of restorative justice]. Taipei: National Police Administration.

Hsu, Hsin-ping, and Hwang Kwang-Kuo. 2016. "Serendipity in Relationships: A Tentative Theory of the Cognitive Process of *Yuanfen* and Its Psychological Constructs in Chinese Cultural Societies." *Frontiers in Psychology* 7: 282.

Hsu, Ya-fei. 2013. "Sterilizing Society: Social Order and Policing Sex Work in Taiwan." *Inter-Asia Cultural Studies* 14 (2): 272–86.

Huang, Hans Tao-Ming. 2004. "State Power, Prostitution and Sexual Order in Taiwan: Towards a Genealogical Critique of 'Virtuous Custom.'" *Inter-Asia Cultural Studies* 5 (2): 237–62.

Huang, Philip C. C. 1993. "Between Informal Mediation and Formal Adjudication." *Modern China* 19: 251–98.

——. 1996. *Civil Justice in China: Representation and Practice in the Qing*. Stanford, CA: Stanford University Press.

Huang Y. 1971. "Liushinianlia de jingcha fazhan jianshi" [Sixty years of police development and foundation]. In *Liushinianlai de Zhongguo jingcha* [Sixty years of Chinese police]. Taipei: Central Police Officers School.

Hwang, Jau-Yuan. 2016. "Transitional Justice in Postwar Taiwan." In *Routledge Handbook of Contemporary Taiwan*, edited by Gunter Schubert, 169–83. London: Routledge.

Jauregui, Beatrice. 2016. *Provisional Authority: Police, Order, and Security in India*. Chicago: University of Chicago Press.

Jennings, Ronald. 2011. "Sovereignty and Political Modernity: A Genealogy of Agamben's Critique of Sovereignty." *Anthropological Theory* 11 (1): 23–61.

Jung Shaw-wu. 2007. "Wenhua, falu yu celue: Xiangzhen tiaojie guocheng de yanjiu" [Culture, law, and strategy: Settlement processes of a district mediation committee]. *Taiwan Shehui Xuekan* 38: 57–104.

Ka, Chih-ming. 1996. *Japanese Colonialism in Taiwan: Land Tenure, Development, and Dependency, 1895–1945*. Taipei: Southern Materials Center.

Kagan, Richard. 1982. "Martial Law in Taiwan." Statement to US House of Representatives, Subcommittee on Asian and Pacific Affairs, Committee on Foreign Affairs. Published in *Bulletin of Concerned Asian Scholars* 14 (3): 48–54.

Kahn, Jeffrey. 2017. "Geographies of Discretion and the Jurisdictional Imagination." *Political and Legal Anthropology Review* 40 (1): 5–27.

Kahn, Paul. 2011. *Political Theology: Four New Chapters on the Concept of Sovereignty*. New York: Columbia University Press.

Kalyvas, Andreas. 2008. *Democracy and the Politics of the Extraordinary: Max Weber, Carl Schmitt, and Hannah Arendt.* Cambridge: Cambridge University Press.

Kant, Immanuel. (1784) 2012. "Answer to the Question What Is Enlightenment." In *Classic Sociological Theory*, edited by Craig Calhoun, Joseph Gerteis, James Moody, Steven Pfaff, and Indermohan Virk, 50–54. Oxford: Wiley-Blackwell.

——. (1785) 1993. *Grounding for the Metaphysics of Morals: On a Supposed Right to Lie Because of Philanthropic Concerns.* Translated by James W. Ellington. Indianapolis: Hackett.

Kaplan, David. 1992. *Fires of the Dragon: Politics, Murder, and the Kuomintang.* New York: Atheneum.

Katz, Paul R. 2005. "Governmentality and Its Consequences in Colonial Taiwan: A Case Study of the Ta-pa-ni Incident of 1915." *Journal of Asian Studies* 64 (2): 387–424.

Keane, Webb. 2002. "Sincerity, 'Modernity,' and the Protestants." *Cultural Anthropology* 17 (1): 65–92.

——. 2003. "Semiotics and the Social Analysis of Material Things." *Language and Communication* 23: 409–25.

Kelling, George, and James Q. Wilson. 1982. "Broken Windows: The Police and Neighborhood Safety." *Atlantic*, March.

Kerr, George H. 1965. *Formosa Betrayed.* Boston: Houghton Mifflin.

——. 1974. *Formosa: Licensed Revolution and the Home Rule Movement, 1895–1945.* Honolulu: University of Hawai'i Press.

——. n.d. George H. Kerr Papers, box 2, folder 3. Hoover Institution Archives. Stanford University (Accession no. XX381).

Kipnis, Andrew. 1997. *Producing Guanxi: Sentiment, Self, and Subculture in a North Chinese Village.* Durham, NC: Duke University Press.

Kuhn, Philip A. 1979. *Rebellion and Its Enemies in Late Imperial China: Militarization and Social Structure, 1796–1864.* Cambridge, MA: Harvard University Press.

Kuo, Yung-Hwa, and Po-Liang Chen. 2016. "Identity Laws and Privacy Protection in a Modern State: The Legal History concerning Personal Information in Taiwan (1895–2015)." *Washington International Law Journal* 25 (2): 223–66.

Kyoko, Matsuda. 2003. "Inō Kanori's 'History' of Taiwan: Colonial Ethnology, the Civilizing Mission and Struggles for Survival in East Asia." *History and Anthropology* 14 (2): 179–96.

Lai Tse-Han, Ramon Myers, and Wei Wou. 1991. *A Tragic Beginning: The Taiwan Uprising of February 28, 1947.* Stanford, CA: Stanford University Press.

Laing, R. D. 1960. *The Divided Self: An Existential Study in Sanity and Madness.* London: Penguin.

Lam, Tong. 2010. "Policing the Imperial Nation: Sovereignty, International Law, and the Civilizing Mission in Late Qing China." *Comparative Studies in Society and History* 52 (4): 881–908.

Lamley, Harry J. 1968. "The 1895 Taiwan Republic: A Significant Episode in Modern Chinese History." *Journal of Asian Studies* 27 (4): 739–62.

——. 1970. "The 1895 Taiwan War of Resistance: Local Chinese Efforts against a Foreign Power." In *Taiwan: Studies in Chinese Local History*, edited by Leonard Gordon, 23–77. New York: Columbia University Press.

——. 1977. "Hsieh-Tou: Pathology of Violence in Southeastern China." *Journal of the Society of Ch'ing Studies* 3: 1–39.

——. 1999. "Taiwan under Japanese Rule, 1895–1945: The Vicissitudes of Colonialism." In *Taiwan: A New History*, edited by Murray Rubenstein, 201–60. Armonk, NY: M. E. Sharpe.

Larkins, Erika R. 2015. *The Spectacular Favela: Violence in Modern Brazil*. Oakland: University of California Press.

Lean, Eugenia. 2007. *Public Passions: The Trial of Shi Jianqiao and the Rise of Popular Sympathy in Republican China*. Berkeley: University of California Press.

Lee, Haiyan. 2007. *Revolution of the Heart: A Genealogy of Love in China, 1900–1950*. Stanford, CA: Stanford University Press.

Leishman, Frank. 1999. "Policing in Japan: East Asian Archetype?" In *Policing across the World: Issues for the 21st Century*, edited by Rob Mawby, 109–26. London: Routledge.

Lentz, Susan A., and Robert H. Chaires. 2007. "The Invention of Peel's Principles: A Study of Policing 'Textbook' History." *Journal of Criminal Justice* 35 (1): 69–79.

Lerman, Arthur. 1977. "National Elite and Local Politician in Taiwan." *American Political Science Review* 71 (4): 1406–22.

Lewis, Margaret K. 2009. "Taiwan's New Adversarial System and the Overlooked Challenge of Efficiency-Driven Reform." *Virginia Journal of International Law* 49 (3): 651–726.

Li Chongxi. 1996. "Riben shidai Taiwan jingcha zhidu zhi yanjiu" [Study of the police system during the Japanese era]. MA thesis, National Taiwan University.

Li Xianfeng. 1998. *Jiedu ererba* [An interpretation of 2/28]. Taipei: Yushan.

Li Zhengchang. 2007. "Cong zhidu yanxu guandian jianshi woguo jingcha paichusuode biange" [Examining the history of Taiwan's *paichusuo* from the perspective of institutional continuity]. MA thesis, National Jinan University.

Liang, Hsi-Huey. 1992. *The Rise of Modern Police and the European State System from Metternich to the Second World War*. Cambridge: Cambridge University Press.

Lin, Diana Yun-Hsien. 2011. "Civil Mediation in Taiwan: Legal Culture and the Process of Legal Modernization." *University of Pennsylvania East Asia Law Review* 6 (2): 191–215.

Lin Meiling. 1991. "Zhian wenti yu jingli yunyong" [Peacekeeping problems and the use of police force]. Taipei: National Policy Research Center.

Lin, Sylvia Li-chun. 2007. *Representing Atrocity in Taiwan: The 2/28 Incident and White Terror in Fiction and Film*. New York: Columbia University Press, 2007.

Lin Thung-Hong and Hui-Jiun Tseng. 2014. "Hukou de zhengzhi: Zhongguo dalu yu Taiwan huji zhidu zhi lishi bijiao" [The politics of *hukou*: A comparative study of the household registration system in China and Taiwan]. *Zhongguo Dalu Yanjiu* 57 (1): 63–96.

Lipsky, Michael. 1980. *Street-Level Bureaucracy: Dilemmas of Individuals in the Public Services*. New York: Russell Sage.

Liu, Fangquan, and Jeffrey T. Martin. 2016. "Policing after the Revolution." In *The Sage Handbook of Global Policing*, edited by Ian Loader, Ben Bradford, Jonny Steinberg, and Beatrice Jauregui. London: Sage.

Liu, Jennifer A. 2012. "Aboriginal Fractions: Enumerating Identity in Taiwan." *Medical Anthropology* 31: 329–46.

Liu, Lydia H. 2004. *The Clash of Empires: The Invention of China in Modern World Making*. Cambridge, MA: Harvard University Press.

Liu N., ed. 1990. *Chongxiu taiwansheng tongzhi baoan pian* [Revised records of Taiwan Province, policing volume]. Taipei: Taiwansheng Wenxian Weiyuanhui.

Liu Shengzuo. 2008. *You guanxi, bie shuo nin buhui: Taiwan jingcha renji guanxi xintan* [There's *guanxi*, don't say you can't: A new exploration of interpersonal relations for Taiwanese police]. Taipei: Rise International.

Loader, Ian, and Aogán Mulcahy 2003. *Policing and the Condition of England: Memory, Politics and Culture*. Oxford: Oxford University Press.

Loader, Ian, and Neil Walker. 2007. *Civilizing Security*. New York: Cambridge University Press.

Lynteris, Christos. 2011. "From Prussia to China: Japanese Colonial Medicine and Goto Shinpei's Combination of Medical Police and Local Self-Administration." *Medical History* 55: 343–47.

Manning, Peter K. 1997. *Police Work: The Social Organization of Policing*. Long Gove, IL: Waveland.

—— 2010. *Democratic Policing in a Changing World*. Boulder, CO: Paradigm.

——. 2013. "Drama, the Police, and the Sacred." In *Policing: Politics, Culture and Control*, edited by Tim Newburn and Jill Peay, 173–94. Oxford: Hart.

Marks, Jonathan. 2012. "The Nature/Culture of the Genetic Fact." *Annual Review of Anthropology* (42): 247–67.

Marks, Thomas A. 1998. *Counterrevolution in China: Wang Sheng and the Kuomintang*. London: Frank Cass.

Martin, Jeffrey T. 2007. "A Reasonable Balance of Law and Sentiment: Social Order in Democratic Taiwan from the Policeman's Point of View." *Law & Society Review* 41 (3): 665–98.

——. 2010. "Volunteer Police and the Production of Social Order in a Taiwanese Village." *Taiwan in Comparative Perspective* 3: 33–49.

——. 2013a. "Police as Linking Principle: Rethinking Police Culture in Contemporary Taiwan." In *Policing and Contemporary Governance*, edited by William Garriott, 157–80. New York: Palgrave Macmillan.

——. 2013b. "The *Hukou* and Traditional Virtue: An Ethnographic Note on Taiwanese Policing." *Theoretical Criminology* 17 (2): 261–69.

—— 2013c. "Legitimate Force in a Particularistic Democracy: Street Police and Outlaw Legislators in the Republic of China on Taiwan." *Law & Social Inquiry* 38 (3): 615–42.

——. 2014. "The Confucian Ethic and the Spirit of East Asian Police: A Comparative Study in the Ideology of Democratic Policing." *Crime, Law & Social Change* 61: 461–90.

——. 2015. "Policing an Occupied Legislature: Symbolic Struggle over the Police Image in Taiwan's Sunflower Movement." *Hong Kong Law Journal* 45 (1): 229–48.

——. 2017. "Affect: The Virtual Force of Policing (Taiwan)." In *Writing the World of Policing: The Difference Ethnography Makes*, edited by Didier Fassin. Chicago: University of Chicago Press

——. 2018. "Police Culture: What It Is, What It Does, and What We Should Do with It." In *The Anthropology of Policing*, edited by Kevin Karpiak and William Garriott, 34–53. New York: Routledge.

Matsumura, Yoshiyuki. 1988. "The Works of Takeyoshi Kawashima." *Law & Society Review* 22 (5): 1037–42.

Mattingly, Cheryl. 2012. "Two Virtue Ethics and the Anthropology of Morality." *Anthropological Theory* 12 (2): 161–84.

Mauss, Marcel. 1966. *The Gift: Forms and Functions of Exchange in Archaic Societies*. London: Cohen & West.

Meskill, Johanna Menzel. 1979. *A Chinese Pioneer Family: The Lins of Wu-feng, Taiwan, 1729–1895*. Princeton, NJ: Princeton University Press.

Miyazawa, Setsuo. 1987. "Taking Kawashima Seriously: A Review of Japanese Research on Japanese Legal Consciousness and Disputing Behavior." *Law & Society Review* 21 (2): 219–41.

Morris, Andrew. 2002. "The Taiwan Republic of 1895 and the Failure of the Qing Modernizing Project." In *Memories of the Future: National Identity Issues and the Search for a New Taiwan*, edited by Stephane Corcuff, 3–24. New York: Routledge.

Moskos, Peter. 2008. *Cop in the Hood: My Year Policing Baltimore's Eastern District*. Princeton, NJ: Princeton University Press.

Mouffe, Chantal. 2009. *The Democratic Paradox*. New York: Verso.

Mulla, Sameena. 2014. *The Violence of Care: Rape Victims, Forensic Nurses, and Sexual Assault Intervention*. New York: NYU Press.

Myers, Ramon. 1971. "The Research of the 'Commission for the Investigation of Traditional Customs in Taiwan.'" *Ch'ing-shi Wen-t'i* 6: 24–54.

Myers, Ramon, and Hsiao-ting Lin. 2007. *Breaking with the Past: The Kuomintang Central Reform Committee on Taiwan, 1950–52*. Stanford, CA: Hoover Institution.

Nadeau, Randall, and Chang Hsun. 2003. "Gods, Ghosts, and Ancestors: Religious Studies and the Question of 'Taiwanese Identity,'" In *Religion in Modern Taiwan*, edited by Philip Clart and Charles B. Jones, 280–300. Honolulu: University of Hawai'i Press.

Naquin, Susan, and Evelyn S. Rawski. 1987. *Chinese Society in the Eighteenth Century*. New Haven, CT: Yale University Press.

Nickels, Ernest. 2007. "A Note on the Status of Discretion in Police Research." *Journal of Criminal Justice* 35: 570–78.

NPA (National Police Administration). 2001. *Jingcha jiguan fenzhu(paichu)suo changyong qinwu zhixing chengxu huibian* [Compiled protocols for common duties implemented by local police substations]. Taipei: National Police Administration.

O'Brien, Suzanne. 2003. *Customizing Daily Life: Representing and Reforming Customs in Nineteenth-Century Japan*. Cambridge, MA: Harvard East Asian Monographs.

Ohlin, Lloyd, and Frank Remington, eds. 1993. *Discretion in Criminal Justice: The Tension between Individualization and Uniformity*. Albany: SUNY Press.

Olds, Kelly B., and Liu Ruey-Hua. 2000. "Economic Cooperation in 19th-Century Taiwan: Religion and Informal Enforcement." *Journal of Institutional and Theoretical Economics* 156: 404–30.

Ortner, Sherry. 1995. "Resistance and the Problem of Ethnographic Refusal." *Comparative Studies in Society and History* 37 (1): 173–93.

Osberg, John. 2013. *Anxious Wealth: Money and Morality among China's New Rich*. Stanford, CA: Stanford University Press.

Ownby, D. 1990. "The Ethnic Feud in Qing Taiwan: What's This Violence Business Anyways? An Interpretation of the 1782 Zhang-Quan Xiedou." *Late Imperial China* 11: 75–98.

Pashukanis, Evgeny. (1924) 1951. "The General Theory of Law and Marxism." In *Soviet Legal Philosophy*, edited by Hugh Babb, 111–225. Cambridge, MA: Harvard University Press.

Pedersen, Morton, and Martin Holbraad. 2013. "Introduction: Times of Security." In *Times of Security: Ethnographies of Fear, Protest and the Future*, edited by Morton Pedersen and Martin Holbraad, 1–27. New York: Routledge.

Peerenboom, Randall. 2004. "Varieties of the Rule of Law: An Introduction and Provisional Conclusion." In *Asian Discourses of Rule of Law: Theories and Implementation of Rule of Law in Twelve Asian Countries, France and the U.S.*, edited by Randall Peerenboom, 1–55. New York: Routledge.

Peng, Ming-min. 1971. "Political Offences in Taiwan: Laws and Problems." *China Quarterly* 47: 471–93.

Penglase, Ben. 2014. *Living with Insecurity in a Brazilian Favela: Urban Violence and Daily Life*. New Brunswick, NJ: Rutgers University Press.

Perkins, Franklin. 2016. "Metaphysics in Chinese Philosophy." In *The Stanford Encyclopedia of Philosophy*, edited by Edward N. Zalta. https://plato.stanford.edu/archives/win2016/entries/chinese-metaphysics/.

Phillips, Steven E. 2003. *Between Assimilation and Independence: The Taiwanese Encounter Nationalist China, 1945–1950*. Stanford, CA: Stanford University Press.

——. 2006. "Identity and Security in Taiwan." *Journal of Democracy* 17 (3): 58–71.

Pitkin, Hanna F. 1969. "The Concept of Representation." In *Representation*, edited by H. F. Pitkin. New York: Atherton.

Potter, Pittman B. 1995. "Doctrinal Norms and Popular Attitudes concerning Civil Law Relationships in Taiwan." *Pacific Basin Law Journal* 13: 265–87.

Puig de la Bellacasa, Maria. 2011. "Matters of Care in Technoscience: Assembling Neglected Things." *Social Studies of Science* 41 (1): 86–106.

——. 2012. "Nothing Comes without Its World: Thinking with Care." *Sociological Review* 60 (2): 197–216.

Rancière, Jacques. 2010. *Dissensus: On Politics and Aesthetics*. London: Bloomsbury.

Redfield, Robert. 1956. *Peasant Society and Culture: An Anthropological Approach to Civilization*. Chicago: University of Chicago Press.

Reed, Bradly W. 2000. *Talons and Teeth: County Clerks and Runners in the Qing Dynasty*. Stanford, CA: Stanford University Press.

Reeves, Joshua, and Jeremy Packer. 2013. "Police Media: The Governance of Territory, Speed, and Communication." *Communication and Critical/Cultural Studies* 10 (4): 359–84.

Reilly, Richard. 2012. "Fingarette on Moral Agency in the Analects." *Philosophy East and West* 62 (4): 529–44.

Reiner, Robert. 2010. *The Politics of the Police*. 4th ed. New York: Oxford University Press.

Richland, Justin. 2013. "Jurisdiction: Grounding Law in Language." *Annual Review of Anthropology* (42): 209–26.

Rigger, Shelly. 1999. *Politics in Taiwan: Voting for Democracy*. New York: Routledge.

——. 2009. "Nationalism versus Citizenship in the Republic of China on Taiwan." In *Changing Meanings of Citizenship in Modern China*, edited by Merle Goldman and Elizabeth J. Perry, 353–74. Cambridge, MA: Harvard University Press.

——. 2011. *Why Taiwan Matters*. Lanham, MD: Rowman & Littlefield.

Rosas, Gilberto. 2012. *Barrio Libre: Criminalizing States and Delinquent Refusals at the New Frontier*. Durham, NC: Duke University Press.

Rousseau, Jean-Jacques. (1762) 2012. "The Social Contract." In *Classic Sociological Theory*, edited by Craig Calhoun, Joseph Gerteis, James Moody, Steven Pfaff, and Indermohan Virk, 38–49. Oxford: Wiley-Blackwell.

Rowen, Ian. 2015. "Inside Taiwan's Sunflower Movement." *Journal of Asian Studies* 74 (1): 5–21.

Schafferer, Christian. 2010. "Consolidation of Democracy and Historical Legacies: A Case Study of Taiwan." *Journal of Contemporary Eastern Asia* 9 (1): 23–41.

Schmitt, Carl. (1922) 2005. *Political Theology: Four Chapters on the Concept of Sovereignty*. Chicago: University of Chicago Press.

Scholler, Heinrich, and Barbara Wagner. 1990. "Police Powers in the Republic of China." *Third World Legal Studies* 9 (6): 153–68.

Scott, James. 1999. *Seeing Like a State*. New Haven, CT: Yale University Press.

Seligman, Adam B., and Robert Weller. 2012. *Rethinking Pluralism: Ritual, Experience, and Ambiguity*. New York: Oxford University Press.

Seligman, Adam B., Robert Weller, Michael Puett, and Bennett Simon. 2008. *Ritual and Its Consequences: An Essay on the Limits of Sincerity*. New York: Oxford University Press.

Setsuo Miyazawa. 1987. "Taking Kawashima Seriously: A Review of Japanese Research on Japanese Legal Consciousness and Disputing Behavior." *Law & Society Review* 21 (2): 219–41.

Shahar, Meir, and Robert Weller. 1996. "Introduction: Gods and Society in China." In *Unruly Gods: Divinity and Society in China*, edited by Meir Shahar and Robert Weller, 1–36. Honolulu: University of Hawai'i Press.

Shak, David. 2009. "The Development of Civility in Taiwan." *Pacific Affairs* 82 (3): 447–65.

Shepherd, John R. 1999. "The Island Frontier of the Ch'ing." In *Taiwan: A New History*, edited by Murray Rubenstein, 107–32. Armonk, NY: M. E. Sharpe.

Sharma, Aradhana, and Akhil Gupta. 2006. Introduction to *The Anthropology of the State: A Reader*, edited by Aradhana Sharma and Akhil Gupta, 1–42. Malden, MA: Wiley-Blackwell.

Shiga, Shuzo. 1998. "Qingdai susong zhidu zhi minshi fayuan de gaikuoxing kaocha—qing, li, fa" [A general investigation into the origins of civil law in the litigation system of the Qing dynasty—sentiment, reason, and law], in *Ming/Qing shiqi de minshi shenpan yu minjian qiyue* [Civil judgment and civil contract in the Ming and Qing period], edited by S. Shiga, 19–53. Beijing: Falu Chubanshe.

Silver, Alan. 1967. "Demand for Order in Civil Society." In *The Police: Six Sociological Essays*, edited by David Bordua, 1–23. New York: Wiley.

Silverstein, Michael. 1998. "The Improvisational Performance of Culture in Realtime Discursive Practice." In *Creativity in Performance*, edited by R. Keith Sawyer, 265–312. Greenwich, CT: Ablex.

———. 2003. "Indexical Order and the Dialectics of Sociolinguistic Life." *Language & Communication* 23: 193–229.

Simon, Jonathan. 2007. *Governing through Crime: How the War on Crime Transformed American Democracy and Created a Culture of Fear*. New York: Oxford University Press.

Sixty Years of Chinese Police, Editorial Committee [Liushinian lai de Zhongguo jingcha, bianji weiyuanhui]. 1971. *Sixty Years of Chinese Police* [Liushinian lai de Zhongguo jingcha]. Taoyuan: Central Police University Press.

Skinner, Quentin. 1989. "The State." In *Political Innovation and Conceptual Change*, edited by Terence Ball, James Farr, and Russell Hanson, 90–131. New York: Cambridge University Press.

Skolnick, Jerome. 1966. *Justice without Trial: Law Enforcement in Democratic Society*. New York: Wiley.

Smith, Richard J. 1991. *Fortune-Tellers and Philosophers: Divination in Traditional Chinese Society*. Boulder, CO: Westview.

Solum, Lawrence. 2004. "The Aretaic Turn in Constitutional Theory." University of San Diego Public Law and Legal Theory Research Paper Series 3. http://digital.sandiego.edu/lwps_public/art3.

Sorel, Georges. (1908) 2004. *Reflections on Violence*. Mineola, NY: Dover.

Star, Susan L., and James R. Griesemer. 1989. "Institutional Ecology, 'Translations' and Boundary Objects: Amateurs and Professionals in Berkeley's Museum of Vertebrate Zoology, 1907–39." *Social Studies of Science* 19 (3): 387–420.

Stolojan, Vladimir. 2017. "Transitional Justice and Collective Memory in Taiwan." *China Perspectives* 2: 27–35.

Stone, Livia. 2015. "Suffering Bodies and Scenes of Confrontation: The Art and Politics of Representing Structural Violence." *Visual Anthropology Review* 31 (2): 177–89.

Su Bing. 1986. *Taiwan's 400 Year History: The Origins and Continuing Development of the Taiwanese Society and People*. Taipei: Taiwanese Cultural Grassroots Association.

Tao, Lung-sheng. 1971. "Reform of the Criminal Process in Nationalist China." *American Journal of Comparative Law* 19 (4): 747–65.

Taylor, Charles. 1979. *Hegel and Modern Society*. Cambridge: Cambridge University Press.

———. 1992. "The Politics of Recognition." In *Multiculturalism and "the Politics of Recognition,"* edited by Amy Gutmann, 25–76. Princeton, NJ: Princeton University Press.

Thacher, David. 2001. "Policing Is Not a Treatment: Alternatives to the Medical Model of Police Research." *Journal of Research in Crime and Delinquency* 38 (4): 387–414.

——. 2014. "Order Maintenance Policing." In *The Oxford Handbook of Police and Policing*, edited by Michael D. Reisig and Robert J. Kane, 122–47. New York: Oxford University Press.

Thomson, Janice. 1995. "State Sovereignty in International Relations: Bridging the Gap between Theory and Empirical Research." *International Studies Quarterly* 39: 213–33.

Tien, Hung-Mao. 1989. *The Great Transition: Political and Social Change in the Republic of China*. Taipei: SMC.

Tipton, Elise K. 2001. *Japanese Police State: Tokko in Interwar Japan*. Honolulu: University of Hawai'i Press.

Tok, Sow Keat. 2013. *Managing China's Sovereignty in Hong Kong and Taiwan*. New York: Palgrave.

Tomlins, Christopher. 2007. "How Autonomous Is Law?" *Annual Review of Law & Social Science* 3: 45–68.

Torpey, John. 1997. "Revolutions and Freedom of Movement: An Analysis of Passport Controls in the French, Russian, and Chinese Revolutions." *Theory and Society* 26: 837–68.

Tronto, Joan C. 1993. *Moral Boundaries: A Political Argument for an Ethic of Care*. New York: Routledge.

Ts'ai, Caroline Hui-Yu. 1990. "One Kind of Control: The *Hoko* System in Taiwan under Japanese Rule, 1895–1945." PhD thesis, Columbia University.

——. 2006. "Shaping Administration in Colonial Taiwan, 1895–1945." In *Taiwan under Japanese Colonial Rule, 1895–1945*, edited by Liao Ping-Hui and David Der-Wei Wang, 97–121. New York: Columbia University Press.

——. 2008. "The Shaping of Colonial Administrators: The Lower Civil Service Examination in Taiwan under Japanese Rule." Paper from the Fifth Conference of the European Association of Taiwan Studies, Prague, April 18–20.

——. 2009. *Taiwan in Japan's Empire Building: An Institutional Approach to Colonial Engineering*. London: Routledge.

——. 2010. "Engineering the Social or Engaging 'Everyday Modernity'? Interwar Taiwan Reconsidered." In *Becoming Taiwan: From Colonialism to Democracy*, edited by Ann Heylen and Scott Sommers, 83–100. Wiesbaden: Harrassowitz Verlag.

——. 2013. "Staging the Police: Visual Presentation and Everyday Coloniality." In *Mass Dictatorship and Modernity*, edited by Michael Kim, Michael Schoenhals, and Yong-Woo Kim, 71–97. New York: Palgrave Macmillan.

Ts'ai, Caroline Hui-Yu, and Wu Mei-hui. 2014. *Guangfu Taiwan yu zhanhou jingzheng* [The retrocession of Taiwan and postwar police administration]. Academia Sinica, Institute of Taiwanese History.

Tsing, Anna. 2010. "Worlding the Matsutake Diaspora." In *Experiments in Holism: Theory and Practice in Contemporary Anthropology*, edited by Nils Bubandt and Ton Otto, 47–66. West Sussex: Wiley-Blackwell.

Tsurumi, Patricia E. 1967. "Taiwan under Kodama Gentaro and Goto Shimpei." In *Papers on Japan*, edited by Albert Craig, 95–146. Cambridge, MA: East Asian Research Center, Harvard University.

Turner, Victor 1967. *The Forest of Symbols: Aspects of Ndembu Ritual*. Ithaca, NY: Cornell University Press.

Umemori, Naoyuki. 2002. "Modernization through Colonial Mediations: The Establishment of the Police and Prison System in Meiji Japan." PhD thesis, University of Chicago.

Valverde, Mariana. 2008. "Analyzing the Governance of Security: Jurisdiction and Scale." *Behemoth: A Journal on Civilization* 1: 3–15.

Von Senger, Harro. 2009. "Looking Outwards: Description of Non-Western Systems, China." Paper presented to Colloquy on Civil Status in the 21st Century, Strasbourg. http://ciec1.org/SITECIEC/PAGE_Colloques2009/fAkAAO_5eEl1SEh3clJESExwGQA.

Wang, Chin-shou. 2016. "Democratic Progressive Party Clientelism: A Failed Political Project." In *Taiwan's Democracy Challenged*, edited by Yun-han Chu, Larry Diamond, and Kharis Templeman, 267–88. Boulder, CO: Lynne Rienner.

Wang, Fei-ling. 2005. *Organizing through Division and Exclusion: China's Hukou System*. Stanford, CA: Stanford University Press.

Wang Fu-chang. 2005. *You "Zhongguo shengji" dao "Taiwan zuqun": Hukou chacha jibie leishu zhuanbian zhi fenxhi* [From Chinese of original domicile to Taiwanese ethnicity: An analysis of census category transformation in Taiwan]. *Taiwanese Sociology* 9: 59–117 (Chinese).

Wang, Tay-Sheng. 2000. *Legal Reform in Taiwan under Japanese Colonial Rule, 1895–1945*. Seattle: University of Washington Press.

——. 2016. "Translation, Codification, and Transplantation of Foreign Laws in Taiwan." *Washington International Law Journal* 25 (2): 307–29.

Weber, Max. (1904) 1949. "Objectivity in Social Science and Social Policy." In *The Methodology of the Social Sciences*, translated and edited by Edward Shils and Henry Finch, 49–112. Glencoe, IL: Free Press.

——. (1917) 1946a. "Science as a Vocation." In *From Max Weber*, translated and edited by H. H. Gerth and C. Wright Mills, 129–58. Glencoe, IL: Free Press.

——. (1919) 1946b. "Politics as a Vocation." In *From Max Weber*, translated and edited by H. H. Gerth and C. Wright Mills, 77–28. Glencoe, IL: Free Press.

Weller, Robert. 1999. *Alternate Civilities: Democracy and Culture in China and Taiwan*. Boulder, CO: Westview.

Wender, Jonathan M. 2008. *Policing and the Poetics of Everyday Life*. Urbana: University of Illinois Press.

Westney, D. Eleanor. 1982. "The Emulation of Western Organizations in Meiji Japan: The Case of the Paris Prefecture of Police and the Keishi-Cho." *Journal of Japanese Studies* 8 (2): 307–42.

——. 1987. *Imitation and Innovation: The Transfer of Western Organizational Patterns to Meiji Japan*. Cambridge, MA: Harvard University Press.

Whyte, William H. 1956. *The Organization Man*. New York: Doubleday.

Wicentowski, Joseph C. 2007. "Policing Health in Modern Taiwan, 1896–1949." PhD diss., Harvard University.

Winkler, Edwin A. 1981a. "National, Regional, and Local Politics." In *The Anthropology of Taiwanese Society*, edited by Emily Martin Ahern and Hill Gates, 13–37. Stanford, CA: Stanford University Press.

——. 1981b. "Roles Linking State and Society." In *The Anthropology of Taiwanese Society*, edited by Emily Martin Ahern and Hill Gates, 50–86. Stanford, CA: Stanford University Press.

——. 1984. "Institutionalization and Participation on Taiwan: From Hard to Soft Authoritarianism." *China Quarterly* 99: 481–99.

Winn, Jane K. 1987. "There Are No Strikes in Taiwan: An Analysis of Labor Law in the Republic of China on Taiwan." *Maryland Journal of International Law & Trade* 12 (1): 35–63.

——. 1994a. "Not by Rule of Law: Mediating State-Society Relations in Taiwan through the Underground Economy." In *The Other Taiwan: 1945 to the Present*, edited by Murray Rubenstein, 183–214. Armonk, NY: M. E. Sharpe.

——. 1994b. "Relational Practices and the Marginalization of Law: Informal Financial Practices of Small Businesses in Taiwan." *Law & Society Review* 28 (2): 193–241.

Winn, Jane K., with Yeh Tang-chi. 1995. "Advocating Democracy: The Role of Lawyers in Taiwan's Political Transformation." *Law & Social Inquiry* 20 (2): 561–99.

Winther, Jennifer A. 2008. "Household Enumeration in National Discourse." *Social Science History* 32 (1): 19–46.

Wolf, Arthur P. 1972. "Gods, Ghosts, and Ancestors." In *Studies in Chinese Society*, edited by Arthur P. Wolf, 131–82. Stanford, CA: Stanford University Press.

Wu, Nai-Teh. 1987. "Politics of a Regime Patronage System: Mobilization and Control in an Authoritarian Regime." PhD diss., University of Chicago.

Wu Yongzheng. 2006. "Zhanhou Taiwan huzheng biange zhi yanjiu: Cong 'jieshou fuyan' dao 'qingxiang jieyan' (1945–1949)" [A study of changes in Taiwan's postwar household registry administration: From "absorption and demobilization" to "cleansing and martial law" (1945–1949)]. MA thesis, National Cheng-Kung University, Tainan.

Xi Xiande. 2012. *Jingcha yu ererba shijian* [Police and the 2/28 incident]. Taipei: Shiying.

Xu Chixiu. 2003. "Taiwan huzheng zhidu zhi yanjiu" [Study of Taiwan's household registry administration system]. MA thesis, National Cheng-Kung University, Tainan.

Yan, Yunxiang. 1996. *The Flow of Gifts: Reciprocity and Social Networks in a Chinese Village*. Stanford, CA: Stanford University Press.

——. 2017. "Civility, Taiwanese Civility, and the Taiwanese Civility Reconstructed by Mainlanders." In *Taiwan's Impact on China*, edited by S. Tsang, 233–58. Palgrave Macmillan.

Yan Zhenzhen. 2014. "Taiwan dixia jingji zhan GDP jin sancheng" [Taiwan's underground economy nearly 30 percent of GDP]. Now News, June 30. https://www.nownews.com/news/20140630/1300335.

Yang Qingjiang. 1993. *Hukou chacha* [Registry inspection (new edition)]. Taoyuan: National Police Officer's School.

Yao, Jen-To. 2001. "Knowing Taiwan: Knowledge, Power, and the Japanese Colonial Governmentality of Taiwan." *Taiwan: A Radical Quarterly in Social Sciences* 42: 119–82.

——. 2006. "The Japanese Colonial State and Its Forms of Knowledge in Taiwan." In *Taiwan under Japanese Colonial Rule, 1895–1945*, edited by Liao Ping-Hui and David Der-Wei Wang, 37–61. New York: Columbia University Press.

——. 2007. "Zhengquan zhuanyi zhi zhilixing: Zhanhou Guomindang zhengquan dui rizhi shidai baojia zhidu de chengxi yu zhuanhua" [Governmentality and the change of regime: The pao-chia system's transformation after 1945]. *Taiwanese Sociology* 15: 47–108.

Yeh, Jiunn-Rong. 2016. *The Constitution of Taiwan: A Contextual Analysis*. Oxford: Bloomsbury.

Zhang Guangming, ed. 2013. *Taiwan jingzheng fazhan shi* [The history of Taiwan's police administration]. Taipei: National Police Administration.

Zhang Rongchun and Ding Weixin, eds. 1987. *Bao an jingcha yewu* [Peace protection police work]. Taipei: Guoya.

Zhu Shaohou. 1994. *Zhongguo gudai zhian zhidu shi* [A history of ancient Chinese peacekeeping systems]. Henan University.

Zhuang Wanshou 2003. *Taiwan wenhua lun* [A cultural theory of Taiwan]. Taipei: Yushan.

Index

CPSIA information can be obtained
at www.ICGtesting.com
Printed in the USA
LVHW090417201219
641189LV00001BA/396/P